A MATTER
OF CONFIDENCE

A MATTER OF CONFIDENCE

The Inside Story of the Political Battle for BC

ROB SHAW AND RICHARD ZUSSMAN

Victoria | Vancouver | Calgary

Heritage House Publishing Company Ltd.
heritagehouse.ca

CATALOGUING INFORMATION AVAILABLE FROM LIBRARY AND ARCHIVES CANADA
978-1-77203-254-3 (pbk)
978-1-77203-255-0 (epub)

Edited by Merrie-Ellen Wilcox
Proofread by Sarah Weber
Cover design by Jacqui Thomas
Interior book design by Setareh Ashrafalogholai

The interior of this book was produced on 100% post-consumer recycled paper, processed chlorine free and printed with vegetable-based inks.

We acknowledge the financial support of the Government of Canada through the Canada Book Fund (CBF) and the Canada Council for the Arts, and the Province of British Columbia through the British Columbia Arts Council and the Book Publishing Tax Credit.

22 21 20 19 18   1 2 3 4 5

Printed in Canada

CONTENTS

ACKNOWLEDGEMENTS

The stories in this book are captured as a moment in time. They are a reflection of the essential moments, and key characters, in an extraordinary period in British Columbia's political history, from 2009 to 2017.

The challenge in writing a contemporary political book about this period is that enough time hasn't yet passed to properly judge the legacy of the three premiers. Gordon Campbell's legacy on carbon pricing is still a work in progress, expanding to a national scale. Christy Clark's legacy is even more complicated, with many of her signature promises either cancelled or shelved. And John Horgan's premiership is in its infancy.

A Matter of Confidence is meant to offer a glimpse into the decisions these governments made, or didn't make, and the actions of those around the premiers during this time. It's too soon to pass judgement on their contributions to the province or how history will remember them.

The authors conducted interviews with seventy people over eight weeks in the research and production of this book. All interviews were completed following the May 9, 2017, BC election, in late July, August, and September. Most interviews were on background, meaning all the information could be used, but not with specific attribution. The information has, where possible, been corroborated by more than one source. Dialogue used in the book was provided either by the participants themselves or by other individuals who were actually part of those specific conversations; in both cases it relies on the best recollection of participants.

The authors conducted several hours of interviews with premiers Christy Clark and John Horgan. We thank them for their candour, opinions, and background. Direct quotes, when used, are prefaced with "... said in an interview for this book." Gordon Campbell declined multiple requests to be interviewed.

We would like to thank the following people for their time and participation: Christy Clark, John Horgan, Andrew Weaver, Sonia Furstenau, Mike Bernier, Brad Bennett, Mike McDonald, Mark Marissen, Laura Miller, Ben Chin, Michele Cadario, George Abbott, Randy Hawes, Sheena McConnell, Liam Iliffe, Craig James, Mike Farnworth, Todd Stone, Rich Coleman, Darryl Plecas, David Eby, Glen Hansman, Jim Iker, Ida Chong, Sherry Dittrick, Terry Lake, Kevin Falcon, Peter Hogg, Maurine Karagianis, Bill Bennett, Adrian Dix, Gordie Hogg, Steve Carr, Dan Doyle, Jasmyn Singh, Stephen Howard, Kimanda Jarzebiak, Mary Ellen Turpel, Kash Heed, Mary McNeil, Bill Vander Zalm, Graham Whitmarsh, Ronna Rae Leonard, Linda Higgins, Jodie Wickens, Colin Hansen, Bob Dewar, Marie Della Mattia, Chris Olsen, Stephen Smart, Bill Tieleman, Dale Steeves, Martyn Brown, Carole James, Mike de Jong, Carole Taylor, Jeremy Brownridge, Peter Fassbender, Kim Haakstad, Shane Mills, Pat Bell, Sam Oliphant, Gabe Garfinkel, Jillian Oliver, Keith Archer, Jenny Kwan, Moira Stilwell, Rob Fleming, Sara Macintyre, and Maclean Kay.

Thank you to Merrie-Ellen Wilcox, our editor, whose keen eye and diligent work made this book much better.

A DAY FOR THE HISTORY BOOKS

The walls of British Columbia's legislature were shaking as the government fell.

The cheers reverberated down the hallway, rattling the stained glass windows inside the historic capital building, as members of the New Democratic Party and the Green Party and supporters in the public gallery burst into a raucous ovation. Together the NDP-Green MLAS had just done the unthinkable—they'd outvoted their political enemies, the BC Liberal Party, and brought the provincial government down on a matter of confidence.

British Columbia has a long history of political intrigue, colourfully wacky characters, and fascinating political events. But June 29, 2017, would rank among its most memorable moments. It was the day sixteen years of Liberal rule crumbled, ending a political dynasty that had started with Gordon Campbell and faltered under Christy Clark. It was the day the province's lieutenant-governor, normally a ceremonial figurehead, exercised rare control of events and rejected the advice of a sitting premier. It was the day an opposition party that had failed to win the last election nonetheless found a way to seize control of power without returning voters to the polls—a sequence of events that hadn't occurred in the province since 1883.

The public gallery of the legislative chamber was filled beyond capacity that day. The House floor was crowded with MLAS and the former politicians and dignitaries seated in chairs along the marble walls. As the Green and NDP MLAS soaked in the cheers, the Liberals filed out after the vote. The last to leave was Premier Christy Clark.

Two dozen journalists were packed into the hallway outside the chamber, waiting for the fallen premier to arrive. She stepped out of the legislative chamber, wearing a dark blue suit, her head held high despite the crushing loss. Reporters started shouting questions, but Clark began to walk. It was a walk she'd done hundreds of times before. This time was different. Her forty-two Liberal MLAS and their staff had packed the building's Memorial Rotunda, creating a gauntlet of cheering, clapping, shouting friendly faces to send off their defeated leader.

With tears in her eyes, Clark smiled, waved, and shook hands with the well-wishers as she walked the route to her office for the last time. It lasted only ninety seconds. BC's major TV news networks, which had carried the confidence vote live, also broadcast the premier's walk to her west annex office through a second-floor breezeway.

As the doors closed behind Clark, the province held its breath.

There was only one hope left for Clark and her Liberals. She'd have to persuade Lieutenant-Governor Judith Guichon to call a new election, and then take her chances again with voters. The same voters who, just seven weeks earlier, had punished her party severely in Metro Vancouver. With anything less than a new election, NDP leader John Horgan would become premier.

After Clark gathered her thoughts inside her office, she was ready to leave. A Vancouver news helicopter buzzed overhead, tracking Clark and her police escort as she was driven to the Government House mansion. It was only a fifteen-minute journey, but it was as breathlessly covered as if it were a high-speed chase.

As that drama played out, John Horgan, the leader of the NDP, paced his legislature office with his favourite lacrosse stick, tossing a squishy stress ball against the walls and catching it, nervously killing time. There was nothing left for him to do other than wait and hope the lieutenant-governor would call and invite him to take Clark's place.

Horgan, though, had a strong feeling that this day was his. He'd received a tip-off that morning from Government House. And he could feel in his bones that victory was within his grasp.

Years of planning and politicking would come down to the next three hours. In the time it takes for a Vancouver Canucks hockey game, the landscape of BC politics would be dramatically altered.

At Government House, Clark made the most important pitch of her political life to Guichon. Inside the lieutenant-governor's private drawing room, Clark spent part of forty-five minutes trying to convince Guichon that calling on Horgan to become premier would be a mistake and would lead to an unstable, unworkable, undemocratic parliament. But she knew almost immediately that her message wasn't getting through. So the end of the meeting was spent drinking wine, two women tied together for nearly five years saying goodbye. The premier would emerge without her trademark smile, utterly deflated.

She collapsed into a chair in one of the building's drawing rooms after the meeting, as her staff gathered around her.

"I don't think she's going to do it," said Clark. "I think she'd made up her mind before I got there. And I think she's going to call on John Horgan."

The iPhone belonging to Horgan's chief of staff, Bob Dewar, started to buzz. On the other end was the lieutenant-governor's private secretary, who said, "This is your million dollar call." And with that, Horgan was out the door, on what felt like the longest drive of his life—to Government House.

The NDP leader had never really wanted to be leader. It was a job thrust on him in a moment of crisis for the party. At first he'd struggled to fit the role. But in the election, he'd risen to the challenge and excelled. After years of self-doubt, he finally seemed like a premier-in-waiting.

NDP leader John Horgan was all smiles when he left his office at the BC legislature on June 29, 2017, just moments after a call from the lieutenant-governor's office requesting that he meet with her. Accompanying him was press secretary Sheena McConnell and her husband and NDP staffer, Liam Iliffe. MARIE DELLA MATTIA

As he walked into Government House and was seated in Guichon's study, Horgan knew, and the province knew, everything was about to change.

June 29, 2017, was a matter of confidence.

The over-confidence of former premier Gordon Campbell, whose harmonized sales tax gave Christy Clark the opening to become premier. The brashness that marked Clark's time in office, until a non-confidence motion threatened to end her political career. And the questionable self-confidence of John Horgan, the man who had struggled to ready himself for the top job.

It was a day for the history books.

This is the inside story.

CHAPTER 1

THE TAX MAN

It took only forty-eight hours for Gordon Campbell to go from career highlight to career lowlight. Just two days between BC's thirty-fourth premier standing on a stage at his May 2009 re-election night victory rally, waving at adoring crowds, and his sitting slumped in a chair inside his office, screaming at a bureaucrat who'd delivered him the worst possible news.

Campbell, it turned out, had serious money problems. He'd spent much of his 2009 election campaign promising voters that, despite a worldwide economic collapse, his BC Liberals were prudent, disciplined managers of the economy. They, and only they, and certainly not the NDP, could deliver to taxpayers a budget that had a small, barely noticeable deficit during a time of global turmoil.

"The deficit will be $495 million maximum," the confident BC Liberal leader had declared on April 23, 2009, mid-campaign. To make matters worse, he'd doubled down on the line the day after winning the election.

Now, just two days after becoming the first premier in twenty-six years to win a third term and strengthening his majority hold on government, a bespectacled civil servant was standing in one of the premier's waterfront Vancouver offices, telling him that he was wrong. And not only was Campbell wrong, but this bureaucrat—the deputy minister of finance, no less—was informing him that he was at least $1.5 billion in the red, with virtually no hope of ever hitting the "maximum" deficit target he'd pinned his credibility on during the campaign. The global recession had pushed BC's economy, like many others, into a tailspin. Revenues were billions of dollars off course. And they weren't coming back anytime soon.

Campbell got mad. Very mad.

"I've just been out and won an election based on $495 (million)," he yelled. "What the hell are we going to do?"

On the receiving end of Campbell's fury were deputy finance minister Graham Whitmarsh and Finance Minister Colin Hansen. After the premier vented, the meeting broke up. Whitmarsh went into a separate room, inside the premier's suite of offices at Canada Place in downtown Vancouver.

There was a flurry of activity among senior Campbell staffers at that point, and it was made clear to Whitmarsh he would have to resign. The figures weren't what the bureaucracy had promised when the budget was tabled in February, and Whitmarsh would need to take responsibility.

No way, said Whitmarsh. Everyone had known all along that $495 million was an aspirational goal, he said. A slim chance. The best, slimmest hope possible. In no way a sure thing. And he'd kept Campbell's deputy minister in the loop on the numbers, he added.

It wasn't his fault, Whitmarsh said, that the campaigning politicians hadn't listened to the warnings of the non-partisan folks inside the finance ministry.

The situation quickly became a standoff.

Everyone went back in to see the mercurial premier.

"Okay," said the boss, who had calmed down slightly. "Give me some options."

From these tumultuous beginnings was born BC's harmonized sales tax. Within seventeen months, Campbell's career would be in ruins and the stage set for the rise of Christy Clark.

THE HST. JUST those three letters are enough to provoke a kind of post-traumatic stress among Liberal politicians and cabinet ministers who served in government at the time and who lived to see the fallout of one the most hated, bungled tax measures in provincial history.

In order to understand exactly how BC got here, you have to first go back to the boss. Gordon Muir Campbell. He was always the smartest person in the room. Or, at least, he thought he was. And he was probably right.

Perhaps it was his voracious reading; he was known to devour books on all manner of subjects at a quick pace, leading to swift policy changes inside his government when an idea caught his fancy. At his cottage on the Sunshine Coast, Campbell's garage was filled with thousands of books, most of which were overflowing with sticky notes and sections highlighted by a premier who didn't just read the text but devoured ideas and repurposed them into actual policy.

Or maybe it was his workaholic tendencies. He was often in his office until very late at night, digesting the briefing books of government ministries. He knew the ministry files better than most ministers. And he had little patience for those who wouldn't keep up.

Or perhaps it was Campbell's pedigree as a former developer-turned-mayor of Vancouver (he was mayor from 1986 to 1993). Or it could have been because, deep down, he preferred policy to people. Ideas to interaction.

Whatever the reason, Campbell did not lack confidence in his own abilities. He'd even survived a public relations scandal that erupted in 2003 after he was arrested for drunk driving in Hawaii.

As premier, Campbell had achieved considerable success. He'd spearheaded the "New Relationship" with First Nations communities, recognizing their right to consultation and accommodation on land title and rights years before other provinces. In 2007, he pivoted the government to tackle the issue of climate change, committing the province to a host of new environmentally friendly projects and a promise of reducing greenhouse gas emissions by one-third by 2020. BC wouldn't achieve that goal, but Campbell's early focus on climate action would make the province an international leader on the file. Earlier in his premiership he'd cut personal income taxes by 25 per cent, the biggest reduction in BC history. And he was part of an ambitious plan to host the Olympics, which paid off in 2003 when Vancouver was awarded the 2010 Winter Olympic Games.

Coming out of the 2009 election, Campbell was the undisputed boss of BC politics. With a small circle of powerful loyalists, and a larger circle of people who feared him, he was unchallenged in his dominance of both the Liberal party and the provincial government. His party had grown its majority by three seats, trouncing the New Democrats yet again, for the third straight time.

But more than that, he'd been proven right on one of the most significant tax shifts in BC's history, the carbon tax. The contentious levy—which most people saw simply as a surcharge on their gas at the pump—had been a Campbell creation and a dominant issue in the twenty-eight-day campaign. BC was so far ahead of the rest of the country on the carbon tax that it would be eight years before Ottawa mandated similar carbon pricing schemes for the rest of the provinces. The carbon tax had also badly divided BC's New Democrats, who had run an "axe that tax" campaign that had blown up in their faces and led prominent environmentalists to abandon ship and support the Liberals.

Voters had ultimately agreed with Campbell. The carbon tax wasn't a needless penalty on drivers; it was an affordable, necessary, and cutting-edge way to protect the environment. And so the policy-wonk premier, who believed he understood tax policy better than almost anyone else, allowed himself to drift into the HST.

The BC government can be a large, unwieldy, slow-moving bureaucratic behemoth. It can take months, if not years, to get a simple permit to start a small project. But when an angry premier shouts urgent orders to fix a political crisis, the civil service moves remarkably fast.

"Go out and find out how we're going to meet the budget target of $495 million," Campbell later recalled himself saying to the bureaucrats.

Fixing this was an important point for the veteran politician. The idea of campaigning on one budget figure, only to unveil worse numbers after winning the election, was unbearable to him. He'd dined out on just that scenario as Opposition leader when in 1996 the NDP government became embroiled in its infamous "fudge-it budget" scandal, promising a balanced budget during the 1996 election and delivering a massive deficit afterward. Campbell and his Liberals feasted on the scandal for years, never hesitating to remind voters that the NDP were incompetent economic managers. The NDP was "the most incompetent, incorrigible and corrupt government in BC history," he'd later say.

Campbell balked at the idea of finding himself in his own fudge-it budget scandal and having similar unflattering monikers etched on his political legacy.

Though by that point it was already too late.

THE 2009 FINANCIAL mess started on January 24, in Courtenay, on central Vancouver Island. Local Liberal MLA and cabinet minister Stan Hagen had passed away suddenly. Family, friends, and Liberal colleagues were in town to attend his memorial service. That evening, after the service was done, Campbell and his chief of staff, Martyn Brown, along with Hansen, Whitmarsh, and outgoing deputy finance minister Chris Trumpy met in a conference room at the nearby Westerly Hotel.

Campbell wanted to table a balanced budget in February, one he could take into the election campaign with confidence to show his party's strong control of the economy. But the worldwide economic situation made that impossible. After a lot of back and forth, the room settled on the parameters of a deficit, somewhere below $500 million, which was, at the time, the most optimistically credible figure that the financial officials were comfortable with given the financial uncertainty.

Even then, it was built on the assumption that the provincial economy would stabilize. It didn't.

"The budget includes a temporary deficit," Hansen said in his budget speech to the legislature on February 17, 2009. "Weighed against the risks to our economy, our communities and our future—it is, quite simply, the right thing to do."

When the election campaign began, the finance officials, minister, and premier broke off day-to-day talks, as is customary during a campaign. But the economic numbers continued to worsen. Hitting the deficit target was looking extremely unlikely without massive cuts to services. When Campbell told the media that the $495 million deficit was the maximum, it made the civil servants inside finance even more uneasy.

Whitmarsh had a close relationship with Campbell, having been recruited into government from the Royal Navy's nuclear submarine program as an advisor on carbon trading in the premier's new climate action office. But as he reflected on the premier's public promises, Whitmarsh was so nervous that, while on a bike ride along Victoria's picturesque Dallas Road waterfront, in the middle of the election, he pulled over and called Hansen, his minister, on his cell phone.

"I just saw the premier talking and I have to tell you I'm uncomfortable," he told Hansen. "When we set that number we knew it was the most optimistic view, and it's just not going to be anywhere close to that." The deficit was now tracking at several billion dollars, and it would take a Herculean effort to tame it.

Hansen does not remember this call. He does remember speaking to Whitmarsh a couple of times, and hearing that there'd be erosion in revenue of a couple of hundred million dollars—a seemingly manageable figure within a $40 billion budget. Regardless, there things stood until just after the election, when Campbell blew his stack on his officials.

The day after Campbell's eruption at Whitmarsh and Hansen, the government's head of tax policy contacted his federal counterpart to ask how much "transition funding" the province could get to sign on to the HST. The answer was $1.6 billion. The federal cash could have been the salvation Campbell was looking for. Enough, at least on paper, to make the pesky little issue of a stubbornly underestimated deficit election promise disappear quietly.

Whitmarsh and Hansen later returned to Campbell's office, where they'd compiled a written list of fifteen things the government could do to cut enough expenses that the $495 million deficit would be achievable. The list included steep cuts to programs and services. It also included the HST, which looked like the most palatable of the options, by far. Campbell was intrigued.

BC was told by Ottawa it would have to act quickly if it wanted to join; Ontario was already in the process of moving to the HST, and Ottawa had the capacity to accommodate BC only if it joined Ontario's process immediately. Otherwise, BC could be waiting for years.

Hansen never questioned that pressure, though in retrospect he regrets not appealing directly to federal finance minister Jim Flaherty for more leniency in the timeline.

BC's plan to use HST cash from Ottawa to salvage its budget might have worked, too, but by early July revenues had slumped further. Personal and corporate income tax revenues were billions off course. Not even the HST could save them. Hansen started laying the groundwork for the rough landing of the new tax anyway.

In early July, the HST was up for debate at a cabinet meeting. It appeared to be the only option available to backstop the slumping treasury. Like they had many times before, the assembled Liberal MLAs put their faith in Campbell to get them out of the sticky situation.

Campbell, too, had come around to liking the merits of the HST. Yes, it was forced on him in a scramble to salvage a financial disaster.

But the policy wonk in him appreciated the elegance of consolidating two taxes into one and eliminating an inefficient provincial sales tax that was long-hated by the business community. So by the time he had to sell it to his colleagues and the public, Campbell was convinced the HST was the right public policy. At one meeting around this time, he was telling senior staff about the decision to proceed with the HST when someone raised the obvious other question: Was it the right move politically?

"That's your fucking job," retorted the premier. "Figure that part out."

Those who worked for Campbell guessed the HST could be the end of their boss's career. And they thought the premier might have known that too.

On July 23, Campbell and Hansen jointly announced that BC had agreed to sign on to the harmonized sales tax. BC would introduce an HST of 12 per cent, replacing the 7 per cent PST and 5 per cent GST, starting in July 2010. Campbell called it the single most important thing he could do to help BC's economy—ten weeks after an election campaign in which he'd never even mentioned it.

They didn't know it at the time, but both men had just ended their political careers.

It would take another four years before another Liberal finance minister, Mike de Jong, would admit the government had "got it big-time wrong" with its 2009 financial figures. But Campbell would be damned if he would admit it at the time.

VOTER OUTRAGE OVER the HST grew quickly. It was built partly on the idea that the Liberals had betrayed the electorate by reneging on a campaign promise not to pursue an HST. But in reality, the HST was never an issue in the 2009 election, and the Liberals had said virtually nothing about the tax. The party's sole commitment had been a response to a restaurant industry survey in late April during the campaign: "The BC Liberals have no plans to formally engage the federal government in discussions about potential harmonization."

Most anger came from the idea that the tax was going to download costs from businesses onto consumers, jacking up the price on some ordinary household items while offering nebulous savings and vague efficiencies to the overall economy. In short, the Liberal-friendly business community would get a break, and everyone else would pay more.

This was the general thrust of the anti-HST campaign that would begin to take form in the months after BC's HST decision was announced. And it didn't help that the tax launched without any validators in the business community, which was pretty much the only sector of the province that actually appreciated the change. Anti-HST advocates would comb through the potential tax code, pointing out a variety of items where the PST had not applied, meaning that item would go from being taxed at a rate of 5 per cent (GST only) to 12 per cent under the HST.

The government countered with a grab bag of high-level economic benefits, such as insisting that the HST would save businesses $1.9 billion on sales tax inputs and that—perhaps hopefully—those savings might be passed on to the consumer.

There is probably no one inside or outside the Liberal party who would argue that government did a good job of selling the public on the benefits of an HST. Only ten minutes after the initial press conference, finance officials found themselves deluged by media requests for specific information. How would the HST affect an average BC family? What would it mean for ordinary items, like diapers? What would it mean for complicated transactions, like homes that were partially built?

The finance ministry did not have the answers. There was no money earmarked to hire a dedicated specialist group of HST communicators, something Hansen later deeply regretted. Worse still, the situation was so complicated that senior advisors to the premier and minister didn't really know how the tax worked.

For every tax expert, or business, government produced to argue that the HST would eliminate the complicated built-in costs of PST applied at every level of a manufactured product, the anti-HST forces would produce an actual living person who was about to get hammered with higher costs for school supplies, restaurant meals, cable TV, and first-aid kits. At one point, the government actually spent $780,000 on a pamphlet it planned to mail to every BC household, extolling the virtues of the HST, but then reconsidered and shredded the whole thing.

Smelling blood in the water, opponents of the Liberals began organizing a formal campaign to oppose the tax. To do it, they'd turn to one of the most unique pieces of legislation in the country.

BC'S INITIATIVE PETITION law was the only one of its kind in Canada. In theory, it gave citizens the power to unite en masse and force politicians to consider new laws at the legislature. All you needed was your own draft bill and fifty dollars for the non-refundable application fee. But in reality, it was believed to be almost unworkable. Since the law's enactment in 1995, six groups had tried to gather enough signatures under the law to actually win a petition. All six had failed, badly. The closest attempt—a 2002 drive for proportional representation—gathered only 44 per cent of the required signatures.

For a petition to pass, it needed 10 per cent of registered voters in each of the province's then eighty-five electoral districts. That high bar was 299,611 voters. And to make it even more challenging, you had only ninety days to pull it all off. On the remote chance someone was ever successful at a petition drive, the result would be that the winning draft bill would go to a legislature committee. There, MLAs would recommend that either the winning bill be introduced in the House for a vote as soon as possible or the issue be put out to provincial voters via a province-wide "initiative vote"—basically, a referendum with different rules.

It was an enormous hurdle that appeared, at the time, to be completely unattainable.

Not to Bill Vander Zalm, though. The former Social Credit premier was at his Delta home when he saw the TV news coverage of the HST. He became incensed, recalling that previous governments, including his, had opposed any attempt by Ottawa to try to encroach on BC's powers of taxation and horn in on the province's revenues. Within a week, he was in a photo on the cover of *The Province* newspaper holding a stop sign and offering to head a revolt against the governing Liberals.

"Short of a revolt, we certainly need to make a huge protest," the seventy-five-year-old Vander Zalm told the paper, urging upset citizens to contact him through his website (which was filled with advertisements promoting his coincidentally timed, recently self-published autobiography).

The defiant Dutchman had always been one of the most charismatic characters in BC politics, even after his resignation from office in disgrace in 1991, when he was found to be in conflict of interest for mixing the private sale of his Fantasy Gardens amusement park with his public office as premier. He was quick-witted, eminently quotable, and willing to appear anywhere a news outlet wanted him, at any time.

Enough time had passed since his resignation that the murky details of his conduct—at one point he accepted bags of cash as part of the sale while premier—had faded from public memory. Nobody seemed to remember that Vander Zalm was responsible for introducing one of BC's other hated taxes, the property transfer tax, which has dinged each home sale in the province for thirty years. He'd been trying to rehabilitate his reputation for years. The veteran politician was quick to wrap himself in the cloak of public righteousness, and soon he was lambasting the new tax for driving up the cost of meals, haircuts, funerals, and other items.

The campaign officially kick-started on September 20, 2009, with nineteen anti-HST rallies taking place simultaneously across the province. The HST plunged the Liberals into a full-out political crisis. The public was furious. The government was on its heels. And the Zalm was stirring up all kinds of trouble.

In Dawson Creek, Energy Minister Blair Lekstrom was watching the HST roll-out with dismay. Although he'd emerged from Campbell's cabinet in solidarity with the tax, he'd heard from residents in his Peace River South riding that they were unimpressed with the idea that the Liberals had said one thing during the election and done the other after winning. Lekstrom had always been outspoken and unafraid to ruffle feathers within his own party. Tall and fit, with a shaved head and trimmed goatee, Lekstrom often wore a skullcap helmet as he drove his '78 Harley-Davidson motorcycle down to the legislature. His first vote in the House after being elected in 2001 was against his own party for ripping up labour contracts. You can imagine how Campbell frowned upon that gesture. It would be seven years before Lekstrom was invited into his cabinet. As a minister, Lekstrom was known as a straight-shooter, unafraid to speak his mind even if it didn't match the script his political masters put in front of him.

Lekstrom arrived for a cabinet meeting in Vancouver on June 11, and, before the meeting started, walked into the premier's office to have a word.

"Gord, I can't govern this way, and I'm making a decision to step back," said Lekstrom. "Unless we put the brakes on and engage the public, I'm not carrying forward."

Campbell was surprised. In different circumstances, with a different minister, he might have blown his top. But Lekstrom wasn't the kind of guy you yelled at, unless you wanted the burly biker to knock you on your ass.

"Blair, my preference is you stick with us," Campbell said diplomatically. But he couldn't offer to halt the tax, because BC needed to move forward with Ontario, he said. Lekstrom respected Campbell and thought he was a good leader. They got along well. So they ended their conversation there.

Lekstrom asked to break the news of his resignation to cabinet, and Campbell agreed. The response from the rest of the beleaguered ministers was cordial but unenthusiastic. They all knew the kind of signal it sent for a popular cabinet minister to quit in protest over a tax everyone else seemed to hate too. Privately, some felt Lekstrom was weak, almost cowardly, for bailing under the same kind of pressure they were all facing.

Ironically, Lekstrom actually believed in the HST as a tax. It had merit as a policy change, he thought, but it had been so badly handled that it was all but dead in the water. Lekstrom would sit as an independent.

One day in mid-2010, Campbell asked Lekstrom's replacement, new Energy Minister Bill Bennett, to his office in Victoria. Bennett, who was not particularly close to Campbell, gave him some blunt advice in a wide-ranging forty-five-minute chat: the Liberal caucus was not healthy. There were some rotten apples causing problems, and dissent was spreading and getting worse. Negative cliques were forming. Things were headed in a bad direction, and the party was going to lose the next election unless something was done, advised Bennett.

"What do you think I should do about it?" asked Campbell.

"I think you've got to resign and take all this stuff with you," said Bennett. "I know it's not fair."

Campbell paused. "Well," he said. "I'm not doing that."

But Bennett was far from the only person urging Campbell to consider stepping aside. As the once-invulnerable premier stumbled, the knives started to come out.

Campbell had successfully held together the Liberal free-enterprise coalition of centrist liberals and right-wing conservatives since 1994, through a mixture of policy smarts, keen intellect, loyal soldiers, and fear. Fear came in a variety of forms. Not just fear of a loss at the polls or the disintegration of the government. But fear of Campbell himself, and falling on the wrong side of both his brilliance and his temper.

Among the many profiles written of Campbell over the years, perhaps the most insightful is one by Frances Bula in *The Vancouver Sun*, just months before he actually became premier in 2001. Bula peeled back the layers of Campbell, then Liberal leader, thus:

> He was and remains, in many ways, a classic introvert, preferring to work one-on-one or in small groups, relating to ideas, not people. At the same time he likes to be in control down to the last neutron . . .
>
> Added to all that, he was hard on people. He could listen to people's opinions attentively while he was still mulling his stance on something, but once he had his mind made up, there was no argument. His decisiveness or opinionated pigheadedness—different people characterize it different ways—could be accompanied by abrasiveness. If someone disappointed him in some way, he acted like a jilted lover . . .
>
> The two Gordons appear everywhere. There's the private Gordon, whose close friendships are marked by long-standing loyalty. The public one, who is ruthlessly expedient at jettisoning the useless or setting aside the no-longer-needed. The public one who appears cool and bland. The private one famous for his screaming sessions with staff or his manic comedy monologues that have people collapsing in hysterical laughter.

As premier, Campbell would govern in largely the same way. It was a style that inspired fierce loyalty in some colleagues, such as ministers Rich Coleman, Shirley Bond, Colin Hansen, and Pat Bell. They saw one side of Campbell, a warm and often funny leader who gave them space to work on their portfolios. When he was upset, to them it was because he was brilliant and frustrated that it took everyone else so long to catch up.

Those who Campbell felt were quick and competent on their files were rewarded. Those he viewed as incompetent or threats to his power were micromanaged out of existence. Those who couldn't, or wouldn't, keep up with his punishing work ethic on their own files he rode mercilessly, sometimes to tears.

Some cabinet ministers could do no right. He'd driven out high-profile women like Christy Clark, Olga Ilich, and Carole Taylor, who'd had enough of his meddling ways. Taylor, a well-connected and popular business leader, had stood up to Campbell's temper, but still found herself cut out of major announcements and left scrambling to find money for promises she didn't know were coming. She quit after one term.

Among Campbell's biggest detractors was George Abbott. Despite his dry demeanour, Abbott held the distinction of being in the rarefied club of MLAs who ever had the temerity to stand up to Campbell publicly in a caucus meeting. That happened in September 2007 at a caucus retreat in Harrison Hot Springs, where Abbott was presenting to MLAs the results of his year-long province-wide consultation on health care.

Campbell, predictably, had strong opinions about the health-care system and started challenging Abbott on certain points, ragging his research and eventually outright riding him through the briefing. After one too many interruptions, Abbott stopped, looked up from his notes and met the premier's gaze directly.

"Would you like to take over, Premier?" he asked.

There was stunned, nervous silence in the room. Everyone held their breath. It was a direct challenge to the boss, in front of the whole caucus. But Campbell backed down and went quiet.

The meeting concluded. Abbott was still furious. He'd had run-ins with the premier before, but he'd begun to suspect their constant differences on the health file were just irreconcilable.

Premier Gordon Campbell was hoping that the 2010 Vancouver Olympics would help the province forget about the HST debacle. But eight months after showing off a gold medal, Campbell was out of a job. PROVINCE OF BC

"I remained pissed off when I awoke the next day," Abbott recalled. "As the old adage goes, 'surly to bed, surly to rise.' I decided to skip caucus without leave and go for a very long walk."

When he got back, Abbott offered his resignation. Campbell refused to accept it, and apologized.

"To his credit, Gordon would realize retrospectively that he had overstepped his bounds and apologize," Abbott said of their disputes. "Unfortunately the apologies didn't always come with long-term warranties."

Clashes like these led Campbell's critics to rally around Abbott as the HST situation worsened. Buzz began to grow that he was organizing a leadership bid behind Campbell's back.

"This is by far the toughest year I've ever gone through as an elected official," Campbell would say publicly at the end of 2009.

"I was under no illusions when we made the decisions that we made, the kind of popularity impacts they would have," he added. "You always want to be popular. But you can't do the job if you worry about being popular."

The Liberals had hoped the 2010 Winter Olympics would divert the public's attention away from the HST. The games, which ran from February 12 to 28, 2010, were a resounding success. And yet when they finished, the HST situation was worse than ever.

"I actually seriously considered leaving after the Olympics and Paralympics," Campbell would later say. "It would have felt great to do that. But it goes back to your sense of obligation to the people you are with. I was the premier when we decided to go forward with the HST and I think it was the right choice to make. I'd still make that choice. But I wanted to stay with our guys and make sure they knew I was with them."

Just over a month later, on April 6, 2010, Vander Zalm would be given the official go-ahead by Elections BC to start his petition drive. Now the clock was ticking, with ninety days to gather the required signatures.

Vander Zalm would later write a book about how he and a loyal group of organizers whipped the province into a frenzy over the HST. It's filled with pages upon pages of detail on how he organized a successful campaign. Co-organizer Bill Tieleman went to Facebook to set up the "No HST" page, which exploded in popularity, growing by more than 6,000 followers a day. It topped out at more than 136,000, more than both the BC Lions and Vancouver Canucks pages had at the time. It was clear that the Fight HST campaign led by Vander Zalm was a resounding success. More than 6,556 canvassers poured out across the province, setting up booths at shopping malls and canvassing neighbourhoods to gather signatures. They had to sign up an average of 3,500 people a day.

MLAs in their ridings got a flavour of the voter outrage in different ways. In Prince George, Pat Bell pulled in to his local Canadian Tire on a rainy day and not only saw Fight HST canvassers successfully gathering signatures from shoppers, but noticed that one of the organizers whipping up voter discontent in the miserable wet conditions was an old golfing colleague, friend, and (Bell had thought) Liberal supporter. Not anymore. For Bell, and many other Liberal MLAs, these kinds of surprise moments showed just how out of touch they were with voter anger over the tax.

On June 30, 2010, Vander Zalm boarded the 11 a.m. Tsawwassen ferry, behind the wheel of a rented Budget flat-panel truck. Inside were eighty-five boxes, containing 705,643 signatures from disgruntled voters in every riding cross the province.

On the Victoria side, as many as fifty supporters wearing yellow Fight HST shirts gathered outside the Elections BC office on Quebec Street, just a block from the legislature, waiting for Vander Zalm to arrive. They swarmed the street as the truck drove up, Vander Zalm playfully honking the horn, bringing any other traffic to a halt as the media gathered around to witness the spectacle. Vander Zalm hopped into the back of the truck and began hauling out boxes, posing for pictures as the supporters chanted "recall, recall." It was a full-blown circus atmosphere.

"We're going to keep fighting!" he declared from his perch on the truck, to cheers below.

And he would. The Fight HST folks quickly moved to target several Liberal MLAs for recall campaigns, the most notable of which was Science and Universities Minister Ida Chong in Oak Bay-Gordon Head.

The recall campaign sent chills through the Liberal benches, as Chong was put through the ringer in her own riding. One long-time supporter, who'd worked on every Chong campaign since 1996, wrote a letter to the local paper disowning her. A home near a local high school that had previously displayed pro-Chong signs now had a giant "Recall Ida Chong" placard. Her phone began ringing with supporters asking her to never contact them again for future fundraisers.

The campaign to fight the HST would be pushed by an unlikely alliance: former Social Credit premier Bill Vander Zalm and long-time NDP strategist Bill Tieleman would deliver enough signatures to force a referendum on the tax. BILL TIELEMAN

Chong's mother, who got her news primarily from Chinese-language media, asked her daughter abruptly one day why people hated her so much. Her mother's Chinese friends were asking too, as if her daughter had brought some sort of shame to the family.

The recall campaigns wouldn't come close to being successful. Canvassers gathered only half the 15,368 signatures needed in Chong's case. But they were still deeply emotional, difficult experiences for the MLAs, and brought fear to the Liberal caucus.

EVEN THE GOVERNMENT knew Vander Zalm had won. BC's business community tried to mount a court challenge, but lost. Elections BC certified the results, revealing 557,383 verified signatures—blowing away the 299,611 threshold that had been required.

Vander Zalm's draft bill to kill the HST went to a legislature committee. The Liberal-dominated committee had two choices: put the bill to kill the HST before the legislature, where they could pass or defeat it quickly, or send it to a referendum. Committee chair Terry Lake felt the best bet, with so many angry voters on Vander Zalm's signature list, was to put it to a province-wide vote and dissipate the anger. This made sense because, under law, the recall act stipulated the vote would be non-binding and would be conducted under strict rules—it required a majority of registered voters across the province to vote in favour of the idea, plus more than half the registered voters in at least two-thirds of the eighty-five electoral districts as well. A massive feat.

But Campbell intervened. Without consulting any ministers or MLAs, he emerged publicly to declare the HST referendum would be binding and he'd accept a simple 50 per cent majority vote to kill the tax.

Lake and the committee were blindsided. Had they known Campbell would lower the threshold and make the vote easier, they would have simply sent the bill to the House and passed it. But the premier was, as usual, marching to the beat of his own drum.

Within Campbell's own cabinet, ministers were beginning to look at their boss and think, The premier's losing his edge.

BEFORE THE VOTE, the premier knew he had to do something. The HST had caught fire on the basis that it would increase costs for ordinary British Columbians. So Campbell took to the airwaves province-wide on the evening of October 27, 2010, to announce a 15 per cent personal income tax cut for incomes up to $72,293—the second-largest tax cut in the province's history.

Campbell phoned several caucus members after he announced the decision, to ask what they'd thought. The results were mixed. Some felt it put the right amount of money back in people's pockets to compensate for the extra costs they'd face under the HST. Others felt it sent the public mixed signals to give money back, when the whole point of the HST was to generate enough revenue to keep government out of deficit.

Lake, who was still incredulous at Campbell's snap decision to lower the referendum threshold, decided to be blunt when the premier called.

"I think," he said, "that it's absolutely the wrong thing to do."

Campbell spent the entire next day travelling the Lower Mainland doing media interviews, trying to sell the tax cut. But instead of getting accolades, he faced questions about whether this was all just a last-ditch attempt to improve his popularity and dismal personal approval ratings. An Angus-Reid poll outlined the crash in Campbell's popularity: only 6 per cent of British Columbians who responded said they'd vote Liberal in the next election if Campbell remained leader.

The premier was dejected—and tired. He went into one of his reflective moods and abruptly announced he was travelling that weekend to spend time with his son Geoff and grandchildren in Los Angeles, where Geoff was working as a vice-president for technology company Sling TV. He asked his staff not to contact him, an unusual step for a premier who always wanted to know what was going on.

Meanwhile, behind the scenes, the Liberal caucus was starting to fracture. MLAs were still petrified of the prospect of facing recall campaigns. There were rumours swirling about a letter signed by dissidents, to be used to force Campbell out if he didn't leave soon. Caucus whip John van Dongen was putting out feelers to MLAs about whether or not they supported Campbell, and if they'd sign a letter calling on the premier to resign. The idea was to present it at the next caucus meeting, on Campbell's return from Los Angeles.

The key players in the dissent appeared to be van Dongen, Abbott, and caucus chair Gordie Hogg, who several people say were agitating behind the scenes to force Campbell out for different reasons but managed to keep just enough distance to maintain clean hands if the situation went sideways.

There were lots of phone calls, though. Conference calls even, where dissidents dialed in to speak to one another as a group. In addition to Hogg and Abbott, the rebels included van Dongen, Energy Minister Bennett, Donna Barnett, John Rustad, Ralph Sultan, Joan Macintyre, and Randy Hawes, to name a few.

Van Dongen continued to encourage people to sign his letter. Whether it actually existed as a printed document during this frantic, messy, mutinous time is a point of contention. Key rebels like Abbott, Hogg, and Bennett insist they never actually saw a letter, and didn't sign it. Campbell loyalist and senior minister Coleman did see it—and the signatures of seven or eight people.

The premier was certainly aware. Friend and former Liberal MLA Gary Collins began his own call-around urging MLAs not to do anything rash and to let Campbell make his own decision on his own time. The feeling among Campbell's friends was that he intended to resign anyway by the next summer, and he wanted to take the entire HST fiasco with him.

Campbell returned to Vancouver, worked from home on Monday, November 1, 2010, and called his staff together the following day to tell them he'd decided to quit. He told his cabinet on November 3, then held a snap press conference.

"When public debate becomes focused on one person, as opposed to what's in the best interests of the province of British Columbia, we've lost sight of what is important," Campbell said to a crowded room of journalists. "When that happens, it's time for a change."

CAMPBELL'S RESIGNATION CAME only seventeen months into his third term, though he said he would stay on the job until February to accommodate the party leadership race.

That decision was not appreciated by all MLAs, some of whom wanted Campbell, the public lightning rod for the HST, gone immediately. The longer he stayed, even as an outgoing leader, the more unpopular he and the party became.

Among those who wanted him gone immediately was Energy Minister Bennett. Bennett had survived an initial attack on Campbell in late October 2010, when he'd sharply criticized the premier in *The Vancouver Sun* for reorganizing the so-called dirt ministries of natural resources, energy, and forests without consulting him or other key ministers. The premier uncharacteristically let the insubordination slide, possibly because he was consumed by his internal debate over his future.

But now that Campbell had decided not to leave immediately, Bennett ratcheted up his game. He went on radio station CKNW to tell guest host Mike Smyth that Campbell should leave sooner rather than later. The comments cost Bennett his job. When he showed up at the next cabinet meeting in Vancouver, on November 17, 2010, he was fired.

That was enough to tip the ostracized, now former energy minister over the edge. He decided to fly to the legislature that day and speak his mind to the press corps stationed there about what it was like to work for the premier. But when Bennett went to book his Helijet, he found out the Liberals had cancelled his credit card. His government-issued phone no longer worked either. Bennett borrowed some cash, arrived in Victoria, convened a hasty press conference at the "blue curtain" media site behind the legislative chamber, and let loose.

Even among veterans with decades of experience covering the legislature, it was a remarkable moment. For almost forty minutes, Bennett ripped in to Campbell as a premier, party leader, and human being.

"I'm going to tell the truth," he said. "I'm tired of the bullshit that goes on in politics and I'm really tired of the way Gordon Campbell thinks he can just run on people. He can run on me. I'm a tough guy. I can take it. But I've seen him do it to other people in our caucus. You have almost a battered-wife syndrome inside our caucus today, inside our cabinet. It's really sad. And all the man has to do to give the BC Liberal party a chance to renew itself is to leave."

The Liberal party was "going down the toilet" and facing implosion as long as Campbell stayed, said Bennett. The premier yelled at people, swore at them, shouted at them until they broke down and cried, and held his caucus together through intimidation.

"He's not a nice man," Bennett said.

Bennett told an extraordinary story about a caucus retreat in Merritt that was followed by a fundraiser in a barn at a ranch for Yale-Lillooet MLA Dave Chutter. Bennett, a rookie MLA at the time, thought the caucus retreat had "seemed a bit lame," without real opportunities for MLAs to contribute. He told some colleagues, who then told the premier, and pretty soon he was summoned behind a barn to meet Campbell.

"He took me behind the barn and started to shout at me and got right up in my face and he was so upset that spittle came out of his mouth and got on my face," recalled Bennett. "Here he is, the premier of the province and he's spitting at me."

The media event with Bennett was so incredible and went on for so long that it prompted spectacularly bizarre questions, like the one posed by Canadian Press correspondent Dirk Meissner: "Did he, like, gob in your face or was it... like spray?" (Let history show, for the record, it was spray.)

The spectacular tirade caught the attention of Christy Clark, the former deputy premier under Campbell who was now hosting her own radio show on CKNW.

"Gordon Campbell is a very, very tough man to work for," Clark said on her show. "He likes control too much. He is profoundly impatient with people who he thinks are too slow to catch up."

Campbell tried to brush off Bennett's critiques in public.

"It's very hard to know how to respond to those kinds of comments," he said in reply. "But let me say this: I've been leader of the party for seventeen years and you don't manage to have that kind of service by being a bully."

WITH THE LIBERALS crumbling, the NDP was poised to take advantage of Campbell's weakness. But New Democrats were once again beset by infighting, this time after the loss of the 2009 election. A group of thirteen internal dissidents—nicknamed the Baker's Dozen—had set about trying to overthrow NDP leader Carole James.

It had all started shortly after the 2009 election, in which the NDP had gained two seats but still lost 35–49 to the Liberals. On election night, May 14, James finished her concession speech at a Victoria conference centre and was walking back to her home in James Bay with chief of staff Jim Rutkowski when she said, "I'm not going to run again. I can't run as leader again. It's going to get tough and I don't know if I have the stomach for that kind of fight."

Rutkowski talked her down, saying she shouldn't make any rash decisions on election night. But in her gut, after losing the 2005 and 2009 elections, James was worried that the knives would come out for her as leader. She was right.

After a month of touring ridings and talking to members, James was persuaded to stay on because of her high profile and how close the party had come in 2009, winning 42 per cent of the popular vote.

Not everyone was willing to give her a third shot. The mutiny started with Bob Simpson, the outspoken former Liberal organizer who joined the NDP and won the riding of Cariboo North in 2005. Simpson penned an opinion piece on the *Welcome to Williams Lake* website in October 2010 that criticized both James and Campbell for their lack of commitments in recent speeches to the BC Union of Municipalities. Simpson had a reputation for being outspoken—some might say a scheming troublemaker—and he fully admitted he expected to get a slap on the wrist from his own leader. Instead, James phoned Simpson the evening of October 6 and told him she was ejecting him from the NDP caucus.

The unilateral decision sent ripples through the party. Later that month, caucus chairman Norm MacDonald resigned his position in protest.

The rebellion was just simmering at that point. But it caught fire on November 17, 2010. Veteran MLA Jenny Kwan set up a meeting with James in Vancouver at the NDP's caucus offices. When the meeting was set to start, Kwan showed up with MacDonald and caucus whip Katrine Conroy. They gave her a letter that contained the signatures of thirteen MLAs demanding she submit to a leadership convention. The other names included MLAs Claire Trevena, Doug Routley, Leonard Krog, Lana Popham, Harry Lali, Robin Austin, Michael Sather, Gary Coons, Guy Gentner, and Nicholas Simons.

Overall, there were a variety of complaints about James and her leadership, ranging from a feeling she just didn't have the popularity to win an election to complaints about her caucus management style as being unaccommodating, closed to criticism, and unilateral.

Two days later, caucus whip Conroy stepped down in a press conference that saw her flanked by MLAs Kwan, Popham, and Trevena. It was one of the first public indications of how deep the infighting had become. Popham and Trevena fled the room without saying much, only serving to bait reporters who then roamed the halls of the legislature confronting any NDP MLAs they could find to try to determine the extent of the problem with James's leadership.

The running gunfight continued into an extraordinary meeting of the NDP's provincial council, set at the Laurel Point Hotel in Victoria on November 20, 2010. James had said it marked "a line in the sand" on her leadership: if she emerged with confidence to continue, then there would be repercussions for those who failed to fall into line.

As dozens of NDP power brokers, local organizers, labour heavyweights, and MLAs gathered inside a conference room at the harbourfront hotel, staff loyal to James began circulating yellow scarves and pins in a show of solidarity with the leader. Soon almost the entire room was full of people wearing yellow scarves—except for the Baker's Dozen, who were publicly outed among their peers in the party as the rebels.

The "night of the yellow scarves," as it became known, was highly influenced by MLA Sue Hammell, a James loyalist. Hammell and MLA Mable Elmore were responsible for handing out the scarves to caucus colleagues. Elmore and fellow MLA Nicholas Simons almost ended up in a fist fight at one point because Simons refused to take a scarf from Elmore.

The provincial council voted 84 per cent to reject a leadership convention. Labour leaders emerged to suggest the rebels fall in line or leave the party. James urged caucus to unite around her. Her strongest supporter at the time was a big outspoken MLA from Juan de Fuca named John Horgan.

"I support Carole James," he told media. "I've always supported Carole James."

Behind the scenes, Horgan had been seething about the betrayals within caucus. He treated the Baker's Dozen roughly, showcasing a quick temper that he'd unleash on the dissidents to their faces. Voices were raised. Egos were bruised. The rebels were being unfaithful to the cause and to their leader, he felt. Some were just looking for attention and their moment in the TV spotlight, Horgan said at one point.

The loyalty Horgan showed James is worth noting. Their bond would go on to influence New Democrat politics in remarkable ways over the next seven years, well beyond the limited impact of the Baker's Dozen. Horgan had James's back. And when the time was right, years later, she'd have his.

But at that moment, even the strong showing at the provincial council failed to quell the dissidents. Kwan escalated the fight by releasing an open letter on December 1, 2010, that called for James to resign. That weekend saw the party's elder statesmen and former premiers dragged into the mess, expressing a variety of opinions to the media about whether James should stay or the rebels be expelled. The situation was deteriorating rapidly. Some warned the party was on the verge of self-destruction.

James called an emergency meeting for Sunday at the Four Seasons Hotel in Vancouver, where she planned to warn that those who failed to follow the will of the majority would be held accountable for their actions—a veiled threat that they would be ejected from the NDP.

But the meeting never happened. Instead, the BC Federation of Labour and United Steelworkers—powerful NDP donors—held a mediation meeting with the thirteen dissidents to see if there was a way to resolve the dispute. Talks went on late into Sunday evening, and James got her last update at 11 p.m. from chief of staff Jim Rutkowski, telling her there was a mix of some MLAs who wanted to keep talking beyond the weekend and others who'd dug in their heels.

James needed to make a decision. She began pacing around the kitchen of her James Bay townhouse, eventually tiring out her husband, Al, who asked if there was any help he could provide before going to bed. Alone, she wrote as many as five lists of pros and cons, preferring handwriting to computer typing because it helped organize her thoughts (James still writes her own speeches by hand).

By 1:30 a.m., James had organized her lists and made up her mind. She woke her husband and phoned Rutkowski, to tell them she planned to resign that morning. Once the decision had been made, she felt a great sense of relief.

A few hours later, at a hastily called press conference inside the Opposition leader's office at the legislature, James broke the news that she was stepping down.

"I know there'll be individuals who see this as a win for the bullies and that goes against any part of my moral fibre," she told reporters. "But I have to tell you that the alternative of having thirteen people walk away, and our party spending time and energy trying to rebuild those ridings, trying to bring back those individuals, and spending another three months divided off, isn't an alternative either."

During her press conference, James was stoic as she pushed back against MLAs who'd ousted her. But when she mentioned her family, she faltered and began to cry. Few knew it at the time, but the personal stress James had been under during the election and its aftermath was immense. Her son, Evan, had battled alcoholism for much of his young life. He'd overdosed on Tylenol several times, in cries for help. The day before the televised leaders debate, James's daughter Alison burst into her room in tears to tell her mom Evan had overdosed again. James immediately flew to Victoria and visited Evan in the hospital, where he was recovering.

But the TV leaders debate—a marquee event in any election campaign—could not be rescheduled. She returned to Vancouver the next day, cried, compartmentalized, braced for the bright lights of the province-wide event, and gave a strong performance against Campbell.

By the time the rebels had come to topple her as leader in the fall of 2010, Evan was making progress in treatment. James had also learned she was to become a grandmother, when Evan's girlfriend (and future wife), Bronwyn, was pregnant. Almost no one, outside of a small handful of trusted aides, knew the full story of James and her son at the time. As pressure grew for her to resign, Evan, who'd required his mother's help for so many years, stepped up to become a critical part of James's support network. After James's resignation press conference, the first email she received was from Evan. It said, simply, "Province's loss, our gain."

The NDP asked what kind of gift James would like, as departing leader. She asked the party to make a donation to the Umbrella Society in Victoria, which had helped her son successfully enter treatment.

Though toppled as leader, James refused to resign her Victoria-Beacon Hill seat. She surprised many by choosing to stay in the party, working alongside those who'd pushed her out of the leadership and providing advice and counsel to two subsequent party leaders (both of whom,

Adrian Dix and John Horgan, were James loyalists throughout the rebellion). Much to the chagrin of those who tried to push her out, James evolved into a kind of beloved elder stateswoman of the party, dutifully working the fundraising circuit for other MLAs, speaking at party events, and continuing in a leading role as both a critic and election platform architect. In the end, James would outlast most of her critics in the Baker's Dozen, half of whom had quit by the time the NDP returned to power in 2017.

When James walked onstage at Government House to be named finance minister and deputy premier on July 18, 2017, she received the loudest applause of the event. The entire room stood and clapped. Even the rebels who remained got on their feet for their deputy premier. The Baker's Dozen may have won the battle on James's leadership in 2010. But Carole James would eventually win the war.

JAMES AND CAMPBELL shared goodbye tributes in the legislature on their last day together. MLAs from both sides of the House rose to pay tribute to the two on February 17, 2011, their final day as premier and Opposition leader. James and Campbell, long-time political foes, also shared compliments about each other.

Campbell, now sixty-two, was reflective about his time in office during interviews that day. He told funny stories, like the time during his first throne speech in 2001 when he'd legislated angry nurses back to work and they showed up to throw shoes at him while he stood on the legislature's front steps waiting for the lieutenant-governor. Nobody was throwing shoes now, but with the sting of the HST still present, Campbell left public office as polarizing and unpopular a figure with some voters as when he'd started.

"People often in the job say, 'Are you having fun?' And I say, 'I'm not particularly having fun but it's a rewarding job,'" Campbell said. "I feel really lucky to have had a chance to do it. But, frankly, I'm really pleased to be leaving."

CHAPTER 2
THE INSIDER'S OUTSIDER

I t was Christy Clark's forty-fifth birthday party, and almost everyone crowded into her tiny half-duplex on Vancouver's West 16th Avenue was happy, having a few drinks, and—as tends to occur when politicos gather—engaged in a vigorous debate about BC politics.

The issue at hand, being batted around by almost fifty guests, was Gordon Campbell's future as premier. Could he withstand the immense blowback over the HST, or would the tax drive him out of office?

Clark was in the minority. As Campbell's former deputy premier, she knew first-hand that the wily former mayor was a political survivor. He'd survived drunk driving and the carbon tax, and, as Clark loudly predicted to anyone who would listen, he'd survive the HST too. He had a gift for political strategy, and he'd find his way out of the mess, Clark argued.

As the conversation lingered on that birthday evening of October 29, 2010, more than one person concluded their opinion with a post-script to Clark directly: You know, they said, you should really consider replacing him as premier yourself. Clark brushed off the overtures as nothing more than the happy musings of drunk party guests who, like her, had spent a lifetime in the trenches of politics.

But five days later, Campbell abruptly announced his resignation. Suddenly Clark's phone started lighting up with calls from stone-cold sober friends and allies to say, seriously, Christy, you should run for Liberal leader.

Clark's reaction to the first wave of propositions was no. She'd been an MLA from 1996 to 2005, when she'd resigned after Campbell, who viewed her as a threat to his leadership, had stuffed her into the perpetual bad-news job of children and family development minister. She'd since signed a five-year contract to continue on as a radio host on CKNW 980 AM in Vancouver, where *The Christy Clark Show* was a popular fixture, giving her a good income, a high profile, and time to spend with her son, Hamish, which was another reason for her resignation in 2005. To go back into politics, she thought, was a step backwards. Though it hadn't stopped her from trying to run for a mayoral nomination in Vancouver in 2005.

Still, her friends and colleagues wouldn't give up. Within Clark's inner circle, phones began to buzz with messages. There were visits from her brother, Bruce Clark, and from her ex-husband, Mark Marissen. Both had heard Clark on her own radio show saying she had no interest in the leader's job. Bruce went to see her first and pleaded with his sister to reconsider. Marissen showed up next.

"It's not often you get to become a premier," he told her.

Despite being exes, Clark and Marissen nonetheless still had a close, trusting relationship. Clark describes Marissen as one of her best friends and a key sounding board for political advice. As the years went by, there was no bigger public defender of Clark on social media than Marissen. Many couldn't understand why Clark's ex-husband would launch himself on attackers with such a vigorous defence of his ex, especially after Marissen remarried. But Clark and Marissen's divorce in 2008 had been largely amicable. They managed to settle it all without lawyers. In the process, they'd formed a tight co-parenting unit for their son. And so Marissen, despite their history, had become one of her top advisors, best friends, and fiercest defenders. He was also a skilled political operator in his own right, having cut his teeth as a major organizer for the federal Liberal party and former prime minister Paul Martin.

Kim Haakstad, Clark's long-time political assistant, was on the beach in Florida on vacation in November 2010 when she started getting texts from Clark and old colleagues about the idea of maybe running for leadership of the Liberal party. Originally from Grand Prairie, Alberta, Haakstad had worked for Clark since her days as a Liberal opposition MLA and was deeply loyal.

Mike McDonald was there from the start too. Long-time friends, they'd worked together organizing the provincial Liberals in the early 1990s under then-leader Gordon Wilson, and McDonald had gone on to help Gordon Campbell become premier. Quiet and soft-spoken, McDonald is nonetheless a brilliant strategist and campaigner with a long memory for facts, figures, and political trivia from BC's history. He's often the most cautious of Clark's group, repeatedly bringing up the risks and potential negatives of a decision, earning him, from some, the affectionate nickname Eeyore.

At first the question was not if Clark should run, but if it was even possible. The group dived into their contacts, identifying possible key supporters and political allies, trying to figure out who they knew that could even make a leadership bid possible.

Clark's friends had hesitations.

Michele Cadario, who'd helped Paul Martin ascend to the prime minister's office as his campaign director, and then his deputy chief of staff, asked Clark out to dinner to talk.

"Are you sure you really want to run?" she asked. "You'd be great, but understand this is a real personal sacrifice for you."

Cadario talked about the bubble that leaders can find themselves in, and how isolating the job can be because everyone wants something from you, always. It would be especially hard for Clark, then a forty-five-year-old single mother, Cadario advised. It would also completely upheave Clark's life. She'd have to commit to a gruelling travel schedule that would take her across the province for events. It would be exhausting.

"Those are good things to think about," Clark said to her friend in return.

But really, they both knew she was probably going to do it anyway.

MARISSEN APPROACHED KEY organizers in the Indo-Canadian community. Bruce Clark, in his first week, secured a million dollars in campaign commitments. But with no money in hand, the team couldn't do any polling. Marissen called his old friend David Herle. The former Paul Martin advisor ran the Gandalf Group and was a regular pundit on CBC's *The National*. Marissen told him he didn't have any money for polling, but if his ex-wife got in the race the bill would be paid. Herle took the job, and what he found was good news for Clark. Among Liberal members in many rural ridings, plus Burnaby, Port Coquitlam, and Vancouver, Clark was the front-runner. But it wasn't going to be a runaway. The polling also showed the possibility that other candidates for the party leadership were tainted by the HST and likely to get slaughtered in the next election by the NDP, and that she, as the outsider, had the best chance of revitalizing the party.

Clark's outside status would be a key selling point of her leadership bid. Angry voters, still looking for someone to blame for the HST after Campbell's departure, would have a hard time pinning it on someone who wasn't even there when the tax was approved. She had just enough distance from the party to be bulletproof to its most recent scandals—even though her political career in Liberal backrooms, which started in 1991, was actually longer than most of her rivals' experiences combined. She was the insider masquerading as the outsider.

Clark needed fresh faces on her team. Marissen introduced her to Ken Boessenkool, an Albertan who'd served as an advisor to Prime

Minister Stephen Harper. Boessenkool had conservative credentials that Clark was desperately looking for to balance her background with the federal Liberals. He agreed to come on and run Clark's leadership campaign.

That didn't sit well with Harper's office, which let Boessenkool know he'd lose his spot on Harper's re-election team if he helped Clark. The federal Conservatives wanted to support Kevin Falcon for leader, and they weren't going to lift a finger to help Clark, a federal Liberal. Frightened, Boessenkool abandoned the campaign before it really even got started.

But none of this deterred Clark. With polling indicating her former party was about to get annihilated in the next election, she decided she was the best person to ride to the rescue.

Yet there were other tactical concerns before Clark launched. She needed to have a serious and likely chance of winning, because no one wanted a repeat of her bid to capture the Non-Partisan Association civic party nomination for Vancouver mayor in 2005, in which the former deputy premier lost a bitter slog of a battle to then–city councillor Sam Sullivan.

By the middle to end of November, Clark was fully committed to running. She publicly announced the campaign on December 8, 2010.

Clark didn't need much help with communications. She quickly showed her chops as a good, positive communicator within the party and the media, generating her own surge in coverage and attendance at events through her skilled public speaking and ability to schmooze.

As he was bailing on the campaign, Boessenkool recommended a friend, Dimitri Pantazopoulos, to help with polling. His right-wing credentials were a plus, and he went on to prove himself a valuable pollster for Clark in future years.

McDonald had to scramble to now direct the leadership campaign. He had been living in Ladysmith but moved to Vancouver, where he spent three months sleeping on a couch at his mother's place and working out of an unglamorous campaign office at the corner of Richards and West Georgia.

The Clark campaign commissioned a public opinion survey in December that showed Clark twenty points ahead of rival George Abbott and thirty points ahead of Falcon. Her supporters felt it was a good reflection of how core Liberals wanted change within the party, because the polling was done before the campaigns signed up tens of thousands of new members.

As the leadership race began, the camps broke down roughly as follows.

George Abbott had the backing of the most caucus members, with twenty supporters, including many of the rebels who were unhappy with Campbell's leadership and had felt neglected under his reign. A serious policy wonk, Abbott was known for his long, drawn-out, professorial speeches, but also a dry, self-deprecating sense of humour. His campaign slogan was "The people are coming!" with a drawing of a flaming torch. It gave the odd impression of some sort of unruly mob coming to burn down the party.

Kevin Falcon had the backing of BC's business community, deep ties to Surrey from his days organizing there, and the backing of the federal Conservatives (including former MP John Reynolds, who warned that if Clark won she'd split the party apart). He was young, smart, well-connected, and politically on the rise to superstardom. For most, he was the odds-on favourite to win. He had the backing of powerful organizer and cabinet minister Rich Coleman, who'd abandoned his own bid earlier in favour of supporting Falcon. On top of all that, Falcon also had nineteen caucus supporters, just one short of Abbott and a clear sign the caucus was divided.

Former attorney general Mike de Jong had no caucus support, and his campaign promise to force MLAs to post their expense forms online was (to put it mildly) unpopular among his colleagues.

Campaigns by cabinet minister Moira Stilwell and Parksville mayor Ed Mayne were short-lived and unremarkable.

Clark had the backing of only one MLA, Harry Bloy, from Burnaby-Lougheed. The rest were either ambivalent about her chances or outright hostile. But what many did not notice at the time was the number of supporters Clark had who were ex-MLAs, especially in ridings the party no longer held. This was the key to her strategy, after the party changed its constitution early in the race to bring in a weighted system of voting in an attempt to be fair to members in ridings across the province. The change capped leadership votes at one hundred for each of the ridings, no matter how many members were there.

It meant that, ironically, to win the Liberal leadership Clark would target ridings held by the NDP. A riding the party had no hope of winning back from the NDP in an election might only have a handful of Liberal members but was still worth one hundred points. Sign up just a few new members and you could win the riding—and the points. That made it just as valuable as expending considerable energy signing up thousands of new members in a Liberal-held, membership-rich riding in, say, Surrey.

The Clark campaign connected with former Liberal MLAs who'd won unconventional ridings for the party during its great sweep of 2001, when the Liberals had crushed the NDP to only two seats. These kinds of ex-MLAs became Clark's unconventional power brokers in the less-travelled corners of the province. Clark found herself visiting Terrace, Prince Rupert, Fort Nelson, and other areas off the beaten path. While some existing Liberal MLAs were openly hostile to her leadership aspirations, others were at least polite enough to show her some hospitality when she arrived. And once they saw her speak and connect with members, some were shocked at how good she was.

Bill Bennett, for example, described it like this in a later *Vancouver Sun* interview:

I supported George Abbott because George was a rural guy and friend and just didn't know Christy Clark that well. I admit to having some questions about her commitment to understanding policy at a deep enough level. I wasn't sure that she had the work ethic. I didn't know her and wasn't based on any objective analysis on my part...

I watched her perform in the leadership contest, and she came to Cranbrook and asked if I could introduce her. I think it was the only place in the province where an MLA supporter of another candidate wanted to introduce her. I thought it was a courtesy thing to do in my home community.

She gave this really thoughtful, genuine and authentic speech to 100 to 150 people in this room which was a large crowd for that leadership contest. She really connected with people.

And that's when I wondered if I'd made a mistake in who I was supporting.

Bennett wasn't even in the Liberal caucus at the time, having been kicked out by Campbell. He asked Clark about whether she'd be an autocratic micromanager like Campbell and received assurances she "wouldn't be having her fingers in the pie all the time." Bennett's riding would end up being an example of a strong Abbott riding that flipped to Clark in the final ballot at the leadership convention.

It was still key for each candidate to sign up as many new Liberal members as they could, to try to flood the vote with their supporters. It sounds complicated, but becoming a Liberal member was simple: fill out a short form and fork over ten dollars. Your membership was good for four years.

As the mass sign-ups continued throughout the province, a few problems popped up.

There was the cat, named Olympia, that someone on the Clark campaign team thought would be a hilarious joke to sign up as a Liberal member. The party claimed the cat would have been caught in vetting. But its registration deepened rivals' suspicions that Clark would play fast and loose with the rules in her attempt to win.

And the Clark campaign was not alone in having membership hiccups. At one point, over-eager Falcon campaigners signed up the entire roster of the Kamloops Blazers hockey team without their knowledge.

Clark's policy platform was a mixture of populist ideas and fiscal conservatism. She wanted a reversal of recent cuts to community gaming grants, a new holiday (later to be called Family Day), and a new auditor general's office to poke around the books of municipal governments. She also promised to hold a town-hall meeting every month and make "increased use of open line radio"—those two promises worth noting if for no other reason than they were later very quickly ignored. In debates, Clark's opponents accused her of not knowing what she was talking about and not thinking through her policies. But none of their platforms were particularly inspiring either.

Campaigning aside, the mechanics of the actual leadership vote had been chosen by the party and would involve more than fifty thousand members getting a personal identification number (PIN) that they could then use to vote online or by telephone. The party was mailing the numbers to each member across BC. But as the vote neared, there were thousands of members, especially in rural BC, who'd yet to get their PINs and couldn't vote. As many as 30 per cent of members in the Peace region and on Vancouver Island still didn't have their PINs the day before the election, and a toll-free line the party had set up to help was overwhelmed with the flood of calls.

The Falcon campaign viewed this as a disturbing sign and suggested the election might need to be extended by a couple of days so all the members could vote. But the party pressed ahead.

Numerous supporters began contacting the Falcon campaign to say they'd tried to vote, only to be told their PIN had already been used to cast a ballot. The Falcon team strongly suspected the security around the PINs had been broken. At one point, a Falcon supporter provided the party with evidence of Clark's campaign having taken stacks of membership forms and matched them using pre-paid ten-dollar Visa gift cards to generate potentially hundreds of PINs.

There were also allegations that operatives would gather at so-called PIN parties at someone's house with hundreds, if not thousands, of dubious PINs they'd collected and use them to cast votes for one candidate over the course of an evening. Some senior figures within the party knew with certainty that the PIN parties were going on, and that they were held for multiple candidates, not just Clark.

Despite all the complaints, the party either couldn't or wouldn't get to the bottom of the evolving mess. And there were other, unconfirmed, allegations of impropriety.

Two years later, a whistleblower who worked on the Clark campaign under the direction of Harry Bloy would tell the RCMP she allegedly saw wrongdoing with the PINs within the Clark leadership campaign. Sepideh Sarrafpour would claim she was hired by Bloy to help with membership sign-ups for Clark and signed up close to seven hundred members without collecting their fees. She alleged she just gathered their membership forms and gave them to Bloy, who allegedly said he'd take care of the money. She further alleged seeing stacks of PINs on the desks of two Clark campaign office workers on voting day, as well as emails being sent to and forwarded by Bloy containing PINs.

Sarrafpour told all this to the Opposition NDP in June and July of 2013—two years after the Liberal race. She also had a larger story to tell, about a host of other unrelated allegations involving work inside the premier's office and on by-election campaigns. The NDP incorporated all of this into a sworn affidavit that they gave to the RCMP in August 2013.

Sarrafpour's allegations sparked an RCMP investigation under the direction of a special prosecutor. Mounties probed the case for three years and charged two Liberal operatives in relation to breach of trust and Elections Act accounting allegations in a 2012 provincial by-election. But there was never any mention of police having found any wrongdoing in the Liberal leadership race, including the misuse of PINS by the Clark campaign.

The party publicly said it was conducting audits of the integrity of the leadership vote, though no such audits were ever made public.

Even years later, a faint whiff of unpleasantness hangs over the 2011 Liberal leadership race. It would be more than six years before the Liberal party ever admitted anything had gone wrong. It did so in a roundabout way, in 2017, announcing its new leadership race would close a series of troublesome loopholes, eliminating personal expense exemptions in campaign spending, banning the use of pre-paid Visa cards for memberships, and alerting the PIN system method of voter authentication to include additional levels of security.

AS THE LEADERSHIP campaign neared its conclusion, the Clark campaign was confident it had the race well under control. A week before the end of the campaign, Mike McDonald reached out to Prime Minister Harper's chief of staff, Nigel Wright, through an intermediary, with a message: We're pretty sure we're going to win, and we want to start things on a fresh page if we do.

The results were announced to a crowd of MLAS, media, and Liberal supporters at the Vancouver Convention Centre on the night of February 26, 2011. Clark and her team huddled around a television in a holding room, watching the proceedings live. In the first round, she won almost 38 per cent of the vote, compared with 28 per cent for Falcon and 25 per cent for Abbott. De Jong was eliminated with 9 per cent. The numbers made Clark's team nervous. They'd hoped to be over 40 per cent and were surprised that Abbott, whom they viewed as stronger than Falcon, was in third place. In the second round, Clark's lead grew to 42 per cent, with Falcon trailing at 30 per cent and Abbott knocked off at 28 per cent. In the third and final ballot, Clark brought the race home with 52 per cent compared with Falcon's 48 per cent.

It took a moment for the results to settle across the room: the outsider with only one caucus supporter had defeated three cabinet ministers to win both the leadership of the party and the premiership. Clark's room broke out in celebration and cheers. As they spilled into the hallway and began walking into the convention centre to meet the crowd, McDonald's phone rang. It was the prime minister. Clark took the call and accepted Harper's congratulations. It proved an important first step in a reset of their relationship after the PMO's meddling in the race.

Clark arrived in the ballroom the triumphant victor and walked up to the stage. There was very little pause before major Liberal heavyweights like Coleman, Bell, and others scrambled up to stand behind her in a show of caucus solidarity. Eventually, all the Liberal MLAs were on the stage together, clapping and waving to the crowd.

"Change begins tonight," said Clark, flanked by the Liberal caucus. "We are going to shape the future of BC together. We are going to build a bigger, stronger coalition starting tonight."

Clark became the thirty-fifth premier of BC, the second female premier in the province's history (the first being Rita Johnston), and the second premier to take office without a seat in the legislature (the other being Bill Vander Zalm).

After the crowds cleared, the first place the victorious Clark campaign visited was Falcon's election party, at the former Shore Club restaurant on Dunsmuir Street. There, she and Falcon climbed up onto the bar to address the crowd in an attempt to bury any hard feelings. Falcon told his supporters to unite around Clark, even though, privately, he was deeply disappointed.

There were strong suspicions within the Falcon campaign that Clark had cheated to win. But Falcon never lodged an official complaint with the party, nor did he appeal the results of the election or speak publicly about the concerns he had with Clark's leadership bid. To do so, he calculated, would make him appear to be a sore loser and, ultimately, lead to a long-running division within the party between his and Clark's supporters. Falcon might not have liked Clark, but he liked even less the idea of doing anything to help the NDP win the next election.

"We're like a big family," Falcon said after the vote. "And at the end of the day, the family comes together and we'll all get behind her."

THE OUTGOING CAMPBELL regime refused to give Clark access to the Vancouver premier's office or any other government space, so Clark managed her transition from hotel rooms, her leadership office (which still had a lease), and her house. She began calling in Liberal MLAs one by one for introductory meetings at her hotel, starting with rival leadership candidates Falcon, Abbott, and de Jong. They also gauged during the chats the party's willingness to invite Blair Lekstrom and Bill Bennett back to the caucus, thereby unifying the party.

Lekstrom came down to Vancouver, where he met with caucus on March 2, 2011. He received more than a few hostile stares from former colleagues who'd toughed out the HST after he'd bailed on the party. The caucus voted to let Lekstrom back in at the premier's urging. But there were some MLAs who, until his retirement two years later, refused to fully forgive him.

After Clark won the leadership, she had asked Coleman to help smooth Bennett's return. The burly cabinet minister, with the nickname "Mr. Fixit" for his ability to solve problems within the party, dutifully helped guide Bennett's return. Coleman had been so mad at Bennett over how he'd treated Campbell that, in the months since, if he saw Bennett in the legislature hallway he'd simply turn around and walk in the opposite direction. He wouldn't speak to him. Pat Bell and Shirley Bond threatened to quit if Bennett was asked back into the party.

Bennett went before the Liberal MLAs in April to plead his case. He told them he regretted going too far in his public campaign to push the premier out, that he'd regret it for the rest of his life and would never do it again because of the impact it had had on his family.

Campbell loyalist Falcon sat in the front row, watching Bennett carefully. After the speech, he came up, shook his hand, and said welcome back.

IN HER FIRST cabinet, unveiled on March 14, 2011, Clark's main leadership rivals all got posts, including Falcon, who had publicly said he didn't want the finance ministry with all its complex numbers and calculations. Taking that into consideration, Clark gave Falcon finance. The new premier felt Falcon was negotiating just for show, and that of course he wanted to be minister of finance, the second-most powerful cabinet post inside government.

Behind the scenes, key members of BC's business community had phoned Falcon to ask that he take the portfolio, because they wanted his steady hand on the treasury while the province figured out what kind of premier Clark would become. Clark would also appoint him deputy premier, a nod toward the conservative side of the Liberal coalition. Despite that, Clark and Falcon would go on to have a strained relationship, at best. Years later, it's clear there's no love lost between them.

Abbott was given the education portfolio, along with the unenviable task of approaching the militant BC Teachers' Federation to work on a long-term labour deal almost no one believed was possible. And de Jong was installed in the massive health portfolio, where his main task was to drive down the growth of spending. The only MLA to support Clark's leadership bid, Harry Bloy, cashed in his chips to make cabinet too as social development minister.

With her leadership cemented and her cabinet in place, the only thing Clark needed was a seat in the legislature. Campbell provided

Christy Clark was sworn in as the second female premier of British Columbia by Lieutenant-Governor Steven Point on March 14, 2011. Her cabinet would include rivals from the leadership race, George Abbott, Kevin Falcon, and Mike de Jong. PROVINCE OF BC

the opportunity by resigning his Vancouver-Point Grey riding, which Clark narrowly won in a May 11, 2011, by-election.

Christy Clark had announced she was quitting provincial politics the first time on September 17, 2004. Now, just five and a half years later, she was back. This time she was the boss. But not everyone was thrilled. A few would do everything they could to make her life a living hell.

CHAPTER 3
CAPTAIN OF A MUTINOUS SHIP

t didn't take long for BC's thirty-fifth premier to realize the job she'd just fought to win was going to be a lot more unpleasant than she'd ever imagined.

At one of Clark's early cabinet meetings in 2011, she experienced what she considers the benchmark for insubordination within her cabinet. The group was discussing its policy platform, something that, at that point, was woefully bare. Then-finance minister Kevin Falcon grew agitated at the lack of substance in the policies, and as discussion drew on he lost his cool. That manifested itself, unusually, in a direct confrontation with Clark in front of the group.

"I can't fucking believe this," he said in a raised voice, hitting his pointed finger hard on the cabinet table repeatedly, surprising the rest of the room into silence. "We are headed toward a buzz saw of political oblivion... This is not leadership. We need leadership in this room."

To Clark, it was not only a breach of decorum in the running of her cabinet meetings, but also a direct challenge to her early authority. She deployed a strategy that would see frequent use in these days of perpetual rebellion: she just waited a minute to see if anyone else backed the criticism up and, if no one did, moved on without acknowledging her opponent's importance, while watching that person deflate. With Falcon, the situation was doubly awkward. She had defeated him for the leadership, and he remained a popular figure within caucus. They'd repaired things amicably enough; after all, he'd accepted the post of deputy premier.

The silent treatment nonetheless worked on this occasion. The cabinet moved on, while Falcon stayed silent. But Clark remembered it for a long time. She recalls the Falcon outburst as perhaps the most disrespectful thing any minister did—to her face—during her time as premier.

Falcon didn't mean it as an outright moment of insubordination. He'd been advocating a bold agenda, something that would set the party apart from the NDP and avoid what appeared to be a looming, crushing electoral loss. He was frustrated by what he saw as Clark's lack of policy detail in her earliest days as premier, compared with the jam-packed agenda enjoyed under Gordon Campbell. It was a common criticism during Clark's earliest days—that she was a skilled campaigner, but once in the job she didn't have much of a vision for the government.

In Falcon's mind, despite his loss in the leadership race, he'd been as loyal to Clark as possible. He didn't leak information or participate in any of the brewing mutinies organized by other MLAS. But Clark was hypersensitive to Falcon's actions, given his status and his support within the conservative side of the party, where she was most vulnerable. Their truce was fragile. In 2012, Falcon wrote an extraordinary letter to fellow ministers warning them not to make splashy funding announcements without his approval first—a veiled reference to the premier's announcement a week earlier of a new $73 million mental health facility at Vancouver General Hospital before the price tag had been approved by treasury board.

Ask Clark to describe these pre-2013 days and she'll come back with one word: terrible. At least half her caucus was a problem. Some were actively undermining her leadership behind her back. Others were agitating for a snap election to replace Clark with a new leader.

It wasn't the job Kevin Falcon wanted, but the man who came closest to defeating Christy Clark for the Liberal leadership was rewarded with the job of finance minister. Here he speaks to the media, on February 21, 2012. PROVINCE OF BC

And still more had mentally checked out of the job, choosing either to resign early or not run for re-election.

CLARK ARRIVED WITH the option of calling a snap election, which would have jettisoned her internal critics and, possibly, given her a refreshed and renewed mandate to govern. The new premier faced two years, two months, and eighteen days between winning the party leadership and the next scheduled provincial election, on May 14, 2013. It was a long haul, given the constant party infighting and backstabbing.

During her leadership campaign, Clark had telegraphed the idea of ending it all early.

"I think two and a half years in government as an unelected premier is an awful long time," she told the CBC. "I think British Columbians might be right to say... 'we want to get a chance to vote for you under the basic principles of democracy.'"

Clark's team was divided internally on whether this was the right move. Some had wanted to skip her by-election in Point Grey and send the entire province straight to the polls. But Clark wanted to see the HST referendum process through, which stretched from the spring to late summer in 2011.

That left a window for a snap election in the fall of 2011, which Clark also examined seriously. But Liberal party troops were tired. MLAs were still scared of ongoing recall campaigns. The party remained unpopular. The HST had fallen to defeat. The PST needed to be rebuilt and reintroduced. And the Liberals were the ones who'd legislated four-year fixed election dates and would be required to break their own law to trigger one early.

Ultimately, Clark went with her gut and didn't take the plunge. Which meant she chose to spend two years without a mandate from voters, facing a barrage of friendly fire from her own MLAs as one scandal after another rocked her party.

One positive effect of all the election speculation for the Liberals was what it did to the NDP. New Democrats got nervous, and leader Adrian Dix was forced to plan a party campaign team before he knew what Clark would decide. The NDP dubbed Clark's snap election deliberations the "false start" of the 2013 election. The party had to lock in its slate of candidates two years early, in the process rushing some less-than-impressive duds onto its roster.

CLARK HAD ONLY one deeply loyal MLA and cabinet minister on her side. Unfortunately for her, he was a failure.

Harry Bloy had been the only MLA to guess correctly who would win the party's leadership race. The MLA for Burnaby-Lougheed signed up early to back Clark's campaign and was her only caucus supporter. After her victory, Clark owed him a similar show of loyalty. So she had appointed him to her first cabinet as minister of social development.

From the moment he took the job, Bloy was in hopelessly over his head. And, unfortunately for him, a massive scandal was brewing inside his ministry. He would be in no way up for the challenge.

Victoria *Times Colonist* reporter Lindsay Kines began a series of devastating stories in June 2011 about Community Living BC, the government agency in charge of the province's developmentally disabled and most vulnerable people.

Kines had chronicled how CLBC was pressuring disabled people and their families to accept less care and less-expensive living arrangements by shuttering some facilities and moving people around. Worse, the agency was misleading the public about it. The core of the problem seemed to be government underfunding, which had left CLBC trying to squeeze savings out of its disabled clients.

Bloy was at a loss to explain publicly what was going on. Though a former businessman who'd created a chain of convenience stores with his brother, he seemed unable to retain extensive briefings in his portfolio, including question period prep.

Former minister Kevin Krueger offered to help, but he was rebuffed.

There were many, at the start, who thought Bloy was a decent guy. He was a devoted volunteer with the Boy Scout movement (he once showed up at the legislature on Boy Scout day wearing the full uniform). But his daily fumbling of the CLBC file exhausted any personal goodwill he might have had left from cabinet colleagues.

Veteran *Vancouver Sun* columnist Vaughn Palmer dubbed it a "sad" performance. "Clark did her supporter no favours by promoting him beyond his abilities," he wrote of Bloy.

In late September 2011, after only six months on the job, Clark shuffled her cabinet and dumped Bloy from the post. The CEO of CLBC was fired as well. The ministry needed someone with better communication skills, Clark said diplomatically.

Bloy was given a junior cabinet job as minister of state for multiculturalism. But even there controversy dogged him and he had to resign six months later. Bloy would leave politics in 2013, embittered at what he felt was unfair treatment at the hands of the media and the lack of recognition of his skills.

Clark's critics watched the flame-out of Bloy with a certain amount of satisfaction. They felt handing over the reins of the third-largest ministry in government to an under-qualified MLA just because he'd happened to guess correctly and support her leadership bid reflected the premier's poor judgement—and blind partisanship.

Meanwhile, the troubles left by Bloy within CLBC proved easy fodder for Liberal MLAS who wanted to find a reason to criticize Clark in public. Many of those critics had been miserable under Gordon Campbell and remained miserable under Clark. But CLBC gave them a reason to step out of line. Backbencher MLA for Abbotsford-Mission Randy Hawes, who'd been one of Clark's most vocal dissidents inside caucus, emerged to snipe at her in October 2011 for underfunding CLBC. Hawes called for a "top-to-bottom" review of CLBC, and suggested Bloy (and by extension his own government) had misled the public about the problems inside the agency.

Hawes and Clark didn't see eye to eye on much. He had supported George Abbott during the leadership campaign. One night during the campaign, when he was on a trip to Hawaii, he had consumed a few beers and was at a barbecue when his phone rang. He looked down and saw the name Lorne. Hawes assumed it was Lorne Valensky, Abbott's campaign manager.

"Christy is up by a little bit," said Lorne. "George is a bit back in second."

"There are bunch of MLAS, several, that have said if Christy wins this thing they will not sit with her," Hawes said. "They will resign before they sit with her. Maybe that should become public in this race. Maybe people should know."

Lorne at the other end of the line started to yell. "We all have to work together," he shouted.

Hawes suddenly realized that it wasn't Lorne Valensky. It was Lorne Mayencourt, a former MLA and one of Clark's strongest supporters and organizers. From then on, Hawes was on the outs with the premier.

But that didn't stop him from raising the prospect of a full-blown rebellion against Clark. He told the media he'd received "quiet support" from other Liberal colleagues about the premier's misguided priorities. Hawes portrayed himself as the first of many inside the party who were genuinely disappointed at the kind of premier Clark had become, and who were upset enough to break ranks and try to take her down publicly.

"They're going, 'Right on, right on. We're with you.' Many, many," said Hawes in late 2011. "Others I hope are about to say what they think. A lot of it will be carried on, I guess, within our caucus walls."

Internally, Clark was furious at the public dissension. She was trying to keep a tight lid on spending after inheriting a cash-strapped treasury that still had not fully recovered from the 2008 global recession, and she didn't feel there was enough money to fully fix CLBC's problems.

The Liberals tried to hash it out internally during a caucus meeting one night in Victoria. But when Clark made a passing reference to her decision to forgo an early election call, some in the room construed it as a threat to either shut up or face a snap election.

Caucus meetings are usually private closed-door sessions where MLAS get to vent and hash out disagreements without fear of reprisal. Even in the most dire of situations, it's rare for members to leak directly to a competing party. And yet, the next day, NDP leader Adrian Dix popped up in question period to bait Clark about leaked comments he'd been given from inside her own caucus room. It was the ultimate betrayal for someone to go squealing to the NDP. Privately, Liberals would confront Hawes for being the biggest leaker.

CLBC proved a slow-moving multi-month mess for the Clark administration in 2011. Bloy's having been given such an important job (and having messed it up) reflected poorly on her judgement. And it ate away at any goodwill she'd had remaining over her idea of a Families First agenda. Here were families of disabled people being mistreated by her government; how could she be trusted to take care of regular families?

Clark considered CLBC and the entire mess the lowest point in her earliest years. As if the infighting in her party weren't enough, Clark's Liberals were facing a serious threat on the right wing of the political spectrum with the upstart BC Conservative Party and its new leader, John Cummins. A former federal Conservative MP, Cummins brought a sense of legitimacy to a BC party that had, for decades, been a virtual non-entity in provincial politics. That worried the BC Liberals, who owed their sixteen years in power to Gordon Campbell's successful efforts to unite the centrist liberals and right-wing conservatives (mainly old Social Credit reformers) under a new free-enterprise coalition banner. If the conservatives broke ranks and joined a new party, all hope would be lost for BC Liberal re-election.

It was a serious risk at the time. And it started with Liberal MLA John van Dongen. On paper, van Dongen's credentials were impressive: a former solicitor general, minister of agriculture, and a four-term MLA who'd spent sixteen years in the political arena. But his most recent years had been spent as an outsider in his own party. The small, wiry, bearded MLA for Abbotsford South was now sitting as a backbencher. He'd fallen out of favour with Gordon Campbell when, during the 2009 election, he'd racked up so many speeding tickets that he'd lost his driver's licence. It was an embarrassing faux pas for the minister in charge of road safety. And it embarrassed the premier during an election campaign. Van Dongen was forced to resign. When Campbell won re-election, van Dongen was pushed out. He never made cabinet again.

Van Dongen had sat and stewed in political exile for years, trying to bring Campbell down. Like the other Campbell mutineers, he now turned on Clark. She hadn't seen fit to appoint him to cabinet either. He'd developed a serious grudge against her as well.

In his basement office in the legislature, van Dongen had accumulated binders of conspiratorial material involving Clark, the sale of the

BC Rail corporation, and government's decision to pay out $6 million in legal fees to two former Liberal aides as part of a plea deal in the long-running case. He'd tied Clark into the conspiracy, somehow, and demanded an inquiry and answers. He got neither.

By March 26, 2012, van Dongen had had enough. He informed the Liberal caucus in a brief two-paragraph statement he was quitting the party later that day. But he didn't tell his colleagues the whole story.

After question period, he rose in the House to make a personal statement. And that's when the other shoe dropped: van Dongen had not only quit, he'd joined the resurgent BC Conservatives. He took a shot at the "honesty, ethics, and personal character" he felt were lacking in the Liberal leadership, in reference to Clark, and raised concerns about the naming rights of a stadium.

"There have been other lapses in proper accountability, and I expect more to come. When more and more decisions are being made for the wrong reasons, then you have an organization that is heading for failure."

The defection to the Conservatives infuriated the Liberals. Now the Conservatives had an actual sitting MLA in the legislature and could claim to be a legitimate player on BC's political scene. Down in the basement of the building, van Dongen's defection was met with loud cheers from the NDP research offices.

Liberal staffers sprang into action—while van Dongen was still speaking they ran to his office and started furiously packing his things into cardboard boxes. By the time he'd finished his speech, all his belongings were sitting in the hallway and the keycard locks on his door had changed.

While staff were packing the boxes, Clark herself was finding out about the move. She was in a cabinet meeting when her executive assistant, Gabe Garfinkel, came in to whisper something in her ear.

"I have to bring you out of this," said Garfinkel. "John van Dongen crossed the floor."

Stone-faced, Clark looked at her cabinet colleagues, packed up her books, and walked out of the room.

In the hallway outside the legislative chamber, Rich Coleman was spitting mad. He went after van Dongen's character, telling the assembled press corps that his former colleague had been fighting significant personal battles.

"I've been concerned about John as a friend for a long period of time. He's been struggling with his role in public life," said Coleman. "He's had a lot of personal issues that he's had to deal with and he's been unhappy since he was no longer in cabinet in 2009. As a friend I know that because we've talked about it at length."

The vague allusions to personal problems caught the attention of journalists. And so, an hour later, when van Dongen stood side by side with BC Conservative leader John Cummins at a hotel across the street from the legislature, attention drifted away from the political importance of the moment and back onto van Dongen himself. What personal issues was he dealing with, reporters wanted to know.

To his credit, van Dongen didn't shy away from the issue. Yes, he admitted, he'd divorced his wife recently. Yes, he was now living with his constituency assistant. And yes, he had set her salary at $78,000 a year (higher than most assistants). But, he claimed, it was all above board. He'd even obtained legal opinions in writing, which he circulated to the reporters. Cummins stood by, glowering, watching his agenda get hijacked by van Dongen's love life.

The immediate effect of the van Dongen defection was a bump in BC Conservative popularity. A month later, polls put the Conservatives and Liberals tied for second place behind the NDP. The Liberals were falling in popularity. The Conservatives were rising. Even a 10 to 12 per cent showing by the BC Conservatives would have been enough to torpedo the Liberals' chances.

Clark spent much of 2012 trying to bolster her conservative credentials and fight off the collapse of the BC Liberal free-enterprise coalition.

To do this, Clark had to bury the hatchet with then–prime minister Stephen Harper's federal Conservative administration, which had been so hostile toward her initial leadership campaign.

Clark made several public appearances with Harper, most notably in January 2012 when she and the prime minister sat in the bleachers at her son's atom-league hockey game, cheering and drinking Tim Hortons like two ordinary hockey parents who just happened to be surrounded by a dozen armed RCMP bodyguards. Harper even stayed for all three periods of the game.

Clark recruited some of his ex-ministers, such as Chuck Strahl, Jay Hill, and Stockwell Day, to try to blunt the attack she faced on her right.

"Either you rally around the Liberals or you're going to have the NDP," Strahl said publicly at the time. He even persuaded his former chief of staff, Laurie Throness, to run for the Liberals in Chilliwack-Hope.

Clark began attending high-profile Conservative events, attempting to explain at an annual conference hosted by Reform party founder Preston Manning that her party was committed to economic growth, balanced budgets, a robust private sector, and natural resource projects like LNG and oil pipelines.

Manning compared Clark to his former deputy leader, Deb Grey, who'd earned the nickname Iron Snowbird—a homage to both Canadian singer Anne Murray (whose song "Snowbird" was one of her biggest hits) and former British prime minister Margaret Thatcher, the Iron Lady.

"I think we've found another Iron Snowbird," Manning said of Clark.

It was an important credential for Clark, though it required swallowing a significant amount of discomfort. She'd been born and raised a federal Liberal, even working for that party for a time in Ottawa. The Conservatives were not her normal allies. But she needed all the help she could get.

Then, on September 21, 2012, Clark received a major boost. Five months earlier, John Martin had run for the BC Conservatives in the riding of Chilliwack-Hope. Although he finished third, his presence was enough for the Liberals to lose this stronghold to the NDP for the first time in history. The Liberals were concerned that BC Conservative candidates across the province would siphon off some of their traditional support. But those fears dissipated, in part, when Martin decided the best way to stop the NDP in the Fraser Valley was for him to quit the upstart Conservatives and join the Liberals. Less than a year later, Martin would win the seat for his new party.

Clark also began to stack her office with conservatives.

Harper press secretary Sara MacIntyre decided to leave Ottawa and come work with Clark in 2012. She arrived to find an undisciplined premier's office, with MLAs sniping at their boss and cabinet ministers making announcements the premier didn't even know about. She locked down communications, trying to provide some sort of structure and planning. But in the process, she also brought an abrasive style to the office. Her clashes with the press became national stories. At one event, in March 2012, she tried to block media from asking Clark questions about her dismal poll numbers, getting into a long confrontation with reporters that went viral. *Globe and Mail* television columnist John Doyle weighed in with a column, calling MacIntyre the country's newest TV villain.

"MacIntyre, all gum-chewing, hair-swinging, finger-wagging, mall-rat malice and attitude, expressed her utter contempt for the reporters and TV crews with aplomb," wrote Doyle. "She was so sharp it looked like she'd even cut herself if she happened to look at herself. The idea that a reporter might want to ask the Premier a question was, to her, so patently outlandish that one imagined her cackling with derision in her dark lair after the event."

The controversy ran counter to the image Clark wanted to portray as open and transparent. But the premier stuck by her press secretary, buying her a gift certificate to the spa the next day in thanks for her hard work.

Clark also brought back Ken Boessenkool, a former Harper advisor, as her new chief of staff in February 2012. She sent long-time friend Mike McDonald from the government to the BC Liberal Party to prepare for the next election. Boessenkool had already flamed out once during Clark's leadership bid, in which he abandoned her campaign under pressure from the prime minister's office. He second foray into British Columbia did not go much better. Seven months into the job, Boessenkool found himself accused, in his own words, of an "incident where I acted inappropriately." It involved touching a female government staffer while in a Victoria-area bar. Boessenkool, who was married with young kids, quit and went home to Alberta. But he left a terrible mess in his wake, with questions about when Clark first knew about the allegations, and why there was not a single paper record of the supposed internal investigation into his conduct. Again, her critics questioned her judgement. How could Clark have entrusted her top staff job to a man who, allegedly, couldn't keep his hands off his junior female subordinates?

One positive aspect of the second Boessenkool flame-out was that Clark finally got a stable, long-term chief of staff. Into the breach stepped Dan Doyle, a veteran bureaucrat, engineer, BC Hydro chairman, former deputy minister, and key organizer of the successful 2010 Winter Olympics, who was now in his seventies. He arrived as Clark's new chief of staff on September 24, took one look around at the various political crises, and thought, what a mess.

He started by reassigning MacIntyre in an attempt to force her out, a move that caught Clark by surprise. Then he cracked down on staff conduct, reining in a culture of drinking and partying that among some Liberal staff had grown to excess.

But Doyle was most concerned about the continued dissent inside the Liberal caucus. He concluded that some MLAs needed, for lack of a better term, their asses kicked. So he started pulling them aside individually and in groups. Some got read the riot act. Others had their complaints broken down and, where possible, Doyle helped find ways to support the projects in their ridings that would shut them up until the election.

By this point, in late 2012 and into early 2013, the lack of conservatives in Clark's office no longer seemed like a big issue. The threat from the BC Conservatives had dimmed. The Cummins–van Dongen alliance had imploded, and the two were at each other's throats. It proved the old political axiom that the smaller the stakes, the more vicious the politics. By late September, van Dongen had quit the party amid a rift with Cummins and, beset by infighting, the BC Conservatives drifted back toward irrelevance.

BY EARLY 2013, with all the dissent, early retirements, and defections inside the Liberals, it wasn't clear the party had the votes required to pass its budget. For the first time in twelve years, the Liberals were worried they might lose a vote in the House. A loss on a budget vote would be considered a matter of confidence and would force the premier to resign or request a new earlier election. Worse, the budget was critically important to Clark's election plans. It couldn't fail. The Liberals were forecasting the first provincial surplus since the economic collapse of 2008, and they wanted to highlight their fiscal responsibility.

Behind the scenes, Doyle and caucus whip Eric Foster were trying to keep the creaky Liberal ship together long enough to pass the budget. The once-mighty Liberal majority of thirteen seats in 2009 had shrunk to only a five-seat lead. After a session in which at least half a dozen Liberal MLAs had spoken out against the direction and policies of their own party, the razor-thin control of the House was in jeopardy.

One example of an MLA the Liberals weren't sure they could count on to support their own budget was Kash Heed, the buff, black-haired, well-spoken Indo-Canadian former police chief from West Vancouver, who was by now fully marching to the beat of his own drum. Once a superstar candidate, Heed had been tapped by Campbell as solicitor general following the 2009 election. During his brief time in the post he was able to spearhead the government's first attempts at new crackdowns on drunk drivers and distracted driving while using a cell phone.

Heed's troubles had begun in the same year, when he'd shot down an early RCMP request for more money to operate its helicopters and catamarans. Then he'd crashed a meeting top RCMP officials had tried to organize behind his back with Premier Campbell, rebuffing their attempts to get early access to the second phase of the inquiry into the RCMP Tasering death of Robert Dziekanski. Ten days later, he got a call while vacationing in San Francisco telling him he was under RCMP investigation for election spending. Heed had to resign as solicitor general twice over the resulting election spending allegations in his riding, involving his campaign manager, Barinder Sall. Two special prosecutors ultimately cleared Heed of any wrongdoing involving a brochure produced by his campaign for which expenses were not declared, but he was forced to pay an $8,000 fine under the Elections Act as the candidate.

To make matters worse, there'd been an embarrassing leak of emails in which Heed had referred to himself to Sall as a "stallion" and a winner stuck waiting on the sidelines. In the emails, Heed also dumped on his colleagues, calling former solicitor general John Les "a goof" and cabinet minister Mary McNeil a "loser" who was "dense." Campbell never put him back into cabinet. Embittered by the whole experience, Heed languished on the backbench.

Clark did not select Heed for her cabinet either. And, like the other Campbell dissidents, he grew to be no fan of Clark. Nor, at that point, did he appear to be a fan of even being an MLA. Regular visitors to the legislature could often spot Heed sitting off in a corner seat in the chamber reading a magazine and refusing to clap with his Liberal colleagues during proceedings.

Heed was now two months from leaving politics for good, and the Liberals weren't sure if he could be counted on to show up to vote with the party on the budget. During all the chaos of his resignations, Heed's then wife had lost a pregnancy. She had to have surgery around the time of the budget vote, and he took personal leave to be with her and skipped the vote entirely.

Even with Heed gone, there were still several others who'd made enough backroom noise that the Liberal brass viewed them as potentially unreliable vote-casters, including Hawes, Hogg, Stilwell, Abbott, Murray Coell, and possibly Ralph Sultan and Joan Macintyre too. Foster, the party whip, was cautiously optimistic he could slide the government through the vote.

"It's certainly a challenge for the members that are retiring, and for us as far as that goes, but they are all loyal to the party and, especially for those who have been here for a long time, they'll be here to help us," he said. "This is not new math. The numbers are pretty simple. They're tight, there's no question about it. We just have to be on our toes."

Three MLAs who might have had to skip the vote, Kevin Falcon (who was expecting his first child to be born), Pat Pimm (who was recovering from knee surgery), and Blair Lekstrom (who was attending his daughter's wedding), were all able to make it in the end. As well, the Liberals picked up the support of two of the four independent MLAs, Vicki Huntington and John Slater.

The budget passed by a vote of 45–38 on March 6, 2013. The mutineers ultimately did not put their votes where their mouths had been. One crisis averted.

But there were several more yet to come.

ONE OF THE biggest problems in Clark's first two years as premier originated in her own office, with one of her closest supporters, and the initial mishandling was all the premier's own fault. Inside the Liberal caucus, a good, old-fashioned staff fight, full of jealousy and revenge, had been brewing.

It centred on Jeff Melland, who worked in Liberal caucus communications. Melland had helped plan and implement a Chinese-language media program for the Liberals, and later helped craft op-eds and news releases that attacked the NDP. By all accounts, Melland was actually fairly well liked. But there was competition with a colleague, Thomas Marshall, who got promoted to a job in the premier's office before Melland. Melland went to Clark's deputy chief of staff, Kim Haakstad, and also asked for a promotion. Haakstad said no. Instead, she tasked Melland with helping strategize on how to engage ethnic media. Melland would play a key role in helping to write and craft the Liberal's multicultural outreach plan, designed to drum up votes for the party in ethnic communities. But his loyalty to the Liberals was non-existent.

Melland was a smoker and, like many who like to light up at the legislature, he took his cigarette break at the rear of the building, on the back steps of the library. Another smoker who also frequented the same area was NDP leader Adrian Dix's chief of staff, Stephen Howard. Under normal circumstances, the conversation between the Opposition leader's chief of staff and a government communications person would be muted at best. But Howard and Melland struck up a rapport while they smoked. Soon Melland would offer Howard his first leak: emails and letters that showed the Liberal government had orchestrated a consultation process for a new Burnaby hospital on the basis of crass political motivations to win the local ridings. The NDP took the documents and leaked them to *The Vancouver Sun*, which published several days' worth of embarrassing stories.

Melland had more ammunition ready. He handed Howard a copy of the Liberal multicultural outreach report he'd helped craft, then stepped back and waited for all hell break loose. Which it did.

NDP house leader John Horgan stood in question period on February 27, 2013, with what he knew was a bombshell: internal Liberal documents, with the name of the premier's deputy chief of staff on them, showing government staffers, ministry officials, ministers, and government communications officials all conspiring to work together, using public time and public money, to plan a database and contact list of ethnic voters that the BC Liberal Party could use in the election. The revelation landed like a bomb on the floor of the House, and sent the Liberals scrambling.

At one point, the plan described using official government apologies for historical wrongs as "quick wins" to get the Liberals ethnic support and help win certain ridings. Multiculturalism Minister John Yap and his executive assistant, Mike Lee, were implicated too, as was former minister Harry Bloy and his then–director of communications, Brian Bonney. Yap would resign his cabinet post and admit he'd tried to use his personal email to avoid getting caught under Freedom of Information rules. Lee would quit. Bloy appeared hapless as usual. Bonney, who'd committed several serious breaches of the rules and spent as much as half the time in his taxpayer-paid job doing partisan work for the party, had already quit. But the Liberal party had to repay $70,000 of his salary to the government.

It was a dumpster fire of a mess for the Liberals and Premier Clark.

When the story broke, Haakstad was just leaving to visit her aunt on a previously planned trip to Grande Prairie in her home province of Alberta. Haakstad was one of Clark's oldest political staffers, having served her boss back in the opposition days and later as a cabinet minister under Campbell. She was deeply loyal, and, as the story broke, she offered to resign immediately to take the pressure off her boss. But chief of staff Doyle wouldn't accept it.

When Haakstad walked out of her office in the west annex of the premier's office later that day for her holiday, she looked back at the historic building and strongly suspected she wouldn't be coming back. She was right.

Haakstad tried to resign a second time. But Doyle, as chief of staff, again refused to accept it. In his mind, there wasn't enough to justify the resignation.

Pressure kept rising. Half a dozen MLAS and cabinet ministers went public, demanding heads roll and Clark act. They represented the rebels who behind the scenes were causing the most trouble for Clark, including cabinet minister Moira Stilwell, Hawes, Heed, and caucus chair Gordie Hogg.

The premier bungled the initial apology. The day after the scandal broke, on February 28, 2013, she was in Vancouver at an editorial board meeting with *The Vancouver Sun*, and failed to attend the afternoon session of the legislature. She ordered an investigation into the "Quick Wins" scandal, as it would come to be called, but left deputy premier Rich Coleman to read a written apology in the House. The Liberals sat silently, stone-faced, as the apology was read. Nobody clapped in support. Coleman emerged from the legislature fuming about the entire affair.

"This is just not acceptable and there will be consequences," he told reporters. "This is not going to be something that's going to languish in any way whatsoever. I expect answers within the next twenty-four hours."

Hogg piled on, announcing that as caucus chairman he would conduct his own investigation into the allegations, in a transparent attempt to keep open a parallel avenue for Clark's biggest critics to keep slagging her character.

Late that day, with the crisis at full boil, Haakstad offered to resign a third time. This time, Doyle accepted.

"Kim Haakstad was the senior person involved in it, so it was appropriate that she resign," Clark would say.

The Liberals convened an emergency cabinet meeting on Sunday to discuss the situation. Outside, it was widely interpreted as a do-or-die moment for Clark's premiership. Some of the cabinet ministers gathered for a drink at the Rogue bar near the premier's downtown Vancouver offices before the meeting, including Terry Lake, Shirley Bond, Pat Bell, Steve Thomson, and others. They basically concluded that Clark was the premier, and it wouldn't do anyone any good at this point to have a big palace revolt. So they decided to just calm the situation down, weather the storm, hear what she had to say, get to a better place, and move on. There was an election in ten weeks to get ready for.

Clark arrived at the emergency meeting to find an ill-shaped piece of cardboard by her seat at the conference table with her name and the word "PREMIER" handwritten in large bold capital letters. It was the work of Bill Bennett, whom Clark had resurrected from Campbell's exile and restored to cabinet as her community, sport and cultural development minister in 2012. It was his public show of support, in capital letters. He considered her the boss, and she was staying the boss.

Clark intended to test her cabinet for loyalty, and, in the process, test whether she could continue in the job. She'd been bracing for the possibility that a minister might resign, which would be the surest sign of all that her days in charge were numbered. But for all the grumbling, murmuring, and whispering that had been going on behind the scenes over her leadership, by the time her cabinet convened for the emergency meeting Clark was unsurprised to find that not a single one of the ministers actually spoke out against her to her face. It became clear to her quickly that no one was quitting. They talked out the issue. The meeting adjourned. And every cabinet minister who left that day, when asked, publicly expressed support for Clark and her continued leadership of the party.

In reality the cabinet was never in doubt. While MLAs were jumping ship, Clark had spent considerable time securing her most loyal supporters. Mary Polak, Terry Lake, Shirley Bond, and Rich Coleman might have all decided to support other candidates in the leadership race, but over time, once Clark was premier, they became her most loyal ministers. Clark was also working behind the scenes to recruit new candidates that would be loyal to her if she won the 2013 election.

Part of the reason why the Quick Wins scandal burned so hot was the perception of Clark's weakness. But in reality, it served to expose the thin grey line that barely separated the work all political parties did at the legislature and the work they did to get re-elected. The NDP had their own creative use of caucus money for political purposes that would later be flagged by the auditor general. When it came to the blurry line between caucus and party work, the rules were simply there to be broken.

But Quick Wins was also more than just the sum of its technical wrongdoings. It left a kind of stench in its wake that fed into a narrative the NDP were trying to build about Clark as a premier: she only wants to be in power and she'll do anything to win.

The scandal would roar back to life on March 14, 2013, when the review that Clark had so quickly ordered in February was complete. Clark's deputy minister, John Dyble, had interviewed twenty-five people and reviewed ten thousand documents, including government records and emails from personal accounts. His review confirmed that numerous staffers had breached standards of conduct and misused government resources in preparing the multicultural outreach plan that targeted ethnic voters.

Clark apologized, again. But she was hammered by the NDP in the legislature's question period. The Opposition was calling for a full-blown corruption inquiry. Luckily for Clark, it was the final question period of the session. It was election time.

The party's popularity was at a crushing low by this point, with the NDP enjoying a twenty-point lead in a March 21 Angus Reid poll. You might think that, with the Liberals on the ropes, a bombshell scandal at their fingertips, and Clark fending off a brewing rebellion inside the ranks, this would be the perfect time for the NDP to swoop in and deliver the coup de grâce on their political opponents, just weeks before the start of the provincial election campaign.

But you'd be wrong. Because that's not what the NDP did at all.

CHAPTER 4
LIQUEFIED NATURAL MIRACLE

If there's one rule in politics worth following it is this: always, always, always kick your opponents when they are down.

In the weeks prior to the 2013 election the Christy Clark Liberals weren't just down. They looked like they were dead. They'd been badly damaged by two years of infighting. The Quick Wins scandal had painted not only Clark but her entire party with the stench of scandal.

It was the perfect time for the NDP to kick.

Instead, the New Democrats did nothing. Leader Adrian Dix was obsessed with the idea of running a "positive" election campaign in 2013, one that would eschew the traditional attack ads in favour of a policy-based race that, he felt, would appeal to the half of the British Columbia electorate who didn't even bother to vote in most elections.

Step one toward that objective was dropping his party's prosecution of the Quick Wins scandal. Instead, Dix busied himself with meeting members of the business community, who by now were watching the beleaguered Liberals with concern and wanting face time with the man who looked like he'd become premier of the next government. This provided ample time for the Liberals to not only flee the legislature but pause, take a breath, and regroup.

It would prove to be an enormous mistake by the New Democrats. We'll let the party's 2013 election director, Brian Topp, explain it in his own words, from the post-mortem report he would write after the election:

> The media didn't want to do more "quick win" stories after a week or two of it. But a more aggressive, bloody-minded campaign than the one we conducted would have nonetheless acted on the traditional political principle that the best time to kick your opponent is when they are down.
>
> We could have strung together Ms. Clark's apologies in a saturation-buy campaign ad and asked if this is the kind of person who should be Premier—the kind of question the Liberals were asking about Adrian Dix in the most grossly offensive terms.
>
> These revelations about Christy Clark and her government could have been politically underlined in many other ways. But we concluded that the work of breaking Christy Clark and the political credibility of her government had been done, that the personal attacks on Adrian Dix had been (effectively) countered, and that the BC NDP could safely return to a positive campaign in March and April in the lead-up to the campaign.
>
> This proved to be a terrible misjudgment. Indeed, by the end of the campaign these events may have, to some extent, helped Ms. Clark. Her government had been confronted by a first-class political crisis. As far as the public could see, she appeared to have reacted to it decisively—firing key aides and apologizing. And basically, as far as the public could see, we accepted this. She had weathered the storm. As awareness of the details faded, what was left was a sense that she was capable of weathering storms—a basic skill required of Premiers.
>
> Many commentators point to our announcement on Kinder-Morgan as the turning point of this campaign... But in my view, this moment in March 2013 was the true turning point of the campaign—the decisive mistake that cost us the election.

Our opponent was on the ropes, and we let her get up. That I didn't see this at the time, and act effectively on it, is my greatest regret in this campaign.

Strong stuff.

So the NDP let the Liberals off the hook of the biggest scandal of Clark's early premiership, at least for the crucial few weeks between the end of the spring legislative session and dropping of the writ on April 16, which signified the official start of the twenty-eight-day election campaign.

The Liberals seized the opportunity to reset the entire election narrative to three simple words: liquefied natural gas.

WHEN CHRISTY CLARK was preparing to name her first cabinet, in 2011, Forests Minister Pat Bell got a call, asking to meet at her home in Vancouver.

He walked into the kitchen of Clark's house, where the newly minted premier was waiting with a new cabinet offer: the jobs ministry. Bell had been lobbying behind the scenes to stay on as forests minister, and he'd been heartened by a campaign from forest companies and unions to pressure Clark to keep him in the portfolio. When he heard about a jobs portfolio he thought, "What the hell is that?"

"Christy, no, you don't understand, I'm the minister of forests," Bell said in a mixture of perhaps pleading and condescension.

Clark smiled, patiently.

"No, no, you don't understand," she said. "I'm the premier. I want you to be minister of jobs."

There was a pause before Bell replied. "Oh, okay. I understand now."

"You know what you did for the forests industry?" the premier asked. "I want you do exactly the same thing for the rest of the economy."

It's here that liquefied natural gas, or LNG, got its political start.

Premier Christy Clark pushed to create a booming liquefied natural gas industry in the province and made many trips to northern BC, including attending a rally in support of LNG on April 26, 2016. BC LIBERAL PARTY

Bell was one of Campbell's top lieutenants by the time the former premier resigned. He'd helped sell a revitalization of the forestry sector, and Clark had set her sights on him working similar salesmanship magic for an idea that had been percolating in her mind—a BC Jobs Plan. The economy was still dogged by global markets, and Clark calculated the public wanted something done to ensure that well-paying jobs were available during turbulent times. The issue of jobs also happened to be a good wedge issue on the NDP, and the milque-toast message was something both the liberal and conservative sides of the free-enterprise coalition could unite behind.

Jobs had always been a key driver for Clark, personally. When asked why, she'd often tell a story about her father. Jim Clark ran three times, unsuccessfully, for the BC Liberals at a time when the party was a virtual non-entity on the political scene. But history will mostly remember him for his decision to drag along his young daughter, Christy, to help knock on doors and pass out campaign literature. Jim passed on the political bug to a future premier at an early age. But he died before

Clark won her first seat in the legislature in 1996 in Port Moody-Burnaby Mountain.

"I was a little baby on my dad's knee when [my father] ran the first time. He got me doing this. My dad really inspired me," Clark would later say, in a 2011 interview. "It wasn't that he was a political candidate, it was that around our dinner table my dad was a school teacher and he believed in debate and discussion... We would all sit around and we all had these vastly different opinions and my dad was all about, 'Bring it on.'"

Jim had another lasting impact on his daughter's life. He had undiagnosed depression, which he self-medicated with alcohol. But it was his thirty-five-year teaching career in Burnaby that kept him alive.

Clark expanded on the influence in an interview with *The Vancouver Sun* much later in her political career:

My father was a public school teacher for 35 plus years and he struggled with a mental illness and the way he dealt with the mental illness was not to go to the doctor, because as men did in those days, it was to drink a lot.

Over the years it got worse. But after his wife left him and his kids had all moved out, he kept going to work every day, sober, packed his own lunch and came home every day feeling like he made a huge difference. When he retired that was when he started to die and he died pretty fast after that, because it was work that allowed him to find the meaning in life and give him an identity in the world. That allowed him to live with his untreated mental illness.

It was after he died, I spent a lot of time thinking about that and that was when I realized how much a job matters. So since then I've looked at all the statistics, incidence of mental illness, suicide, going on social assistance, having healthy kids, involvement in crime—every single one of those statistics changes when someone has a job.

My experience very directly was seeing how much a job matters in somebody's life in ways we don't even quantify. It's not just to provide for the people we love, it gives us meaning, identity, a place in the world, colleagues to see every day, a reason to get up, a chance to make a difference. All of those things. That's why I'm so focused on job creation because I saw what it did for my dad.

And so Clark spent the earliest days of her premiership thinking about a jobs plan for her new government. She turned over the details to Bell.

Bell decided to base his jobs plan on what he considered the most influential book he'd ever read, *Good to Great* by Jim Collins. It was a five-year study of twenty-eight high-performing companies in the 1990s, focused on identifying why they had become high-performing companies with large returns. Bell zeroed in on Collins's recommendation to pick the things where you have a strategic advantage over others and narrow your focus to avoid distraction. One of the first things he did was buy ten copies of *Good to Great* and hand them out at a meeting of senior bureaucrats in his ministry, saying, "Read this. This is our jobs plan. This is what it's going to be based on."

The jobs plan would eventually focus on eight industries in BC where there was some type of unique advantage for the province against competing players. Among those was natural gas. Within that a new term emerged that would soon transform the provincial government and come to define Clark's premiership: liquefied natural gas.

The jobs plan was officially unveiled on September 22, 2011. It included a focus on mines, a commitment to Asian markets, and the goal of moving the province into the country's top three in job creation.

But the cornerstone was LNG. On paper, at least, BC looked like it had the ability to be a major player in the LNG game. There was the province's direct shipping route to Asia, via the Pacific Ocean, which would give it key access to the hungry markets, where China, Korea, and Japan needed more gas. There were the massive natural gas deposits in the province's northeast, which stretched into Alberta, presenting companies with access to probably the top two or three gas basins in the world. And there were little things, like the lower temperature of BC's coast, which would help cut costs on the cooling required to get the gas to liquefy into its much smaller form so it could be transported via massive supertankers. Yet the idea also came with no shortage of risks. BC's analysis concluded there was room for roughly eight to ten new LNG plants, globally, before the market became saturated in Asia and India and prices began to fall. And companies from around the world were banging on the government's door to bid on building facilities in the province.

BC had access to huge amounts of cheap natural gas, but fewer and fewer markets to sell it in as the United States ramped up its own production. In 2006, the province brought in more than $1 billion in natural gas royalties and in 2008, $2.5 billion in drill lease revenue from natural gas companies. But when government officials analyzed the industry trends, they saw the money drying up, fast, as the markets shrank and more gas flooded the system. The officials would eventually be proven right: by 2016, natural gas royalties had fallen to less than $150 million, and lease sales at one point hit a projected mere $14 million.

It looked like the answer to BC's natural gas woes would be the LNG industry.

When Clark assumed her premiership in 2011, neither she nor her top officials had any clue what LNG was or why it was important. A national public relations firm tried to set up a meeting with the premier and what was described to her chief of staff, McDonald, as "these guys from Malaysia and these guys from Calgary" about something called LNG.

The Malaysians turned out to be Petronas, the state-run massive oil and gas company that would become the leading proponent in BC's LNG race. They missed the meeting at the last minute, but the guys from Calgary, Progress Energy, a major player in BC's natural gas industry, showed up to discuss LNG. Petronas would later buy Progress Energy for $5.5 billion.

At the meeting, McDonald wasn't exactly sure what they were talking about. But within a year, the LNG file would go from awkward encounters like this to full-out overdrive within the premier's office, with Clark herself soliciting the meetings and breaking down doors to get audiences.

As the Clark government began to clue in to the opportunity presented by LNG in 2012, it also began ramping up the rhetoric. Some attribute this to Clark's ability to seize on an aspirational opportunity that both fit well in the jobs agenda she was creating and provided the kind of big, bold vision for economic growth she wanted to run on in the 2013 election. Others, including her less charitable rivals at the cabinet table, watched a premier who was great at running election campaigns finally win control over government and then have very little in the way of policies to offer. When LNG came along, Clark's skeptics viewed her sudden enthusiasm as akin to a drowning person seizing on whatever they could to keep from sinking in the water.

As 2012 drew to a close, the government commissioned consulting firm Grant Thornton to analyze the potential economic impact of BC's LNG aspirations. As many as 100,000 jobs could be created, the firm concluded, if the province were to realize its dream of five operational LNG plants. This number would later be picked apart in great detail by critics, including the fact that it was based on the government's own data and a series of borderline-ridiculous assumptions by the province. But at the time, everyone in the government just went with it.

A new addition to Clark's office would soon begin to make his mark in a big way. Ben Chin was hired in her communications division in December 2012, and he'd go on to become one of Clark's most influential advisors during her premiership. Chin was a familiar face to many Canadians, having been a CBC TV journalist who'd risen to anchor of the flagship newscast, *The National*. His father had served as the South Korean ambassador to Canada, and Chin had always had a keen interest in politics. He quit broadcasting to get involved in Ontario provincial politics, first joining then-premier Dalton McGuinty's communications staff and then running unsuccessfully in a provincial by-election. He'd also served for a time as a vice-president in the Ontario Power Authority.

By the time Clark became premier, Chin was living in Predator Ridge in BC's Interior and working as a vice-president for Air Miles. Many of his colleagues in McGuinty's old office, including Laura Miller and Don Guy, were being tapped by Clark's Liberals to help out in the impending BC election campaign.

Mike McDonald reached out to Chin for communications advice in the run-up to the campaign, which led to him joining Clark's office in December 2012. During one of their earliest conversations, Chin began to write communications messaging that would carry Clark into the campaign. He started by asking why she wanted the job. What was she here to do as premier?

The goal was to craft the premier's messaging around her own core beliefs. It's a lot easier to remember your speaking points, effectively ad-lib, and stay on message if that message is something you actually believe in. Clark told Chin that, for her, it all came down to job creation. She wanted to create well-paying jobs for people. She wanted to balance the provincial budget and control government spending. She wanted to leave her son, Hamish, a province that was in better shape than when she became its premier, a story she illustrated with the term "intergenerational equity." They were the premier's core beliefs, ones she'd carried with her since she was in the legislature's model parliament as a youngster in the 1980s, where she'd railed against what she felt were out-of-control federal deficits that had left her generation behind the eight ball.

Okay, thought Chin, I can work with that. He crafted a speech for Clark to read at a Liberal party provincial council meeting a month later, in February, heavy on references to "intergenerational equity" and the responsibility to do something that leaves a better future for the next generation. Fantastic speech, Clark told him when she received it.

Then she got on stage and didn't read a word of it. Instead, she ad-libbed the entire thing. She took the speech as a kind of launching pad, on the fly rejigging it all in her own words. Clark told a personal story about her modest middle-class upbringing in Burnaby with her parents, Mavis and Jim. Her dad refused to leave his kids with a penny of debt, she said, going so far as to prepay his funeral costs before he died. She asked the crowd, What makes it right to leave our kids with a government that spends today but has to borrow that money from the future in the form of debt? Despite a speech heavily loaded with the term she had wanted, Clark didn't use "intergenerational equity" once. But in her ad-libbing, she did coin LNG as a "generational opportunity" that would clean up global warming, create jobs, build more hospitals and schools, and leave the province a better place for their children.

Chin was standing at the back of the room with Don Guy and Mike McDonald as Clark broke down the "intergenerational equity" doctrine and rebuilt it on the fly under her LNG agenda.

"We've got to get working on the platform," McDonald said to Chin and Guy.

Guy pointed at the stage. "I think that was the platform," he said. "There's your platform right there."

Chin agreed. He began translating Clark's "generational opportunity" LNG speech, delivered to party insiders, as the Liberal government's next throne speech, tapping the Grant Thornton study and the provincial bureaucracy for figures to include in the throne speech. At the same time, the party sifted through it to develop aspirational catch-phrases like "Debt-Free BC" and "Strong economy, Secure tomorrow" that it would test through focus groups.

Lieutenant-Governor Judith Guichon arrived at the legislature on February 12, 2013, settled into the throne chair at the front of the legislative chamber, opened up the speech, and began to read to the assembled MLAs, dignitaries, and media. It quickly became clear that Clark had not only staked her reputation on LNG, but she had gone all-in on that one sector saving her political career and propelling her to re-election.

BC could earn enough from LNG to fill a special $100-billion "prosperity fund" over thirty years that would erase the province's entire $56-billion debt by the 2020s, read the speech. The LNG industry would be up and running by 2020. It would generate $1 trillion in economic growth. The province would see up to $8.7 billion in extra revenue each year. As many as 100,000 people would get well-paying, family-supporting jobs. On and on the numbers tumbled out of Guichon's address in a seemingly never-ending barrage of good news.

The speech was an enormous political gamble. By tying her fortunes to an industry she'd known nothing about just two years prior, Clark was showcasing either the kind of aggressive visionary leadership her supporters lauded her for or a kind of cynical political showmanship that bordered on the outright dishonesty her critics suspected she was capable of. Either way, the speech was what it was: a carefully crafted and elevated take on Clark's core vision of jobs and economic growth, using LNG as the sharp end of the spear to drive the message home to voters about what was possible if you dreamed big.

Reaction was not kind. Pundits declared it an act of political desperation, with an LNG vision so fantastic as to be miraculous.

"With a government capable of this many miracles, the Liberals had better keep all this stuff secret from the Vatican," wrote *Province* columnist Mike Smyth. "If the conclave of cardinals gets wind of this, they might elect Christy Clark pope before she gets re-elected premier."

The speech's promises were simply unbelievable, wrote *Vancouver Sun* columnist Vaughn Palmer. "Eliminate the provincial debt! Wipe out the sales tax! Why not use the money to cure cancer, build a fixed link to Vancouver Island or colonize Mars?" he wrote. "Still, one could readily grasp the Liberal predicament as they sat down to craft their legislative agenda. The remainder of the throne speech was the thinnest gruel imaginable, recycled promises from past years, new promises so negligible as to be pathetic… Seriously, judging from the contents of the throne speech, the tank has run dry for the Liberals. So perhaps it is not all that surprising that Clark and her colleagues decided to escape into the throne speech equivalent of virtual reality."

Clark doubled-down on the promises of her throne speech when unveiling her party's election platform in April, in advance of the May provincial election. "On May 14, we will have a once-in-a-lifetime chance to eliminate the debt for our children," she declared.

When it came time to wrap the Liberal campaign bus with the pictures and logos that would carry the Liberals through the campaign, there was a brief pause. McDonald was nervous about the "debt-free BC" slogan that would become ubiquitous in the campaign. Perhaps it was just a bit much, he thought. How could they sell to British Columbians the idea of eliminating the entire debt, and what happened if they fell short?

Ontario strategist Guy, now firmly entrenched in the BC campaign, calmed him down. Bald, with dark-rimmed black glasses, Guy earned the nickname "the godfather of Queen's Park" during his time in Ontario. In 2011 the *Toronto Star* called him "the mystery man of politics, mythologized at 46 and described as scary smart, intimidating, inscrutable, and not to be crossed."

Guy told McDonald the campaign had to be aspirational, and LNG was the way into that vision. What is the Liberal party's "moonshot"? he asked. What ambitious, ground-breaking goal, like launching a spacecraft to the moon, was the Liberal government trying to achieve?

McDonald gulped, and agreed.

When the Liberal campaign bus rolled out during the election, emblazoned on the sides were the words "Strong Economy. Secure Tomorrow. For a Debt-Free BC."

DESPITE ALL THE hype, LNG did very little to improve Clark's dismal popularity in the short term.

The Liberals would start their election campaign twenty points down in the polls to their NDP rivals. Clark did not appear worried, at least on the outside. She viewed her chances at re-election as favourable once the public got a look at her versus NDP leader Dix on the campaign trail.

As the election grew nearer, more than one pundit was surprised to survey the BC Liberal candidate list and see a collection of top-tier names on the ballot. Mayors. Councillors. Prominent business owners. Even an Olympic gold medalist. Couldn't they read the polls? Didn't they all know the Liberals were about to be slaughtered? From the outside, running for the Liberals at this point looked a bit like chaining an anvil to your ankle and diving into the deepest part of the ocean: no matter how great a candidate you were, the party was dragging you down with it.

But as the media focused on the many scandals and challenges besetting the party, most had missed a key event in late 2012 that would pay major dividends in the May 2013 election.

The annual Liberal convention in Whistler on the weekend of October 26, 2012, had been, by all accounts, a resounding success. More than a thousand delegates had convened at the convention centre, where they heard a surprisingly strong message from the conservative right that the party needed to stick together, buck up, and start fighting back. Former Conservative MPs Stockwell Day, Gerry St. Germain, and John Reynolds were working the floor, shoring up support from those who were considering jumping ship to the BC Conservatives.

Brad Bennett, the son and grandson, respectively, of former Social Credit premiers Bill Bennett and W.A.C. Bennett, took the stage to discuss how his family's political dynasty now manifested itself in Clark, and to pledge to fight with her for the values of free enterprise. While he spoke, projected behind him were large pictures of the legendary premiers, who, combined, had ruled the province for more than three decades.

Delegates were given hope by political operatives Stephen Carter, from Alberta, and Guy, from Ontario. They argued that the electorate was volatile and wouldn't make up their minds who to support until just before the May 14 vote. There were plenty of comeback examples in the long history of Canadian politics. The strategists also said not to listen to the negative commentary from pollsters, pundits, or political scientists, because they are "the holy trinity of incompetence" and don't know what they are talking about. That line would prove a favourite of Clark's and she'd dust it off in future years with relish whenever someone underestimated her.

The highlight of the event, for many, was the opening session, in which anyone who wanted it was given a minute to speak about their vision for the future of the province, in an event dubbed "Free Enterprise Friday." It seemed to excite the room, with everyone taking a stab at a quick statement from the floor. Co-hosting the event were three-time Langley City mayor Peter Fassbender and Paralympic gold-medalist Michelle Stilwell. Both had been recruited by Clark to run the segment and both walked away feeling maybe the Liberals were not quite as hopeless as they looked from the outside.

Clark was spending a lot of her time behind the scenes, making personal appeals to candidates to run with her in the election. The convention seemed to cement the decision for many of them.

"We have a plan for British Columbia," she told her convention. "But what do we do next? Help us."

The weekend concluded with the entire Liberal caucus on stage singing Queen's "We Will Rock You" in a type of pre-election war chant.

If you ask rookie Liberal candidates about why they threw their credibility behind what many thought was a lost cause at the time, almost all will at some point reference the positive feelings they got from the party convention. Fassbender and Stilwell would sign on officially in the months after the campaign, making considerable news as superstar candidates. Mostly the good news was overshadowed by the bad press the party was attracting. But it was critically important. By the time the election rolled around, the party had defied the odds by attracting a roster of competent, eager, highly motivated community leaders to fly its flag to the electorate.

Meanwhile, after passing on an opportunity to finish off the Liberals on the Quick Wins file, the New Democrats were struggling. Expectations of Dix were high, as was the pressure to prove that his positive campaign could actually work. His party was so far ahead in the polls, it was already facing a bad case of front-runner's disease.

The March 7, 2013, cover of *The Province* newspaper in Vancouver summed it up in this all-caps headline, accompanied by a photo of Dix: "IF THIS MAN KICKED A DOG, HE'D STILL WIN THE ELECTION." Inside, columnist Mike Smyth (who, for the record, did not write the infamous headline) interviewed seven political scientists and pollsters. They were split on the issue and, unlike the headline, mostly hedged their bets that the Liberals were done for.

"The BC NDP has a long history of snatching defeat from the jaws of victory," said Dennis Pilon, a York University professor who'd studied BC politics and lived in the province until recently. "They excel at losing." Though, for the record, Pilon also added he thought Dix would win.

The Province's headline will live on in infamy within BC political circles because it was so big, so bold, and so flat-out wrong.

The NDP election campaign started on April 16, with a planned eight days of big-ticket announcements from the party platform. Campaign director Brian Topp had a further idea: why not make the announcements in the ridings of the Liberal cabinet minister whose portfolio the NDP was criticizing and proposing to change? The party could then detail how the government had failed on that item, point to the minister whose riding they were in, and offer a positive alternative, all in one stop.

As an idea, it wasn't horrible. But in reality, the strategy provided bizarre results. Dix and his campaign team would often find themselves standing in a field, or at a gazebo, or in some far-flung location with a background that didn't match the topic they were discussing. A prime example was the NDP plan to freeze BC Ferries rates. A popular proposal that struck at the heart of a mismanaged government file, it was sure to drum up votes in Vancouver Island ridings and coastal communities. So where did the NDP announce the ferry freeze on April 17? At the landlocked Fraser Valley riding of Finance Minister Mike de Jong, in Abbotsford West. There wasn't a glimpse of the ocean for at least fifty kilometres.

To Dix's credit, he did raise the issue as a concern at one point, asking via conference-call to the NDP war room a day or so before the ferry announcement if it truly made sense to do it so far from Island voters. But, as Dix was learning, it's almost impossible to micromanage an election campaign from inside the leader's bus. That's why there's a separate campaign director and team to keep an eye on the bigger picture.

The campaign director, though, was not without controversy. Brian Topp was a long-time NDP strategist and backroom operative at the federal and provincial levels. In 2011/12, he'd run in the federal NDP leadership campaign, finishing second to Thomas Mulcair. Former NDP leaders Carole James and Dawn Black had endorsed Topp in his campaign. And Dix would eventually ask him if he would come to BC to serve as campaign director during the election in 2013.

The Topp hire rubbed some people in the party the wrong way. Dix had gone outside the established group of traditional BC NDP campaign directors. At the beginning, the grumbling was subdued. Then, three months before the 2013 election, Topp announced he'd formed a new consulting firm: Kool Topp & Guy. The firm saw Topp partner with Ken Boessenkool and Don Guy to provide political advice across the country.

"We offer the most senior level longitudinal, vertical and horizontal public affairs counsel available in Canada today," the trio confidently announced in a press release steeped in head-scratching jargon.

For such supposedly brilliant public relations strategists, they caused a real mess with their announcement. BC New Democrats were incredulous. Furious might be an understatement. Boessenkool was Clark's former chief of staff, who'd had to resign several months earlier in disgrace after inappropriate conduct involving a female staffer in a Victoria bar. Guy was an Ontario Liberal operative who was already actively working for Clark on the BC Liberal campaign and its LNG narrative. All three were now in bed together in a consulting firm—just before an election in which Guy and Topp would be slugging it out for opposite teams.

Dix faced intense, heated pressure to fire Topp immediately. But with three months left in the campaign, Dix kept Topp in place if for no other reason than the NDP didn't know who else to turn to at such a late date. The consequence of Topp's political foolishness was that many NDP candidates immediately distrusted and disliked their election campaign director before he'd even started the job.

Dix took even more heat when it was later revealed Topp didn't want to use long-time BC NDP advertising firm NOW Communications to do the election ads, which added several more names to a growing list of alienated New Democrat supporters.

The NDP would soon face a different type of advertising problem. Vancouver businessman Jim Shepard, a former CEO of forestry firm

Canfor and an advisor to Clark, began hammering Dix in a series of early pre-election radio and television ads in January and February, using his organization Concerned Citizens for BC. He zeroed in on Dix's tenure as chief of staff to then–NDP premier Glen Clark in 1998 in which Dix was fired for backdating a memo to save the premier from controversy. In another ad, an animated storm dubbed "Hurricane Adrian" threatened to "blow out" the energy sector, evaporate megaprojects with a "swirling front of punitive legislation," and crush businesses with "a sweltering heat wave of pummeling labour legislation."

Shepard's group had $1 million to spend on the ads, and blanketed the airwaves. For many in the public, it was their first introduction to Dix, and the negative impression influenced what people thought of him. The NDP internally debated suing Shepard and the group, but got bogged down in how to do it and eventually simply did nothing at all.

It was doubly hard for the NDP to strike back for two reasons: Dix refused to allow the NDP to run a negative campaign or attack ads, and he refused to allow his personal life to become part of the election campaign. That one-two combination would prove an insurmountable disadvantage for the NDP.

"A lot of people think the way to respond to negative ads is to run negative ads ourselves," Dix told the *Parksville Qualicum Beach News* in 2012 about his strategy. "The reason we are not going to do this is very simple. First, 1.7 million people didn't vote in the last provincial election. We are not going to bring anybody back to politics by deciding the winner of an election is the person with the best ad agency to run the nastiest negative ads. We need to bring people back to politics and that means offering some hope that change will happen."

Throughout the campaign, Dix's closest advisors would ask him to reconsider his decision not to go negative, but he never came close to doing so. They'd also beg him to show some kind of personal side, through his wife or parents. But he would simply say, "My personal life is my life." In Dix's mind, the many visuals of Clark with her son,

Hamish, where she invited TV cameras in to see her as a single mother, was crass, fake, and transparently obvious. He thought the public would see that too.

For a while, the public clearly did see Dix as the winner. He was ahead in the polls. He was as popular as an NDP candidate ever could be in the business community. And he was scoring points for his strategy to run a positive campaign that stuck to the issues, not to personal attacks against Clark.

But the NDP's defining moment in the 2013 election campaign would likely come on April 22, in what's now referred to, colloquially, as the NDP's "Kinder Surprise." Dix had gone into the election campaign saying that his party would not take a stand one way or another on the proposed twinning of the existing Kinder Morgan Trans Mountain pipeline between Alberta and Burnaby. It was a "matter of principle" that the NDP would wait until the developer submitted a formal application for the project, Dix said.

Environmentalists wanted the oil pipeline expansion scrapped, for risk of spills both on land and in the ocean, where tanker traffic would dramatically increase in the coastal waters off Vancouver. But several communities in BC's Interior stood to benefit over the long term from the pipeline work in the form of high-paying jobs. It was the classic environment-versus-natural-resource-industry, or green-versus-brown, debate that had long divided the NDP internally.

Dix had managed to straddle the fence with his position not to take a position until some point in the distant future, certainly after the election campaign. So everyone was surprised when, in the second week of the campaign, on Earth Day, while standing on the banks of the North Thompson River, Dix suddenly announced he was opposed to the pipeline expansion because the expanded oil tanker traffic would turn the Port of Vancouver into a major oil export port.

Not only were journalists and voters surprised, but senior New Democrats like Carole James were as well. Dix had consulted with almost nobody before the move. Party veteran Mike Farnworth was gobsmacked. He called Jim Rutkowski, James's former chief of staff, who was a senior advisor in the campaign war room.

"Jim, what is going on?" asked Farnworth. "I thought we had a position."

Rutkowski, who was also blindsided, said HQ was working on a way to explain it. "We're going to be getting nuanced language," he told Farnworth.

"This is an election campaign, not a negotiation," Farnworth spat back. "What the fuck is nuance?"

The first draft of history in subsequent 2013 post-mortems recorded the Kinder Surprise as something Dix made up, on the fly, during the election. The reality was a bit more complicated. Topp, Howard, and Dix had first come up with the idea of switching positions in February—three months before the election—as a kind of back-pocket, mid-campaign manoeuvre that would provide an injection of bold excitement into the race if needed. They'd looped in prominent environmentalist Tzeporah Berman, to the extent that she was one of the first out of the gate after Dix spoke to publicly support his move. Yet they had not been prepared for the sudden blowback that occurred in the form of people accusing Dix of flip-flopping on his position. The reality was that the NDP had also done no polling on this new position, nor had it consulted with its caucus or key supporters.

"Given some very clear statements our leader had made on April 11th on a cable interview program with Vaughn Palmer, objectively we had no room to pivot like this, and no reason to believe it could work," Topp wrote in his post-election report. "One of the key underlying motives to make this announcement, which was to cure the problems of our first week by shaking up the campaign, thus led us to make some pretty bad decisions."

"The political consequences soon became clear," Topp added. "Our move on Kinder Morgan gave the Liberals a very helpful two-pocket pool shot that they played right through to the end of the campaign. It gave them an opening to turn our apparent inconsistency into a character issue about our leader—surfacing their heretofore flimsily disguised personal attack strategy and bringing it into the core of the debate. And it simultaneously allowed them to build on their argument that changing the government was too economically risky—their core case for re-election."

The Liberals began to hear from the business community—which had to a certain extent begun to get comfortable with the idea of Premier Dix—that the sudden reversal reignited their hesitancy over the unreliability of an NDP government.

Clark came out swinging against Dix on the flip-flop. But in the days that followed, her attacks actually seemed to flatten Liberal polling. The war room suggested Clark stop talking about Kinder Morgan at one point, but she refused, saying it was an important character moment for Dix. Results would later prove Clark right.

The NDP's move did play well in Metro Vancouver, including Vancouver-Point Grey, where civil rights lawyer David Eby was making significant ground on the premier in her own riding. But it probably also contributed to eventual losses in rural communities like Fraser-Nicola and Williams Lake. In Fraser-Nicola, long-time outspoken NDP MLA Harry Lali, who was known for the loud colours of his suits and even louder opinions, blasted his own party for the decision after the election, when he came back to the legislature to clean out his office in defeat.

"The real kicker was Kinder Morgan," he told *The Vancouver Sun*, while he packed his personal belongings into boxes. "When the announcement about the Kinder Morgan pipeline was made, it basically decimated Interior and northern BC for us—rural BC, basically."

Lali added, "You can't be against (Enbridge's) Northern Gateway, you can't be against Site C, you can't be against Kinder Morgan and all of that because the message from the blue-collar worker is: 'Those are my jobs. I'm in construction, I need that job.' The blue-collar worker virtually abandoned the NDP in this election, mostly by staying at home."

Lali would go on to make one of the more ironic statements inside the NDP caucus after the 2013 campaign concluded. When the NDP reconvened for its first caucus meeting post-election, Lali stood up in front of the MLAS and declared, "If only Carole had been leader, we would have won!"

Lali, of course, had been one of the Baker's Dozen MLAS who rebelled against James and forced her out of the job. Now he was complaining that she'd given in to his demands to leave.

CLARK ENTERED THE campaign certain that the public would be far less interested in the recent scandals of her government than in directly comparing her with the NDP's Dix. And it was a comparison she was comfortable with.

"I won't be running against perfection any more the minute the writ is dropped," she told the Victoria *Times Colonist*. "I'll be running against Adrian Dix."

The idea that the public doesn't expect perfection would be tested in the campaign. On April 27, *Vancouver Sun* reporter Jonathan Fowlie published a lengthy profile of Clark. This section, written near the end of the piece, describing the relationship between Clark and her son, Hamish, would provide the premier with days of headaches:

> At times, the two seem more like sidekicks—siblings even—than they do mother and son. And especially so the morning when the two were on their way to Hamish's goalie clinic.
>
> "Let's see you go through this red light," Hamish challenged as they pulled up that morning, at 5:15 a.m., to an abandoned Vancouver intersection.
>
> "I might. Don't test me," Clark replies.

"Yeah. Go ahead."

"Should I?"

"There's no one."

"Would you go through? You shouldn't because that would be breaking the law," she says.

And with that the car has already sailed underneath the stale red stoplight and through the empty intersection.

"You always do that," says Hamish.

Tiny things can become huge problems during an election campaign, and this was one of them. Critics piled on Clark over the lack of judgement she'd shown in running a red light with her son in the car—even though it was at a deserted intersection at 5:15 a.m. Perhaps the most stinging critique of the incident came from within Clark's own cabinet. Moira Stilwell, a doctor, used the opportunity to try to bury the premier. She told media that breaking the law on purpose was unacceptable, and then talked about how her husband, Sam, a surgeon, had often had to operate on car-crash victims, sometimes harvesting their organs for donors. Clark's team would never forgive or forget Stilwell's decision to take a run at the premier in the middle of an election campaign. Her words carried significant weight as Clark's own minister of social development.

Stilwell, the MLA for Vancouver-Langara, proved to be fascinating character over the years. Arguably one of the legislature's most intelligent MLAs, she was a nuclear medicine physician and former head of that division at St. Paul's Hospital. But she clashed with Clark almost from the moment she became premier. Their dislike of each other became widely known throughout the legislature. Consequently, whenever a controversy erupted—Quick Wins, CLBC, and so on—reporters would run to Stilwell for comment, and Stilwell would deliver a quietly scathing and artfully constructed rebuke of the premier and her policies.

Nonetheless, the new premier, desperate to keep control of the situation, had elevated Stilwell to cabinet in late 2012. But the old adage that you should keep your friends close and your enemies closer had not worked in Stilwell's case. The Liberals suspected her of leaking cabinet information—at one point giving only Stilwell the wrong time of a key cabinet meeting to see if it would leak out that way in the media.

Even with Stilwell fanning the flames, the red-light incident proved to be but a momentary blip of controversy in the election campaign. It failed to gain traction, in large part because the NDP and leader Dix were still insistent on running a positive campaign and refused to criticize her over the issue.

"There are more important matters to discuss," said Dix.

Clark shook off the controversy and headed into the televised leaders debate, which she considers the turning point of the campaign. There were no "knockout blows," as the media often says after such debates, but without the media filter Clark felt she was able to directly connect with voters. She thought the public would see Dix as shifty, untrustworthy, eccentric, and a little weird, in contrast to her smiling, gregarious self. Clark hit her usual themes in the debate—job creation, leaving more money in your pocket, controlling government spending, and "putting BC on a path to be debt-free in fifteen years." No matter the question lobbed at her during the debate, Clark pivoted back to jobs and the economy. The last question, in which a viewer asked whether the leaders were in favour of decriminalization and/or legalization of marijuana, was illustrative of the debate.

"Yes," answered Dix, who then described in detail the federal-provincial jurisdictional issues on marijuana.

Clark simply ignored the question and started talking about jobs again.

At the time, New Democrats found Clark's performance laughable. She ignored entire questions. Rejected the premise of others. Pivoted everything back to jobs and the economy. But they would later realize (too late) that she had done what Dix had not: hit home a single key message to voters.

Clark would go on to keep up a gruelling schedule during the campaign. She frequently hit construction sites, where, in custom-fit overalls and hard hat, she'd chat up the construction workers and point out the importance of job creation, LNG, and natural resource projects.

It was clear within the Liberal party that momentum was building, and it accelerated rapidly after the leadership debate. Liberal polling, led by Dimitri Pantazopoulos, internally predicted the party was doing far better, in far more ridings, than public polling was indicating. Campaign director McDonald even sent out a memo to supporters shortly before election day, indicating victory could be within grasp with a final big push. Most people on the outside thought he was crazy.

When the results came in on election night, May 14, 2013, all their hard work paid off. The BC Liberals had won again. Not only that, but Clark had grown her party's majority by four seats to forty-nine. The NDP had lost two seats, to close at thirty-four. The Greens were now at the table with one.

On election night, Clark and a small group of senior staffers sat upstairs in their private suite at the Wall Centre in downtown Vancouver. They had several draft speeches in front of them. They'd prepared for a variety of outcomes. When it became clear they were going to need the speech that outlined a stunning victory, but a loss of her seat in Vancouver-Point Grey, the room's printer jammed. As supporters cheered and chanted her name downstairs, and TV stations waited live to carry her address, Clark and the staff wrestled with the broken printer trying to get a copy of the victory speech to print on fickle technology. Her arrival was delayed by at least fifteen minutes.

Over at the NDP headquarters, Adrian Dix was understandably crushed. He had gone from heir apparent to the throne, to loser, in just one evening.

"Go ahead and call it what it is: the most amazing political come-back British Columbia has ever seen, and the biggest political choke in BC history," wrote *Province* columnist Mike Smyth.

The Dix campaign had not crafted a concession speech in advance—though in some ways that was not unusual for Dix, who most often just took a small piece of paper with him to the stage filled with key facts and then largely improvised his speech as he went along, using his almost-photographic memory. In that way, and perhaps only that way, he and Clark were alike—both used their speaking materials as launching pads for speeches they often made up on the fly.

Dix made his way to the stage at the Vancouver Convention Centre, where a deflated crowd perked up at the arrival of their leader. He shared one last hug with his wife, Renée Saklikar, a poet and writer—though you could be forgiven for not knowing who she was, given Dix's insistence she never be introduced to voters. Then he walked onstage, as the crowd shouted "NDP, NDP" in a half-hearted attempt to put the best spin on the evening.

"Never a dull moment in BC politics," Dix opened with. "A few minutes ago I called Premier Clark and congratulated her on her victory in this election. Elections belong to the voters, and the voters have decided and it's our responsibility, our duty, to accept that decision, and to accept responsibility for that decision."

Dix told the crowd he was very proud of the campaign New Democrat candidates, and volunteers, ran across British Columbia.

"If there's one disappointment I have, other than the obvious," he said, "it's that we haven't managed to address issues of participation in our democracy yet. But I don't know about you, but I haven't given up trying."

Dix's refusal to go negative in the election had entirely failed to yield the results he'd hoped. The gamble had been that a positive campaign would appeal to the 1.6 million eligible voters in British Columbians who didn't show up to vote in 2009 (half the eligible total). Unfortunately, voter turnout barely rose. That half of the population still stayed home.

The 2013 election is notable not only for the surprising collapse of the NDP, but also for the emergence of a new player on the political scene: the BC Green Party. After several years of failing to win a seat, the BC Greens had turned to University of Victoria climate scientist Andrew Weaver as their best hope. Weaver surprised many with a spirited election campaign in the riding of Oak Bay-Gordon Head that toppled Liberal cabinet minister Ida Chong by a vast margin. The Greens had eaten thousands of votes from both the NDP and the Liberals.

"We didn't split the vote, we are the vote in Oak Bay-Gordon Head," Weaver said in his victory speech.

Back at the BC Liberal party election night party in Vancouver, Clark and her supporters were enjoying the hard-won results of one of the most stunning come-from-behind victories in BC election history. Clark had finally printed her speech and made her way to the ballroom floor, where her RCMP security detail, as well as key aides, had to push and pull the boss through the crowd of outstretched hands and cheers as it surged toward her. Clark took the stage, approached the podium and waited for the applause to die down.

"Well," she deadpanned. "That was easy."

The Liberals would spend the night partying and celebrating their victory. It didn't matter that she'd lost her own seat to rookie New Democrat David Eby in Vancouver-Point Grey. (She'd later return to the legislature as the MLA for Kelowna-West in a by-election.)

Away from the TV lights on the Wall Centre convention floor, dozens of Liberal staffers, local campaign workers, and volunteers gathered in a conference room several floors up.

The party was in full swing later that night, when the door opened and Clark strode triumphantly into the room. She grabbed a chair and a champagne bottle, and, in front of a crowd that was now jumping up and down and screaming, climbed on top of the chair, nonchalantly popped the champagne cork with one thumb and started to shotgun the bottle. It was a messy, enthusiastic scene as the premier took a long draw. The room went wild.

"Tonight we celebrate the biggest political comeback in BC history," she said, on the chair.

The crowd began chanting, "Christy, Christy!" Clark hopped off the chair, gave a bear hug to a nearby supporter, and proceeded to do what she always does: she started working the room. That night, anyone who wanted it got a one-on-one moment with the premier and a personal thanks for their work on the campaign. Staffers were in tears.

Clark's BC Liberal party won a historic fourth consecutive majority. She'd defied all her many critics, rebellious internal MLAS, and pollsters. She survived the blowback over the HST that had toppled the once-invulnerable Gordon Campbell. And she'd made the pundits look foolish for the fact they'd long since written her off as the expected loser on May 14.

"I think people are going to re-examine the truthfulness of polls," she would say, shortly after the election. "If there is any lesson in this, it's that pollsters and pundits and commentators do not choose the government. It's the people of British Columbia that choose the government."

CHAPTER 5
DOING IT MY WAY

The day after Christy Clark's stunning come-from-behind election victory, she held a press conference in Vancouver that left no question about what she really thought of all the people who'd thought she was dead in the water going into the May 14, 2013, election.

"I wasn't as surprised as everybody else," she told a packed room of journalists in her waterfront premier's office. "I said this to you guys from the very beginning: the polls do not tell us how people are going to vote, because voting day is the only day that they vote. It's like me asking you what you're going to have for dinner a month from now. Maybe it's chicken maybe it's steak, I don't know. You don't know. You might make a guess at it, but your decision could change before then. I've always been a skeptic of the polls."

Pollsters themselves would do extensive soul-searching following the election, questioning how the methodology that at one point predicted a twenty-point NDP win could have been so wrong. Here, too, Clark had an immediate opinion.

"You guys get this stuff for free," she said of the polls for media. "And you should take it for what it's worth."

She added, "Pollsters do not get to choose the government. The people of British Columbia chose the government, and guess what? It turns out that people make their own choices, despite what the pollsters tell us. People make their own choices, and it's a private personal choice."

When a columnist at one point expressed surprise at her margin of victory, Clark was quick with a withering comeback, suggesting if journalists had spent less time on the golf course and more time out on the campaign trail with her, they too would have seen the momentum she saw building in the campaign.

You can perhaps forgive Clark for a brief period of gloating. She had suffered through two years of mutinies and infighting in her party, overcome widespread predictions she was destined to lose the election, and almost single-handedly clawed the Liberals back from the brink of oblivion.

A WEEK LATER, Clark would gather her forty-nine-member Liberal caucus for its first meeting since election day.

"So many people said it could not be done, so many people said that British Columbians would not choose a government that was going to put the economy first," she told the new and returning MLAs. "So many people said economy wasn't the issue for British Columbians. And they were all proven wrong."

This was the start of Clark's golden period of governance. She had vowed to do it her way, to lead in the manner she'd always wanted before being saddled with the HST and the baggage of Gordon Campbell's administration. Clark was fortunate to be able to utilize the fastest-growing economy in the country, bolstered in part by her jobs plan and tourism numbers that had climbed in the aftermath of the 2010 Olympics. But she'd have to address looming labour negotiations, budget pressures, First Nations legal challenges, and Alberta's insistence that more pipelines be pushed through British Columbia.

Clark had not only saved the Liberals from extinction in 2013, but she'd strengthened the party from forty-five to forty-nine seats. Half of the old caucus had been out to make her life miserable, and those MLAs had either quit or retired. The other half had rallied behind her and now owed their political lives to Clark's campaigning. The new MLAS were, of course, loyal to the boss who'd recruited them. So as Clark surveyed the caucus room before her, she now saw a friendly, united team. Unquestioned loyalty. Reverence, even, in certain cases. She had complete control of her troops.

Two dissidents who had stayed on soon found themselves exiled to the political equivalent of Siberia by the premier—former caucus chair Gordie Hogg, who'd tried to conduct an investigation into Clark over Quick Wins, and former cabinet minister Moira Stilwell, who'd been running a guerrilla campaign of leaks and criticism against Clark for months and who'd spoken out against the premier for running a red light during the election campaign. Hogg was stripped of his caucus chairmanship. Stilwell was treated like a pariah. Clark's friends like to speak about her capacity for forgiveness, even to those who've done her wrong. But that did not, it appears, extend to Stilwell.

With total control of her caucus and cabinet, Clark was finally free to govern the way she wanted. The newly re-elected premier's style was immediately compared with that of her predecessor, Campbell. There were many differences.

The most obvious was temperament. Clark never yelled or lost her cool. When she was upset, her ministers knew it, but more often in a quiet way, similar to a parent telling a child they are disappointed in them. She relied on the self-motivation of her ministers, and she gave them rope to run off and figure things out—at least, during the earliest days of her term.

Cabinet veterans who'd served under both premiers say Clark was more willing to change her mind or be persuaded of a decision she wasn't sure was correct, after a debate within cabinet. Campbell stated his opinion first in cabinet, and couldn't be moved off it except in rare circumstances.

Clark's cabinet meetings always started on time and ended when scheduled. Though many ministers appreciated the punctuality, it often meant the kind of lengthy debate on serious issues that had existed under Campbell were cut short under Clark.

If Clark was more willing to keep an open mind, it might also have been because she didn't know her ministers' files as well as Campbell did. The former premier was well known for devouring the briefing books of his own ministers, and working, in some cases, harder to understand their files than they did. If he didn't like what he was seeing, he'd just bypass the minister and get the job done himself. Clark didn't continue the trend of micromanaging her ministers. What's the point, she would say, of putting smart people into cabinet if you aren't willing to listen to them and let them do their job?

Clark also wasn't the policy wonk that Campbell was. She didn't come back after Christmas break to radically shift her government in a new direction after reading a new idea in a book, like Campbell did, nor did she frequently shuffle her cabinet to freshen up the faces and portfolios. Her mantra became stability. Clark's critics would accuse her of having no ideas or ambition. Clark would simply say she was focusing on her election promises of jobs and the economy.

Not everyone was a fan of the changes. For MLAS who wanted to participate in policy making, they found caucus meetings reduced, in their mind, to simple sessions in which the day's agenda for the House was often the priority versus giving backbenchers a chance to chime in with ideas. Cabinet ministers appreciated the chance to debate issues with a premier who wouldn't yell at them, but more than a few also noticed that their opinions sometimes carried less weight than the crew of advisors Clark surrounded herself with, including those who weren't even working at the legislature, like Clark's ex-husband, Mark Marissen.

CLARK'S TOP PRIORITY after winning re-election was to get moving on the LNG tax and environment regimes that would allow companies to make final investment decisions to build plants in the province.

There was a lot riding on the Liberals being able to deliver the LNG industry. After all, it was that miracle vision that had propelled the party campaign machine into such lofty promises as "debt-free BC." Unquestionably, it was a major influence in the party's victory.

Clark got to work on developing an LNG tax structure that would provide the BC government with at least a small slice of the profits from the industry. In its next full budget, in February 2014, the Liberal government released a "framework" for an LNG tax of up to 1.5 per cent on profits until the multi-billion-dollar capital costs of the plant had been recovered, then up to 7 per cent on profits after that. The throne speech also promised a "reengineering of our secondary and post-secondary institutions to ensure our students have the skills for the jobs of the future" in an abrupt push to focus more on trades training, instead of artsy degrees, to train a workforce for the jobs required in the LNG industry.

Full details of BC's LNG tax were set to be released in November. But by October, Malaysian state-run energy giant Petronas, which was proposing a $36 billion LNG facility and pipeline in Prince Rupert, had grown frustrated. Oil prices had fallen dramatically, and companies that were proposing LNG facilities had seen the bottom-line profits from their oil divisions, used to fund LNG exploration, take a serious hit.

Petronas had picked a bad site for its LNG project, on Lelu Island near Prince Rupert. The location had caused persistent environmental concerns because the sandy area called Flora Bank, between the proposed facility and the marine terminal, was a crucial juvenile salmon location for the nearby Skeena River estuary. Premier Clark's chief of staff Dan Doyle had been telling Petronas for years that they had chosen a poor location. Petronas was scared that if it tried to change it would be sent back to square one for new environmental approvals, so the company began working on the idea of a ludicrously expensive $1 billion suspension bridge to cross the Flora Bank.

Petronas waited until October 6, 2014, the day the Liberal government was planning to deliver its new speech from the throne, to start playing hardball. Just hours before the speech, the Malaysians released a rocket of a statement that cut the Liberals down at the knees and threatened a fifteen-year delay without a better government deal.

The Liberals sprang into action. On October 21 they announced the 7 per cent LNG tax had been cut in half to 3.5 per cent for the next twenty years.

"The thud you heard early Tuesday afternoon was the sound of the BC Liberal government dropping back to Planet Earth after a heady trip through clouds of speculation on the liquefied natural gas file," observed *Vancouver Sun* columnist Vaughn Palmer.

There were, by now, few mentions of the $100 billion prosperity fund promised by the Liberals in the election, or of a "debt-free BC." When pressed, de Jong said it could still be done in forty years. At that rate, most of Clark's cabinet would die of old age before fulfilling their election promise to make BC debt free.

On July 11, 2015, Petronas announced a "conditional final investment decision" that appeared to give a green light to the project, subject to a project development agreement passed by BC in the legislature and a positive federal environmental decision by Ottawa.

The Liberals reconvened the legislature that fall to pass the deal. But Prime Minister Harper's Conservative government punted a decision until after the federal election on October 19, 2015. This added a year's delay and was a significant blow to the project.

The federal Conservatives lost to Justin Trudeau's Liberals. The new Liberal government took one look at the potential pollution levels of the Petronas project and also punted its decision. It would take the Trudeau Liberals almost another year, until September 27, 2016, before they were ready to green-light Petronas. Even then, it wasn't without drama.

Federal environment minister Catherine McKenna had made the approval conditional on BC joining Ottawa's announcement for a

Canada-wide carbon tax. BC's carbon tax had been in place for years, courtesy of the forethought of Gordon Campbell, and Clark would only agree to increase the provincial levels once other provinces caught up. Ottawa agreed.

On September 27, 2016, Ottawa announced a snap press conference in Metro Vancouver that caught even Clark by surprise. She was in Kelowna at the time, touring the Duke and Duchess of Cambridge through the province, and had to scramble to fly back to Vancouver to make the event. She was late because no plane is allowed to leave the tarmac until after the royal couple leave.

Once Clark arrived, McKenna tried to jam her in a final meeting in an aerocentre meeting room. She demanded BC drop its request for an equivalency test on Ottawa's new pan-Canadian carbon pricing scheme, which would have let BC bail on the deal if an independent review showed the cap-and-trade system used in Ontario and Quebec gave those provinces an unfair advantage. At first, McKenna tried to say BC had agreed to those terms, which Clark denied. Then the federal minister started yelling, and said Clark's staff had told federal staff it was okay (which BC staff flatly denied). Clark used her finely honed skill at sizing up opponents, took one look at McKenna and, quite literally, laughed in her face.

"I'm not doing it," Clark said to McKenna's demands.

"Well, we're not going to announce this then," replied McKenna.

Clark crossed her arms, leaned across the table, and looked right at the minister. "I'm pretty sure you are," she said.

McKenna's clumsy negotiating had nowhere to go.

Ottawa had called the press conference and sent three cabinet ministers to the announcement. The media was already outside waiting for them. The feds had lost their leverage. Further, Trudeau's cabinet had passed the approval order. What was McKenna going to do—unapprove a cabinet order on her own? Lie to the press?

"Are we going to do the announcement or what?" asked Clark.

Everyone left. McKenna was forced to follow and grit her teeth through the subsequent press conference.

But by then, Petronas was in a crunch. It only had until December to make the project work using gas contracts it had previously locked in with customers at favourable rates. Clark's chief of staff, Steve Carr, had friends within Petronas, and he soon heard the company's auditors had swept in to close the books on the project. When a decision wasn't announced by December, and Petronas's gas contracts lapsed, BC knew the project was as good as dead.

Petronas officially announced the cancellation of Pacific Northwest LNG on July 25, 2017. BC's dream of LNG was all but over, with the exception of one small facility in Squamish called Woodfibre LNG. BC still sits on one of the largest natural gas deposits in the world, and perhaps, some day, the idea of LNG will be resurrected in a way that actually flourishes.

The consequences of BC's obsession with LNG won't be known for some time. Not only did the province abruptly shift its focus to a single industry for many years, but it re-engineered the education system and overhauled trades training to try to facilitate jobs that would never exist. History may one day regard Clark's infamous 2013 LNG throne speech with something more than the derision it has since elicited in political circles. But as of 2017, virtually none of the promises she or her government made about LNG ever came true. Clark's speech was a complete and utter misfire.

Still, it accomplished one very important point at the time it was read in 2013: it inspired voters. They glimpsed an ambitious dream. One they'd conclude was worth the risk of voting for.

AT HER FIRST caucus meeting following the 2013 election, Clark also had this line for the new Liberals, which would foreshadow one of their toughest fights ahead: "We will make sure that every one of our children has the chance to fight and win on the world stage because we are going to find labour peace in our classrooms."

Long-term labour peace with the BC Teachers' Federation had been an election promise from Clark. She tasked rookie MLA Peter Fassbender with the job.

After the election, in June 2013, Clark invited Fassbender to her downtown premier's office to offer him the post as education minister.

"I'm going to ask you to come into cabinet," she told Fassbender.

"Well, I'm honoured and willing to do that," replied Fassbender.

"You might be surprised at what I'm going to ask you to do," said the premier. "I'd like you to take on the education portfolio."

"Really?" replied Fassbender. "I thought you liked me."

A former mayor of the City of Langley, he'd recently helped municipalities and the province negotiate a long-term policing contract with the RCMP, and Clark thought he could use his gift of the gab and political experience to hammer out a deal.

It did not quite work that way. Instead, teachers launched the longest strike in BC's history. Within ten months of Fassbender taking on the job, in March 2014, BCTF members had voted overwhelmingly in favour of job action, after receiving what they considered an "insulting" wage offer from the province of a two-year salary freeze and no movement on smaller classes or more teachers.

The Clark government had surprised many by achieving labour peace with negotiated new contracts for all other public-sector unions except the BCTF. The premier, who was no fan of the union, intended to bring the teachers to heel by flexing the muscle of her recently won majority mandate.

But it was the teachers who remained in early control of the dispute. By April 2014, they had started phase one of job action by not communicating or meeting with school administrators. In May they began a series of rotating strikes lasting three weeks. Fassbender responded by offering a $1,200 signing bonus if the teachers would sign a new deal before the end of the school year, and threatening as much as a 10 per cent wage rollback if they kept up their strike activity.

The BCTF scoffed, and on June 17 started a full-scale strike, shutting down schools, except for provincial exams, which were designated an essential service. The strike technically continued throughout the summer, though with no kids in classrooms only summer school and international programs were affected. By September 2014, though, with picket lines still up outside schools, parents were getting angry with both sides. Veteran mediator Vince Ready started helping in talks around that time.

The central issue of the strike, outside of wages and the usual matters, was a contentious government proposal called E80, which the teachers felt would have undone their previous court victories on class size and composition. The government steadfastly refused to budge on the clause, and the two sides were deadlocked.

The key to settling the dispute originated in a hotel lobby in Charlottetown, Prince Edward Island, in late August, where Clark was attending a premiers' conference and happened to see Jerry Dias, president of Unifor. The two had met earlier in the year, when Clark and Dias managed to hammer out a deal between striking container-truck drivers, the province, and the federal government at the Port of Vancouver in a flurry of negotiations at the legislature. It was one of Clark's early wins on the organized labour front.

In Charlottetown, Dias introduced Clark to Hassan Yussuff, the new president of the Canadian Labour Congress, who offered to help try to broker talks with the BCTF back in BC. Several weeks passed before Clark would take Yussuff up on the offer. By then, it was the second week of the new school year, classrooms were behind picket lines, and the Liberal government was experiencing an intense backlash from irate parents who wanted the situation resolved. Half a million students weren't in school. Their parents were scrambling to find child care. Nerves were frayed on all sides.

Yussuff had suggested to BCTF president Jim Iker that he meet with Clark in late August in a neutral province like Ontario, but Iker wasn't interested. By the second week of September, though, the teachers' union too was under immense pressure to get a deal because it was broke. Iker was frustrated by negotiations that he felt were getting nowhere with the government's bargaining agent, the BC Public Sector Employers' Council, and so after a particularly fruitless exchange over the issue of binding arbitration, he called Yussuff to ask if he could still get a meeting together with the premier.

First, Iker would have to meet with Clark's chief of staff, Dan Doyle, a veteran civil servant with a reputation for being a plain-spoken straight-shooter. They met for two and a half hours at a hotel near Vancouver's airport, where Iker explained why the teachers wouldn't give away their court victories by agreeing to the E80 clause but would be willing to find other ways to reach an agreement. It was an awkward meeting, but the two men eventually hit it off.

Iker is a mustachioed, soft-spoken character from Topley, a remote BC town of fewer than 120 people near Burns Lake in BC's Interior. He likes chopping wood, riding his ATV, and playing old-timer hockey with his friends, where his trademark long-flowing, grey-streaked mullet hair would drop around his goalie mask as he dived around in the net. Iker likes classic rock, and took breaks during pressure-filled days during the strike by slapping on headphones and walking around the BCTF's office listening to the Rolling Stones, Neil Young, and AC/DC. He is not a screamer or a shouter. His two kids say they've never seen their dad lose his cool. He's a hippie at heart, more likely to get watery eyes in a debate than kick over a table in frustration.

Doyle liked Iker. He left the meeting and suggested Clark agree to a sit-down.

The BCTF and government bargainers were setting up meetings for the weekend of September 20, in a last-ditch effort to get some sort of deal with the help of mediator Vince Ready. Doyle phoned Iker back before that weekend started and offered a meeting with the premier on Friday, at 9:30 a.m.

The location for the secret rendezvous between Iker and Clark was the Delta Suite Hotel in downtown Vancouver. Clark and Doyle sneaked in the back route with a police escort. When Clark and Iker sat down, the premier opened with a familiar anecdote about how her father was a teacher and she knew the hardships of the job.

Iker responded with, "It's time to get a deal."

For around forty-five minutes, the two tried to outline some of the issues, and Iker hit the elephant in the room head-on at one point by saying to Clark he wondered if she was just trying to find a way to legislate them back to work. Clark admitted to Iker she was feeling the pressure from her supporters to end the strike. The premier concluded the meeting by saying she'd instruct her side to try to do something different in the weekend talks. Iker felt hopeful. Both sides agreed to keep the meeting secret.

Behind the scenes, Clark, through Doyle, told government bargainers to abandon clause E80 and "get moving" on settling this thing. Yussuff, on the teacher side, exerted similar pressure.

A marathon weekend of bargaining stretched into Monday. The government finally took E80 off the table late Monday night. Both sides started to make concessions on wages, benefits, calendars, and a new education fund proposed by government to be spent on teachers.

Iker took what he thought was a workable proposal away from the main meeting room at the Pacific Gateway Hotel in Richmond and back downstairs to a room where his bargaining team was waiting. He asked what they thought. They gave it a unanimous approval. Iker went back upstairs, and at 3:30 a.m. Tuesday told the government negotiators, "We have a deal."

Teachers would later vote 86 per cent to ratify the proposal, which included a 7.25 per cent salary increase, a $400 million education fund to hire specialist teachers, and a $105 million fund for retroactive grievances. It didn't deal with the court appeals, instead giving both sides an opportunity to renegotiate depending on the outcome. At six years, it was the longest teachers' contract ever reached, expiring in 2019.

Doyle called the premier at home at 3:30 a.m. to tell her about the deal. She was wide awake, and had been sitting up waiting for a call. She too was relieved that the longest teacher strike in BC history was over.

Clark had campaigned on long-term labour peace with the teachers. It wasn't quite the ten-year time frame she'd once proposed, but six years was still enough to label it a rare and "historic" settlement with teachers. It was only the third negotiated contract with teachers since provincial bargaining began in 1994. The Liberals marked it down as a win in their books.

THE MANY PROGRAMS and policies that crossed Clark's desk during these years would be dwarfed by the sheer size and scale of one proposal in particular: the Site C dam. Weighing in with an estimated $8.8 billion price tag, it was the most expensive project in BC history. It was also one of the most contentious.

The dam, to be located on the Peace River near Fort St. John, had a long history in the province. Its earliest consideration dates back fifty years as the proposed third of five major dams on the Peace River, following the construction of the W.A.C. Bennett Dam and the Peace Canyon Dam.

Gordon Campbell was the latest to approve moving the project forward, in 2010. At the time he even had the support of climate scientist Andrew Weaver, who would later go on to become Green Party leader. Campbell chose to exempt the project from review by the BC Utilities Commission, because the pesky independent agency had an annoying habit of reaching its own conclusions on projects that sometimes did not align with the wants of the government of the day. The agency had, for example, reviewed Site C and rejected the idea in the 1980s. Campbell also set in motion federal and provincial environmental reviews before he was forced to resign.

Site C chugged along quietly behind the scenes until Clark became premier. At the time, Dan Doyle (later Clark's chief of staff) was chair of BC Hydro's board, and he put Site C through an internal review, whipping the proposal into shape before it ever saw the light of day in front of the premier and her cabinet. Doyle knew, and had seen first-hand, how quickly a project that doesn't have its ducks in a row could find its chances for approval collapse in front of cabinet scrutiny.

After Clark won re-election in 2013, Site C landed on her desk. The allure was simple: clean, environmentally friendly, sustainable, cheap, reliable hydroelectric power that, while maybe not needed right at this moment, would almost certainly be needed sometime in the province's future. But at the beginning, the new premier wasn't sure the dam was worth the time, effort, money, or political capital it would take to fight with critics and local First Nations. In one of their first private meetings on the file, Clark turned to Energy Minister Bill Bennett and said, "I just want you to know, I'm not a big fan of the Site C project." And she left it at that.

Clark would play her cards close to her chest on the file for months. And she'd take advantage of some simmering personal tension between key ministers and officials to try to grind the project down and stress-test it before a final decision.

The two main combatants on Site C were Bennett and Finance Minister Mike de Jong. They did not particularly like each other. Bennett was a bombastic, outspoken, quick-tempered, highly intelligent hunter and lawyer from rural BC who had pissed a lot of people off in his own party with his scorched-earth mutiny against Campbell. De Jong was a cautious, hard-to-read, slow-spoken, thoughtful, conservative lawyer known for his frugality and ability to stretch a dollar.

Bennett thought de Jong was a Machiavellian manipulator. The finance minister's tendency to sit quietly during meetings, not giving away his true opinion until the very end, after everyone else had spoken, rubbed Bennett the wrong way. Bennett is a plain speaker, and he says what's on his mind.

De Jong eyed Bennett with wary suspicion, at best, given his pedigree as a loose cannon. To a man like de Jong, Bennett was unpredictable and unreliable.

Clark pitted the two of them against each other on the file. Bennett needed to get treasury board approval for Site C from de Jong. De Jong needed to keep the budget balanced and the AAA credit rating intact. They spent many months debating the project, with de Jong challenging BC Hydro's accounting, assumptions, methodology, forecasting, and overall fiscal competence, while also unleashing his ministry's small army of bureaucrats to go to BC Hydro and pore over the Crown corporation's books.

Another complicating factor was BC Hydro CEO Jessica McDonald, who had a reputation for being a tough-as-nails negotiator, First Nations consultant, and civil servant. She also brought her own baggage to the fight, stemming from her seemingly meteoric rise through the civil service under Campbell to become his deputy minister and head of the civil service. Doyle began picking up lingering notes of resentment among some cabinet ministers and top deputies who remembered McDonald from Campbell's days in power. She'd been his tough enforcer at times, undercutting cabinet ministers at the order of the premier by simply going to their deputies and getting things done without their involvement. Though arguably brilliant, and certainly a keen administrator of the Site C file, she ruffled feathers around cabinet and these had to be occasionally smoothed over by Doyle as well.

Doyle also had to do significant work with cabinet members just to prepare them to understand how to make a decision on Site C. The cabinet had several rookie members, like Amrik Virk, a former Surrey RCMP inspector, and Coralee Oakes, a former Quesnel councillor. They had no idea how to begin to handle a decision of the magnitude of Site C, with a price tag larger than anything they'd ever seen, a construction schedule that would last almost a decade, and an energy analysis that stretched a hundred years. Doyle held his own seminars on business case analysis and decision-making strategies, to give the cabinet ministers the tools they'd need to participate meaningfully in the debate.

There were two points when the Site C proposal looked like it was going to fail.

The first was in 2014, when Bennett himself was still not convinced BC needed a mega-dam when it could just go to the private sector and achieve the same energy through numerous other small-scale projects, like wind, solar, river, and geothermal. He'd struck up a friendship with key private power folks, and it took him half of 2014 to be convinced that, despite their arguments, the reliable power of a dam was more desirable than that of smaller projects. Whether Bennett actually reached the right conclusion on that particular point remains a matter of contention among critics.

The debate continued when, on May 8, 2014, a joint review panel for the provincial and federal government concluded that Site C was the best and cheapest way for British Columbia to get new energy, but that BC Hydro "has not fully demonstrated the need for the Project on the timetable set forth" and that its forecasts for demand and load be given to the independent BC Utilities Commission to analyze. The report was filled with the kind of vague bureaucratic double-speak the Clark administration hated. Its authors would in one paragraph praise Site C for its comparatively low cost of power and in another say they didn't have the tools to analyze BC Hydro's financial calculations. They'd conclude BC Hydro hadn't made its case for the power on its timetable, but didn't make any conclusions of their own, couching the report's fifty recommendations in terms like "if ministers are inclined to proceed" and "if the project is to proceed."

The report did contain at least one idea the Clark cabinet agreed with, though: "The decision on whether the Project proceeds is made by elected officials, not by the panel." The Liberals had no intention of reversing Campbell's decision to exempt Site C from review by the BC Utilities Commission, fearing it would generate similarly frustrating reports and ultimately delay the project even further.

The second point at which the mega-dam proposal almost failed was in early 2015, when de Jong cracked down so hard on BC Hydro and Site C that it looked like the project would simply fall apart. He suggested at cabinet that BC Hydro still hadn't done its due diligence on the numbers. He pushed, and prodded, and made it very clear Site C wasn't up to snuff. Jobs Minister Shirley Bond, also not a fan of Bennett's, backed him up in his rigorous dissection of the project.

But by then, Clark and the rest of cabinet were warming up to the idea of Site C. De Jong probably could have killed it, had he really wanted to, say those who were there. But he pulled back and instead suggested adding $600 million to the price tag in the form of contingency money and to accommodate provincial sales tax payments.

In the end, cabinet gave unanimous approval for Site C. It required decades of conceptual work, years of actual planning, and at least six months of intensive cabinet deliberations to reach the conclusion.

Clark came around to fully backing Site C. It was the kind of forward-thinking visionary project Clark liked to pride herself on being able to champion. She fashioned herself as a modern-day W.A.C. Bennett, who, in the 1950s and '60s, had shrugged off his short-sighted critics to build the hydro dams and provincial highways that would form the backbone of the province today. With the cost ground down by de Jong, the contingency fund increased, the argument over cheaper power settled amid weeks of debate, and BC Hydro pushed to justify the smallest details, Clark felt comfortable revealing, by the end of the debate, that she too was now in favour of Site C.

"In the life of any province, there are moments where each of us have an opportunity, a responsibility, to make big decisions, ones that are going to matter, in this case, for a century," Clark said when announcing Site C's approval at the legislature on December 16, 2014. "Today is that day."

For some, the Clark Liberals didn't give enough weight to the idea that the smaller wind, solar, and geothermal projects would become more efficient and cheaper in future years. Environmental groups and First Nations have challenged that Site C will irrevocably harm farm land, destroy traditional Aboriginal territory in the Peace River Valley, and unfairly lead to the eviction of a small number of local landowners. Energy critics, including former BC Hydro CEOs, have argued the government should have let the utilities commission back in so the experts could have done a better analysis of Site C's merits than Clark's cabinet did.

Putting Site C back to the utilities commission was never an option Clark seriously considered. She and Bennett shared a similar philosophy here: politicians were elected to lead and make the tough decisions on a project the size of Site C, not a bunch of unelected, unaccountable, bureaucrats in some review agency. Site C had been studied to death, they felt. And voters had entrusted them to govern, with a sizable majority. It was their call on whether to proceed, and they'd face the consequences with the electorate.

THE EARLY DAYS of the post-2013 Clark administration were filled with references to balanced budgets, spending prudence, and a focus on cutting costs within government. Internally, a lacklustre economy was threatening to evaporate the razor-thin 2013/14 surplus on which was built the first balanced budget since 2008. Clark, who'd just won a campaign by portraying the NDP as a bunch of tax-and-spend reckless financial mismanagers who would drive the province to economic ruin, couldn't very well allow deficits now on her own budgets.

"There will be calls to spend money," Clark told her MLAs. "For the next little while, our answer to most of those questions has to be no, not now... It's difficult to say no, but we have a mandate from the people of British Columbia to make sure that we're controlling government spending. It's what we promised we would do."

Finance Minister Mike de Jong steered government into its fifth straight year of austerity measures and cutbacks. The Liberals had been taking an axe to government spending since 2009, cutting millions. They'd reduced the advertising budget. Banned all but essential travel. Slashed office expenses. Cancelled service contracts. Fired some government employees. Instituted a hiring freeze within the civil service. Cracked down on compensation and bonuses for Crown corporation executives. And sold more than one hundred surplus government properties and assets. Clark would add to that a sweeping "core review" of the entire government, designed to hunt down red tape, eliminate duplication, and remove barriers to economic growth and job creation.

Overall, de Jong said the government would sharply curtail its average spending growth to 1.6 per cent, and throttle health spending—its largest expense—to just 2.6 per cent annually from a high of more than 6 per cent. On the health file alone, curbing the growth of health costs proved a Herculean task, but one accomplished by Health Minister Terry Lake after considerable effort.

Some saw the cost-cutting as grim. But being prudent managers of the public penny played well within the Liberal base. And cracking down on government waste was what they'd told voters they would do.

Clark and Liberals who suffered through this period of austerity will point out that balanced budgets then were tough, gruelling slogs. They required deliberate work and focus. They remain, in the minds of many Liberals, an accomplishment worth celebrating. Though you could argue the Liberals became obsessed with the idea of balanced books, AAA credit ratings, and being perceived as fiscally prudent, to the point that the government became scared to take a risk on big spending promises for voters—something that would haunt the party in its next re-election bid.

THERE WERE A few early, unique policy wins for the Liberals.

Finance Minister de Jong proposed spending some limited funds to create a $1,200 grant for every child's RESP account if they were born after 2007. It was classic de Jong, a frugal farmer from Abbotsford, to come up with a forced savings plan for parents that, while they might not appreciate it initially, would certainly accrue benefits by the time the child was ready for post-secondary education.

Children's Minister Stephanie Cadieux approached the premier with an idea about doing something for poverty-level moms who were having trouble getting back into the workforce and earning an income for their kids. Clark took up the task with her, and they developed a $24.5 million plan to pay for the school fees, daycare, medical costs, transportation, and tuition for single parents on welfare who wanted to go back to school and train for an in-demand job. The idea, announced in 2015, would help boost someone out of poverty while also helping fill jobs in sectors that needed workers, including carpentry, welding, office support work, retail, cooking, social work, early childhood education, heavy equipment operation, security, plumbing, marriage counselling, and baking, to name a few. Almost four thousand people would go through the program by 2017, and not even the New Democrats had a critical thing to say about it.

That's not to say everything was rosy in the early days for the new premier. Her government continued to face accusations that it was too miserly on social services, and a barrage of bad press over "clawbacks" to maternity benefits and bus passes for those on welfare and disability.

The centrepiece of the Clark administration for quite some time was the jobs plan, first developed in the earliest days of her premiership in

2011. The Liberals tried to make the plan a living document, refreshing it annually, holding frequent updates to celebrate its accomplishments. The government would repeatedly trumpet the plan for growing BC's GDP to the leading rate in Canada, reducing unemployment, diversifying the economy, increasing investment, and boosting the number of international students.

More time will have to pass for the true impact, or lack thereof, of the jobs plan to be known. The Liberals liked to pat themselves on the back for job growth statistics that may or may not have had anything to do with the plan, especially as the province's hot housing market led to a dramatic rise in jobs in the real estate sector and housing construction—neither of which was in the jobs plan. When the jobs numbers were up, the Liberals took credit. When they were down, they pointed out how government can't create jobs, only the private sector can. The plan also suffered from its early association with LNG, which, as time went by, kept failing to materialize. For many, the jobs plan was just another part of an LNG dream that never became a reality.

The Enbridge Gateway Pipeline was a different story. Prime Minister Stephen Harper was desperate to get more raw bitumen out of the ground in northern Alberta. One idea that had a lot of traction was the Gateway pipeline that would carry crude from Alberta through a pipeline across British Columbia to a terminal in Kitimat. Harper had an ally in Premier Alison Redford in Alberta. For months the premiers squared off in the media, Clark not willing to support the project and Redford demanding BC make way for the project she was pitching, which was in the best interest of the country.

As the debate around the pipeline continued in 2013, Clark travelled to Edmonton and Regina. She wanted to deliver some news in person. She met first with Premier Brad Wall in Saskatchewan, and then with Redford on her home turf, to reveal her so-called five conditions. They included BC getting a fair share of royalties in the project and boosted environmental protection. Clark explained to Redford in a meeting that any BC royalties would come from Enbridge and not cut into Alberta's share of oil revenues. Redford still wasn't happy with BC's power play. She emerged to blast Clark in the media for trying to horn in on Alberta's proceeds, despite Clark's explicit denials of any such plan. Then Redford's office tipped off the Alberta legislative press gallery on Clark's schedule, so reporters could ambush the BC premier on her way out of town.

After Clark's stunning re-election in 2013, the two premiers would find a way to hash out their disagreements. It was the first of several times Clark would issue ultimatums and win on the national stage.

EVEN WITH A united team, a large majority in the legislature, and a clear runway to accomplish what she wanted, Clark could not accomplish all her goals.

One of her ambitions had been to improve the health-care system for those who were trying to care for their ill and elderly parents. It was an intensely personal goal for Clark. In 2006, her seventy-five-year-old mother, Mavis, was dying of brain cancer. She was in hospital at the time, but it wasn't a workable scenario. Mavis wanted only her daughter to help her shower, for example, and when Clark wasn't there she'd sometimes wander around the facility.

Clark didn't know what else to do, so she took her mother out of hospital to care for her at home. It was the most challenging experience of her life, caring for her mother and Hamish, and also working full-time on her own talk show on CKNW. Her mother was disoriented and slipping away. She would sometimes just scream as the cancer got worse. Clark would climb into bed with her mother and hold her while she was crying and disoriented, just trying to calm her down. Mavis Clark would die on March 19, 2006.

Clark told the story of her mother often while running for the party leadership in 2011. She wanted to reform the health-care system to help others who needed to care for their sick and ailing parents. It was the kind of raw, honest, emotional story that attracted supporters to Clark during the earliest days of her leadership and her "families first" agenda. But as the years ticked away during Clark's premiership, reform never happened.

The goal, in Clark's mind, was to come up with a way to pay people something if they chose to stay at home with their loved ones, or, at the very least, support them somehow through a generous tax credit. Her government started its transformation toward home care in 2014, beginning to move some of the almost $18 billion spent annually on health care into better services to help seniors and the elderly stay at home for as long as possible. The idea was that it's cheaper and provides better care to have the system send nurses and care aides to a person's home to help them shower, cook, and take their medicine than it is to have that same person occupy a bed in a hospital.

Yet the change occurred slowly inside the massively complicated health system. Everything required enormous time and money. Plus there was resistance from some in the system who said, these people are going to stay home with their loved one anyway, so why pay them?

In the end, despite all her power, influence, and complete control of government for four unopposed years, Clark ultimately failed to enact the reforms she'd promised in the wake of her mother's death.

Nonetheless, Clark was able to use the strong majority she won single-handedly in 2013. She passed legislation to protect the Great Bear Rainforest; achieved labour peace through new deals for teachers, nurses, and government employees; and put in place conditions that would benefit BC and some First Nations on natural resource projects, LNG, and oil pipelines. But what she was most proud of was holding the line on balanced budgets every year. It would be up to voters to decide if all this was enough to reward her party with another term in power.

CHAPTER 6
MADAM PREMIER

When Peter Fassbender went knocking on doors during the 2017 election campaign, the smooth-talking former ad salesman and mayor could handle pretty much any criticism thrown at him on the doorstep. Except for one. It almost always came from the woman of the household. And as the campaign went on, it grew in frequency until it was a regular occurrence whenever he hit the doorbell.

"I like you," the female voter would say. "But I don't like your leader. And I can't vote for you because of that."

There wasn't enough time in the day for Fassbender to try to argue his way through Christy Clark's popularity problems. And besides, neither he nor his fellow Liberal candidates, nor party HQ for that matter, really understood the many layers of the anger she was facing among women in Metro Vancouver during the campaign. In the end, Fassbender lost his Surrey-area riding for a variety of reasons—bridge tolls, Uber, school portables, and housing affordability, to name a few—but top of his list, if you ask him, was the surprisingly visceral hostility he and other Liberal candidates faced on the doorstep from female voters whose outpouring of negative opinions over Clark caught everyone by surprise.

Among the many paradoxes that surround Clark, this one stands out: how the longest-serving female premier in BC history, who blazed a trail for women leaders in her administration, who became the first female first minister re-elected in Canadian history, could be so disliked by female voters. But there it was, again and again in Liberal polling and on the campaign trail, a puzzling hostility between Clark and women that stretched across her six years as premier, from start to finish.

Gender politics was a persistent and fascinating undercurrent of Clark's time in office. Considerable time and energy went into fostering a Liberal women's network and opening job-shadowing placements for girls in the premier's office. Yet the public debate only became more fractured as her premiership continued.

The overarching problem in charting the issue of female leadership and Clark's premiership is quite simply this: the longer she was in office, the more disliked by the public she became. And so, as she increased her efforts to speak out about the obstacles faced by women leaders, or the need to encourage them to enter public life, her credibility was simultaneously eroded by the growing, visceral, negative reaction she elicited from voters—especially, and ironically, women.

The problem was there from the beginning. Clark's leadership was fashioned around a "families first" agenda, which began by helping low-income families, raising the minimum wage, and creating a new Family Day holiday. They were pocketbook issues that resonated well with voters, and women in particular. But it was also quickly clear she'd be getting the kinds of questions her predecessor, Gordon Campbell, never did. On the night she was elected leader, Global TV anchor Chris Gailus asked her if her new job would still give her time to date, a question that was repeated the next morning in her first media scrum as premier-designate. Nobody had ever asked Campbell about his love life (though he was not immune to rumours).

Still, it was not totally unfamiliar territory for Clark, whose personal life, previous marriage, and son had proven irresistible fodder for news coverage—which she encouraged—when she was deputy premier in the early 2000s Liberal government. She was the first BC cabinet minister in history to bring her infant son to work and care for him in a nursery created out of an old office at the legislature. Since then, the idea that a woman cabinet minister could balance having a baby and working at the same time has not even been an issue.

After Clark won the Liberal leadership, her first post-leadership media event was at a hockey rink, where she wanted to be photographed watching Hamish play hockey like an ordinary mom. The premier's staff clearly saw political points to be gained from playing up certain parts of her life, where it suited her image.

The first true debate over gender politics arrived, without warning, on October 5, 2011. Clark had shown up for question period in the legislature, ready to take on NDP leader Adrian Dix in debate. She was wearing a knee-length navy dress and a khaki-coloured blazer over top. You could see, if you really focused on it, a bit of cleavage in the way the V-neck dress crossed her chest. Clark had worn the dress to her swearing-in, and no one had said a word. To almost everyone, it was the kind of appropriate modern business attire worn by thousands of Canadian women every day. But not for David Schreck. The former NDP MLA, now self-styled pundit, used his overactive Twitter account to kick-start what would become a firestorm about the premier's appearance.

"Is Premier Clark's cleavage revealing attire appropriate for the legislature?" Schreck tweeted that day.

In the resulting uproar, many people called him sexist.

"I beg to differ," Schreck tweeted, doubling down on his critics. "She crosses the line and needs to be called on it."

Media descended on him for an explanation.

"I was watching question period and noticed the premier was showing a lot more cleavage than normal. I've got nothing against cleavage, but there's appropriate dress for appropriate occasions. And I thought the way the premier was dressed was inappropriate for the legislature," Schreck was quoted as saying at the time. "It could be that I'm just an old fogey, but it was my wife who originally raised the question."

Schreck is an old fogey. Now a senior citizen, he spends an inordinate amount of time on Twitter.

One Victoria *Times Colonist* reader did pen a letter in support.

"Where is the limit?" wrote the reader. "Is it one inch of cleavage, two inches, three inches? Perhaps a more dignified approach for the leader of our province would be to raise the bar, as well as the level of her blouse, for those of us who believe in self respect. The legislature is not the place to expose one's bosom."

The paper subsequently gave Schreck its weekly "thumbs down" award for his claim that Clark dressed too provocatively. "She wasn't; it was none of his business; and there are real issues to discuss," declared the editorial board.

Province columnist Mike Smyth won the day with the witty conclusion to a subsequent column: "I've got a message for David Schreckosaurus: The dinosaur age is over, pal. Stop ogling the premier's goodies like a dirty old man, and get back to the real issues of the day."

It was a low point for political discourse in the province. You'd be hard pressed to find anyone who remembers the substantive questions that day in the legislature. (It was actually a debate about funding for group homes for people with disabilities.)

To the NDP's credit, it disowned Schreck at the time.

"I'll tell you this. Schreck's comments were wrong," Dix told reporters. "I completely disagree with him."

Clark was stung by the criticism. She did, in fact, change her wardrobe. Gone were the V-neck dresses. Her blouse line went up a few inches. She would later put significant thought into her clothes, choosing different colours for different reasons (for example, she felt blue made her look fresher and younger). It wasn't about what she wanted to wear, but about how other women would notice the little details, like her necklace choice, and size her up immediately using a different matrix than they'd apply to a man.

Michele Cadario, a friend and the then chief fundraiser for the Liberal party, started hearing business leaders discussing Clark's dresses and cleavage during business meetings. She'd push back hard but was surprised at how men she'd respected, who were loyal to the Liberal party, were so quickly sucked into the sexist debate.

Former NDP leader Carole James also publicly defended Clark over her wardrobe, telling media she'd suffered similar oafish critiques of her attire while leader, and whether she dyed her hair. James had been told she wasn't tough enough, or she took too much time to make decisions, or she was too consultative. When she forced her MLAs in 2005 to stop heckling their opponents in the legislature, she was called weak and too nice. When Dix did it in 2012, he was praised for his courageous decision to better the tone of debate.

Examples of sexism continued to affect the early days of Clark's premiership. In May 2012, Virgin CEO Sir Richard Branson arrived in Vancouver, hosting a press conference with Clark to announce his airline's non-stop service from Vancouver to London. Days later he'd post online a photo of himself kitesurfing while a naked supermodel clung to his back, with this caption: "When in British Columbia a few days ago, the delightful Premier Christy Clark accepted my invite to come for a kite-surf ride on my back. One thing though—I forgot to tell her about the dress code! Well, here it is. The offer still stands Christy!"

Clark was quick to respond.

"I think when you meet with the CEO of a billion-dollar company who wants to do business with your province, you can get a little more respectful treatment than that," she said. "I think it was very disrespectful. Somebody said to me as a joke that if that is his best pickup line, then maybe there is a reason he called his company Virgin."

The aggressive pushback and zinger at Branson's expense earned Clark kudos on social media. Branson would later apologize. Yet she did not always respond to a sexist comment with an outright counterattack. And it was the times in which she tried to defuse the insult with humour—if for no other reason than because she was put on the spot—that public reaction was divided.

Seven months after the Branson incident, in December 2012, Clark was on an FM radio show in Courtenay when host Justin Wilcomes (who went by the on-air name Drex) asked her, on behalf of a listener, what it was like for her to be the premier and a "MILF" (a crude pop culture term popularized by the 1999 film *American Pie* that stands for "Mother I'd Like to Fuck"). BC's thirty-fifth premier laughed and paused briefly as she tried to compose a reply on live radio.

"You know, I take that as a compliment," she said, chuckling. "Better a MILF than a cougar."

The cougar reference is another pop culture term for an older woman who prowls bars for younger men. Her response was divisive. Some insisted she should have pushed back and put the DJ in his place, while others said she did the best she could to make a joke out of an inappropriate question that would never have been asked of a male politician. In the resulting backlash, the radio station took down the interview and fired Drex.

Around this time, Liberals began to make the gender attacks against Clark a public issue. BC Liberal supporter Diamond Isinger even created a Tumblr page online called "Madam Premier" to catalogue the running collection of items and commentary the Liberals deemed sexist. The Liberal pushback came as Clark's popularity tumbled following her honeymoon period. In the months leading up to the 2013 election, as her government grappled with the growing Quick Wins scandal, her popularity, including among women, tanked. An Ipsos Reid poll in December 2012 appeared to indicate that women approved of Dix's leadership over Clark's by a score of almost two to one.

"There is a personal element to it," observed veteran *Vancouver Sun* columnist Vaughn Palmer in a column at the time. "Often voiced by women as a lack of authenticity to the Clark style of leadership."

Authenticity would be a constant undercurrent of the gender debate during Clark's premiership. To those who disliked her, the ever-present smile was a sign she was constantly faking it. And the mounting government scandals, such as underfunding child care and exploiting the ethnic community for votes, gave the impression, to some, that she was mean and ruthless.

Fake and mean. Out to win at all costs. Difficult criticism to overcome.

Clark and the Liberals believed that the problem was not unique to her, and that Campbell too had been unpopular among women before elections. The Liberal theory is that women voters drift away while the party governs, and they have to be lured back with pocketbook household issues, like children's arts tax credits, during the campaign; Clark was not a particular factor one way or another for female voters. In the 2013 campaign, the Liberals did bring enough women voters back to the fold to help grow the party's majority. But female voters turned against her shortly after, and Clark was unable to lure them back home for the 2017 election.

The debate over how Clark was treated is made more difficult by the fact that, at times, she used gender politics to her advantage to score points against her political opponents. In a November 28, 2014, interview with *The Vancouver Sun*, she said that Horgan used a dismissive tone with her during the legislative session in part because she's a woman. Clark didn't come out and say it outright, but the insinuation was clear: Horgan doesn't respect women. He's sexist.

"I think that the NDP, some of the members of the NDP, do have a tendency to see women differently from men," she said. "It's something women experience all over the place. Any woman watching this will be going, 'Uh huh, I've felt that.' So I think I experience a little bit of that from John Horgan, and Adrian Dix, as well."

Horgan read the paper the next day and was furious. Former leader James went to visit him in his office the morning the story ran, to try to calm him down. The accusation was especially galling to Horgan because his father had died when he was young and he'd been raised by his mother and sister (his brothers were much older and had left the house during his formative years). He felt deep respect for the strong female leaders in his life and in no way considered himself sexist.

"It's not fair she can make those comments about me," he fumed. "Because it's not true. And there's no way for me to defend myself, because then I sound defensive."

Indeed, Clark's comments boxed Horgan in. He could say nothing, and let the allegation stick. Or he could try to defend himself and appear, in the process, suspiciously over-defensive.

"You've got to let it go," advised James. "These are the things you've got to let go and can't let bother you because it will get you off your game, and get you off your message."

Don't take the bait, other advisors told Horgan. It's a game, and Clark is trying to draw you in. But in the fast-moving, twenty-four-hour news cycle of the Internet age, the media wanted a response from Horgan and he was hounded until he gave one three days later.

"I didn't want to dignify it with a response because I think it's ridiculous," Horgan said. "I was offended by it, to be quite honest with you."

Horgan acknowledged, first, the obvious.

"I'm passionate and I'm big and I'm male and there's not a damn thing I can do about that," he said.

Then he tried to frame his critique.

"I have to tell you that I have tremendous respect for Premier Clark's abilities as a politician," he offered. "I have serious misgivings about her abilities to manage the various files that I'm raising in the legislature. That's my job, whether she's a man or a woman."

Then he gave Clark faint praise.

"Is she a formidable campaigner? Absolutely. Is she a partisan animal? Absolutely. But the public have a different set of interests than just partisan debates and who won the day. They want their political leaders to respond to the issues of the day in a meaningful way, rather than a glib and irreverent way. And that's not a gender issue, that's an approach, that's a perspective."

All in all, about as good an answer as he could have given in the situation.

The sexist Horgan insinuation had ramifications through the NDP ranks as well. The party's powerful women's caucus sat down during a weekly meeting shortly after the story came out to try to figure out a way to backstop Horgan's reputation. Should they have female MLAs come out publicly and tell people how supportive of women he is? Should they share stories about how supportive he'd been for their careers?

The women's caucus was a strong behind-the-scenes force in the NDP, and able to influence the party's policies and directions through its unified action. Its members decided to make sure the NDP didn't look like it was, in turn, going after Clark because of her gender. And so it made a concerted effort to snuff out the remaining lines in public NDP speeches that referenced how Clark was always smiling and how she was obsessed with photo ops rather than governing.

References to Clark as a "cheerleader" for projects like LNG needed to be dampened too. Other phrasings had also crept into the speeches in the legislature from NDP MLAs, such as calling Clark's throne speech "a bunch of fluff" and saying that her LNG promises were similar to "unicorns and butterflies and flowers and fairies." It wasn't, perhaps, overtly sexist language. At least not yet. But it was clearly headed down a path toward something worse, until the NDP altered course.

Another line the NDP kept using was that Clark was "all politics all the time." It was Horgan's new chief of staff, and incoming campaign director, Bob Dewar, who finally put a stop to some of the language in 2016, as he tried to focus New Democrats on the looming election. To the line that Clark is all politics all the time, he had this snappy retort for MLAs: "You guys are all politicians. And you are all doing politics."

Both the NDP and the Liberals knew that in the 2017 election, at some point, Clark was going to play "the gender card" to try to make Horgan look even worse. How that would manifest itself, no one was yet sure. But the idea that her status as a female leader would become a weapon with which to attack Horgan and the NDP during a twenty-eight-day election campaign also undermined the sincerity of her earlier attempts to champion the cause of female leadership.

For the Liberals, gender issues could have been good politics in the campaign. It presented a political opening to frame the trailblazing strength of their own leader and garner attention in the media cycle. Yet despite months of what must have been preparation on the file, the Liberal execution of gender issues in the campaign was remarkably clumsy.

The launching point was the April 20, 2017, radio debate, in which Horgan snapped at Clark for touching his arm and, his frustration boiling over during a particularly testy exchange in which Clark spoke over him, leaned sideways with an unpleasant grin on his face and said, "If you want to keep just doing your thing, I'll watch you for a while—I know you like that."

It was a bungled counterattack by a frazzled leader. Provoked, Horgan had walked into another trap.

The Liberals were quick to seize the opportunity. If gender was to become an issue in the campaign, it would be now. The party got Pamela Martin, a former TV news anchor who now did community outreach for the Liberals, to pen an op-ed in *The Huffington Post* that blasted Horgan for his "casual sexism" during the radio debate.

"I recoiled slightly as those words were spoken, as I imagine many women did who were tuning in that morning," wrote Martin. "I wasn't the one being patronized, but I still felt it. Women everywhere have at one point or another endured condescending, dismissive, creepy remarks designed to 'put us in our place.'"

The Liberals also used the hashtag #CalmDownJohn to try to drive up interest on Twitter about Horgan's angry outburst during the debate.

And so the gender card was played.

But by this point the public's opinion of Clark appeared baked in. If you were a BC teacher, social worker, childcare worker, or health-care worker, or you were First Nations or on welfare or disabled, you probably already disliked Clark intensely for some type of harm inflicted by her government on your profession, industry, or community during her premiership. She remained intensely unpopular. And so Horgan's outburst, though clumsy and possibly sexist, didn't elicit as much outrage as that which people already felt toward Clark and the Liberals. Some people actually praised Horgan for his aggressive tone.

CLARK DID TRY to use her office during her six years as premier to reach out to the young women who would form the next generation of female leaders.

She opened the 2016 We For She conference in Vancouver by telling the school-aged girls in the audience of 1,500 delegates that they would have to fight harder than men and push for everything they wanted, because even she, as the province's top leader, still faced sexism on the job. Clark told the crowd she still faced men who came into her office and spoke to her male staff before her, cutting her out of the conversation while the boys did the talking. It was so persistent that Clark at one point changed the seating configuration in her Vancouver premier's office, making sure she always sat in a particular wingback chair, so that no matter how sexist the official visitors might be, they had no choice but to look at her when they addressed the room.

Clark had also taken to mentoring young teenaged women who were interested in politics, having them job-shadow her at the legislature in what she said was a deliberate attempt to show them that a strong female leader could be attacked in question period but still emerge smiling and confident in her abilities.

It was all laudable work. But if your view of Christy Clark was that she was a scheming politician willing to do anything to win—by 2016 a view reinforced in the minds of thousands of female teachers, for example, who had endured a lengthy strike and bitter labour dispute with the province—then no amount of work the premier did to mentor young women or encourage the next generation of female leaders was credible. It was all just a game.

Clark tried to point out, often through surrogates, that there were more women now than ever before in leadership positions within her government. Women occupied the senior leadership ranks of the parliamentary system, including Lieutenant-Governor Judith Guichon (who was appointed by Prime Minister Stephen Harper, not Clark), Speaker of the Legislature Linda Reid, BC Hydro CEO Jessica McDonald, deputy finance minister Athana Mentzelopoulos, and deputy minister to the premier and head of the civil service Kim Henderson. But this, too, failed to garner much public interest.

Clark has long felt that women were harder on her than they would have been on a male premier. They had high expectations, so high that she felt they were impossible to meet. Women, Clark believed, generally wanted to see likability in other women. And the opposite of likeable is competent, striving, and ambitious. For men, those things can coexist. But women in the corporate and political world are rarely able to have it all.

Whenever she was under attack, Clark also lamented how few defenders there were among academics and feminist media commentators. A successful woman from a centre-right political party couldn't always count on the left-wing members of the feminist establishment to rush to her defence.

THE PREMIERSHIP TOOK a large toll on Clark's personal life as a single mother, though she rarely talked candidly about it. Her friend and, later, deputy chief of staff Cadario had warned Clark from the first moment she considered running for leader that being the premier would heavily influence her relationships too.

In fact, Clark wasn't able to have much of a personal life for six years as premier. She didn't go on any dates, partly because she was worried that people, and the media, might obsessively talk about it. She was once asked out by one of the dads at a hockey game of Hamish's and replied, "Yes. This is it. Let's get popcorn. Because I don't have any other time." Every free moment she had was dedicated to Hamish, out of a sense she was somehow cheating him otherwise. But these were not things the premier spoke publicly about. She wasn't sure how it would be perceived. And worse, she worried it might dominate the discussion about her. She wanted people talking about the important things she had to say, on governing, policy, and the province, not about her personal life.

Clark did have a support network of women friends that she could talk to on tough nights, but admitted she saw them so irregularly due to her schedule that she was a lousy friend over six years. The core group, consisting of seven or eight people, dated back to Clark's high-school and university days, as well as the years when Hamish was in daycare. One friend, Sarah, kept the premier afloat by sending late-night emails that would compare her to ass-kicking singer/songwriter Beyoncé and offer other funny jokes. The premier used her friends to escape work, not to vent about how hard the job was.

Clark's son, Hamish, was drawn into the bitter sexist commentary as well. Throughout her premiership, there had been constant whispers about whether Clark as a mother was dragging her son into the media spotlight for political gain and to soften her image. Hamish was the focus of international media attention in 2016 when he stood beside his mother at the airport with Prime Minister Justin Trudeau and welcomed Prince William, Kate Middleton, and their two children to the city on their royal tour. Still just a teenager, with immense pressure on him at the moment, Hamish put his hands into the pockets of his tan suit while he waited. He was subsequently roasted on social media for appearing to have no manners. Recognizing the awkwardness, Clark and Hamish appeared the next day on Global TV to explain.

"I was so nervous, and having my hands in my pockets, I just didn't really know where to put my hands," Hamish told Chris Gailus. "Social media was mad at me for it and I felt really bad."

Privately, Clark felt Hamish, who was fiercely protective of his mother, was more worried he'd embarrassed her than himself.

During the 2017 campaign, Hamish had also spent a few days with her, main-streeting and shaking hands with voters. At his first stop, outside an ice-cream shop in Maple Ridge, the Liberal campaign bus pulled up to find a bunch of placard-waving NDP protesters already waiting for the premier. Hamish was nervous and quietly asked his mother what to do if they shouted questions at him or physically confronted him. Clark was sitting beside him on the bus, and leaned in close to reassure him. They aren't bad people, she said, they are just with the other party and they are trying to make a point during an election. Stick with me, stay close, and you'll be fine, she said. Clark led him out of the bus, and Liberal supporters crowded out the New Democrats. Hamish went inside and helped scoop ice cream for the cameras. They got back on the bus without incident.

Some might wonder why you'd put your son through such a stressful spectacle at all. If you asked her, Clark had a clear answer for involving Hamish in her political life. She was Anglican, raised on the value of public service for others, and she wanted to instill that value in her son. As a politician, that meant involving him in her job, showing him the good and the bad, in the hope he'd contribute to society as a young man too. It didn't have to be politics, necessarily, but Clark wanted Hamish to learn the value of giving back to society.

Throughout her political career, Christy Clark never shied away from appearing with her son, Hamish Marissen-Clark, on the campaign trail or mentioning him during speeches. JOHN LEHMANN/BC LIBERAL PARTY

It's a legitimate argument and a laudable goal. But politics is full of cynics. And outside of Clark's inner circle, very few people ever believed her explanation. More saw her using her son as a partisan political prop, whether it was true or not.

ONE OF THE more difficult moments of Clark's premiership came when she went public with a story of sexual assault in an op-ed in *The Vancouver Sun* on June 10, 2016. She described being dragged into the bushes by a strange man, thirty-five years earlier, when she was thirteen years old, on her way to a job washing dishes at her family's Burnaby restaurant:

> Over the last few weeks, I've shared this story with female friends and colleagues. Almost every single one of them also had a story. Like me, none of them had said a word.
>
> That's why the stories of so many women who stay silent have struck me so deeply. Many of their stories are much worse; horrifying events will take

years of determined effort to heal. Nonetheless, many of us share something in common: we have never spoken about it, not to the authorities, or our parents or spouses...

Sexual violence is common. Unfortunately, so is staying silent about it. Our silence makes it easier for those who wish to harm us. We don't share our stories, we don't think anyone would care much if we did, and then we live with the warped impression that we are alone in our fear and shame.

I'm not speaking out for sympathy; I don't need it. I am speaking out because as Premier of British Columbia and BC's first elected female premier, I am privileged to have a public platform.

I want women who have never said anything about sexual violence in their lives to know they are not alone.

It was a powerful piece. She followed it up with emotional interviews, explaining how that experience was why she later decided to support Green Leader Andrew Weaver's private member's bill to boost sexual assault reporting practices at post-secondary schools. But when she appeared on CBC Radio, she was lambasted by a steady stream of critics who went on air to point out her government wasn't doing enough to actually help women who were victims of assault. They said that transition houses for women fleeing abuse were still underfunded, welfare rates hadn't been raised, legal aid was cut to women who might need help fighting violence in the courts, rape kits weren't readily available for victims in small rural communities, and there'd been little progress in increasing charge approvals for sexual assault. The backlash clearly caught Clark by surprise.

Coverage quickly morphed into outlining her government's lack of action to help women. While it's admirable to speak out publicly, said advocacy groups, it'd be even more admirable to actually do something to make the system better. The blowback exemplified how, for some, Clark's words and actions did not match up. It would become a persistent problem for her re-election campaign.

CHRISTY CLARK MADE it further in BC's political game than any woman before her. She held the top job in the province for six years—an extraordinary feat, regardless of gender.

There is no doubt she faced a great deal of sexism on the job. She fended off her attackers, while also using the prominence of her position to mentor young women, tell intensely personal stories about her own experiences, and show her son the value of public service. But Clark also wielded gender politics as a weapon against her political opponents, muddying the sincerity of her advocacy work. And in the end, it was her larger credibility issues, and her dismal popularity among all voters, on which she was ultimately judged at the ballot box.

That is illustrative of the entire problem she faced on gender issues as premier. No matter what she did or said, or what causes she championed, there was always a portion of the population who saw her as a ruthless, partisan, mean-spirited, political operative with a fake smile who'd do anything to win, including using women's issues and her own son as a prop.

It wasn't the real Christy Clark. But politics is perception. And by the end of her premiership, one of the most divisive political figures in BC's history was simply too unpopular in some minds to be given the benefit of the doubt.

CHAPTER 7
CRACKS EMERGING

Christy Clark leaned across her cabinet table in the early spring of 2016, sized up the assembled ministers and finance ministry bureaucrats, and let loose her frustration.

The premier had had enough of the foot-dragging by her finance minister, Mike de Jong, and his staff on the issue of foreign buyers in Metro Vancouver's real estate market. Her political instincts had been telling her to act for the better part of a year, but de Jong, her most senior minister, whom she'd grown to trust implicitly, had insisted there wasn't enough data to make a move. Clark was mad at de Jong, and partly at herself, as she looked at yet another finance ministry report on options to address skyrocketing housing prices. There still wasn't enough information from de Jong's civil servants to make a decision, despite her repeated requests to get on with it.

"Look," she began. "Here is what you need to understand. We need to deal with this issue if we're going to win the election.

"And it's not just us who are going to lose our jobs," she added, pointing at the finance staff, "you are going to lose your jobs. They are going to fire you. So get me this fucking information. Because we are going to do this."

After that, things moved quickly. By June, at a cabinet retreat in Quesnel, there was enough information for Clark to push the 15 per cent surcharge on foreign buyers in Metro Vancouver up for a decision. Not surprisingly, with the boss's foot planted firmly behind the idea, it passed.

The issue of the foreign buyer tax had stretched one of Clark's closest relationships. She and de Jong had proved a formidable duo at the cabinet table—the whip-smart premier with a highly developed political antenna who was bold and impulsive, and the slow, methodical, cautious finance minister who liked to pinch pennies. Together, they were the political odd couple.

De Jong's frugality was legendary. His Dutch parents had been liberated from the Nazis by Canadian soldiers before he was born. At the time they were saved, they hadn't eaten in ten days. The elder de Jongs raised young Mike not to leave food on his plate or spend money unwisely. He still drives a Mazda Miata that's more than twenty years old, with an odometer approaching 500,000 kilometres. When the linoleum floor cracked in his family's farmhouse, de Jong found the receipt and got the store to honour the lifetime guarantee to replace it, even though the lino was now decades old. "They said lifetime guarantee; I'm still alive," he recounted.

Clark saw him as an iconoclast who was comfortable doing what he thought was right and who was unconcerned about what other people thought of him. Nowhere was that more evident than on the issue of MLA expense accounts, which de Jong fought to make public online, despite enormous internal criticism from his caucus colleagues (including MLAS in the NDP) who would have preferred that their food, travel, and housing allowances remained secret.

The working partnership between Clark and de Jong served them both well for the bulk of her premiership. Their decisions were driven by both instincts and data. It was similar to Clark's long-standing political relationship with Mike McDonald; where she was positive, he was negative, and together they were often an unstoppable force.

Clark had watched de Jong rag the puck on the housing file with growing exasperation. She trusted his cautious instincts, and she respected his ability to second-guess an easy solution. But on the issue of housing affordability, the premier was worried. She couldn't understand why de Jong and her Metro Vancouver MLAs weren't as concerned as she was. Housing affordability, she predicted, would be a defining issue of the 2017 election campaign. Her government had faced months of criticism that it wasn't doing enough.

The average price of a detached home in Greater Vancouver had shot up from $1.2 million in 2011 to $1.8 million in 2016. The sharpest rise occurred around 2015/16, when home prices increased more in one year than they had in the previous five. The NDP were hammering the Liberal government on the file, accusing the party of not protecting average homeowners from the cruel forces of the market because the Liberals didn't want to upset their many donors within the real estate, business, and development communities, who were making a killing on the sales. An undertone of racism often crept into the debate over Vancouver's housing prices, because it seemed that many of the most expensive, high-profile homes were being purchased by wealthy Chinese residents, as well as, in some cases, foreign investors who kept the homes empty as investments. The longer Clark's government waited, the more the issue festered. Maybe there wasn't a silver bullet to address affordability, but there was a strong perception the province was doing nothing.

Ideologically, the Liberals generally believed in a free market, and they didn't feel it was the job of government to intervene in what they felt was clearly an issue of supply and demand within the housing sector. Nowhere was that view more prevalent than with de Jong. He had other concerns too. He'd spent much of his career, and numerous trade trips to places like India, trying to encourage foreign investment in BC's economy, and he felt that cracking down on foreign buyers sent the wrong message and could hurt the economy. He also had a bone to pick with local mayors and municipal councils, who were too slow and timid to approve new housing projects, and who had thousands of applications stuck in the queue.

De Jong's concerns were all legitimate. But they didn't change the stark political reality that Clark saw, which was that government needed to be seen to be doing something to help people or it was going to face a punishing blowback from voters at the polls.

The housing issue cut across generations of voters. It wasn't just young millennials who couldn't afford to buy their own home. That group doesn't vote in large numbers anyway. It was their parents, the baby boomers, who were frustrated at seeing their children get good jobs and be ready to start a family and yet also be unable to afford to buy a house. The aging parents would then either need to help out financially or watch their children and grandchildren move away to more affordable cities. The baby boomers were some of the most reliable, sought-after voters a political party could hope for. And even they were conflicted. Because while they were angry that their kids couldn't afford homes, they also generally didn't want to see government do anything that would sink the value of the properties they had owned for decades and one day wanted to be able to cash in for millions to help fund their retirement.

Whipping up voter discontent on the issue was rookie NDP MLA David Eby. A lawyer and former executive director of the BC Civil Liberties Association, Eby was quick on his feet and no stranger to drumming up press coverage of activist issues. Eby unleashed a devastating public prosecution of the Liberal government, which went on for months, for its inaction on the housing file. He scored major points both in the legislature and out on the street on a file that was top of mind for voters.

Stung, the Liberals did eventually act to take away the real estate sector's self-policing powers, ban the practice of "shadow flipping" (where a realtor sells a property multiple times before closing), and give the City of Vancouver powers to tax vacant homes. But the biggest arrow in the government's quiver was a tax on foreign buyers. It had been debated internally for the better part of a year by the time it reached that tipping point with Clark in spring 2016.

Around the cabinet table, it was well known that de Jong was dragging his feet on the file. His ministry kept asking for more data on real estate ownership and sales trends. In retrospect, de Jong admits he waited too long to get moving on the issue of housing affordability. He should have collected the data sooner, at the very least. Clark didn't personally blame de Jong, and the two did manage to smooth out their relationship. De Jong is who he is. She gave him some rope on a key file, and he ran with it for far too long before she pulled him back. That's as much on her as it is on him. If the best parts of our character are why we fail, then de Jong's cautiousness got the better of him, and Clark's trust in a key advisor did too.

What Clark still steams about, however, is the lack of political smarts among her Metro Vancouver MLAS and cabinet ministers on the issue of housing. That's not an assertion shared by her Metro Vancouver MLAS, some of whom insist they were trying to raise the issue to a premier who was long criticized for paying more attention to her staff than her MLAS. But it did expose a larger problem with Clark's cabinet that was never addressed: the Metro Vancouver ministers didn't speak as loudly or as forcefully on issues as the ministers from the Interior and the north. The cabinet was out of balance on rural and urban issues.

After Clark's cabinet blow-up, she and de Jong jointly announced the 15 per cent tax on Metro Vancouver homes purchased by foreign citizens, on July 25, 2016. The changes took effect August 2. There was an immediate drop in the number of foreign buyers, from 13 per cent of sales in June to fewer than 1 per cent in August. But any corresponding cooling on the actual prices of homes was temporary. By February 2017 prices had begun to rebound, and later in the year they exceeded pre-tax levels. Still, the tax was a win politically. It was popular among voters and led to a bump in Clark's approval rating as premier. It also had the NDP worried. Housing was one of their key issues and the tax took away some of that momentum.

The premier's instincts had been proven right. But the fact that she was frustrated within her own cabinet on the issue for months is illustrative of the cracks that had begun to emerge in her administration heading into the 2017 election. Clark had enjoyed four years of unchallenged power and authority. Now the baggage of her Liberal government—extending back sixteen years under Campbell—was piling up. To get a better handle on things, Clark turned to an unexpected ally.

The premier and former finance minister Carole Taylor had had a chance encounter at an event in the fall of 2015 in Vancouver. They struck up a friendly conversation after Clark's speech and spent more time than either had expected, in a corner of the room, talking about the issues of the day. Taylor and Clark weren't friends and didn't travel in the same circles. Taylor flew among the elite in BC's business community and academic worlds. She was highly respected and plugged in among the movers and shakers in Vancouver, far more than Clark and her top advisors. But the two shared a common political history—both had survived Gordon Campbell's premiership as top ministers, and both had hated his style and temperament.

A short time later, Clark phoned Taylor to ask if she could offer her any type of work that Taylor would find interesting.

"No, I'm happy," said Taylor. "But if you want to ask me a question, I'll tell you what I think."

Clark persisted, laying out a plan to make Taylor a kind of bridge between the premier's office and the business community, where Taylor had done policy work for the BC Business Council and Board of Trade.

"I'll only do it if I talk directly to you," said Taylor.

Agreed, said Clark. Taylor got a one-dollar-a-year salary and a small office behind Clark's inside the Vancouver cabinet offices at Canada Place, and once a week, on Mondays, the two would spend an hour talking. Taylor used her connections in the business world to give feedback Clark might otherwise not have heard. It was valuable intel. And it went straight to the premier.

Taylor also offered advice—most of which Clark didn't act on. As the weeks went by, Taylor became slightly frustrated. But the premier is the premier, and what she wants to do is ultimately her call.

Taylor kept hearing about housing affordability as the big burning issue in Metro Vancouver, and at one point suggested to Clark that the government bring in a speculator's tax on profits made if someone was to flip a house for resale within, say, a year of purchase. But Clark didn't seem interested. Like many of Taylor's suggestions, this one just went nowhere. Later, the NDP would raise the same idea as part of a housing action plan that caught the public's attention and picked up significant voter support in Metro Vancouver, at the Liberals' expense. The Liberals countered with a first-time home-buyers loan program that, while clearly welcome, failed to excite the public.

Clark and the cabinet felt a speculation tax was too hard and would ultimately be a waste of time. Clark felt if you set rules that penalized a person for selling their home within, say, a year, then people would just wait a year and a day to get around the impediment.

Taylor kept dutifully reporting back and offering up ideas to Clark. But the relationship between these two dynamic, powerful, charismatic political allies never yielded any spectacular results.

PERHAPS NO FILE was more damaging to the Clark government's reputation on social issues than the continued deaths of children in care within the child welfare system.

The Ministry of Children and Family Development, with its incredibly complicated interconnections with the issues of poverty, social supports, foster care, and adoption, have haunted successive provincial governments for decades. Key to the file had been Mary Ellen Turpel-Lafond, the fierce and outspoken former judge who spent ten years as BC's independent Representative for Children and Youth from 2006 to 2016.

At the beginning, Clark and Turpel-Lafond found common ground. From her time as a radio talk show host, Clark had been intensely critical of the government's handling of child welfare issues, and her leadership bid's theme of "families first" promised wholesale change within MCFD. After she became premier, Clark sat down with Turpel-Lafond for a face-to-face chat on how to begin fixing the many problems in the system.

Clark offered an olive branch, in the form of the head of one of Turpel-Lafond's enemies within the ministry. Clark fired deputy children's minister Leslie du Toit, whose restructuring of MCFD under Campbell had turned into a blundering and confusing exercise, and whose uncommunicative relationship with outside critics had provoked the ire of Turpel-Lafond. In du Toit's place, Clark appointed Stephen Brown, a soft-spoken British change-management expert, with a background in child services, whose star was on the rise within the government bureaucracy as an effective manager of complex files. As well, Clark shuffled the polarizing figure of Mary Polak out of the minister's chair and installed Mary McNeil, a conciliatory former CEO of the BC Cancer Foundation.

McNeil, Brown, and Turpel-Lafond hit it off from the start. For eighteen months, there was a level of peace and harmony within the system between its minister and watchdog that BC had not seen for some time. Clark and the representative collaborated on hiring a new provincial director of child welfare. When Turpel-Lafond raised the issue of domestic violence after withering reports on the murder-suicide of five people in Oak Bay by estranged husband Peter Lee, and Allan Schoenborn's murder of this three young children inside a Merritt trailer, the government actually acted. It created the Provincial Domestic Violence Office in 2012, tasked with improving provincial coordination on supports.

It helped that, unlike many of her predecessors, McNeil loved the work as children's minister. And it showed. But McNeil had found politics a weary experience. In only one term, she'd survived the HST, Gordon Campbell's resignation, and Christy Clark's arrival, and she was now facing the prospect of a hopeless 2013 election campaign. She resigned from the post on August 31, 2012, announcing she wasn't running again in the provincial election campaign in nine months.

In McNeil's place, Clark slotted Stephanie Cadieux as minister. And that's when things began to deteriorate. Cadieux was a well-regarded minister who had spent the bulk of her adult life advocating for the rights of people with disabilities. She'd been using a wheelchair since a car accident at the age of eighteen, and was only the second MLA who uses a wheelchair to be elected to the legislature.

It would be a drastic oversimplification to lay all the blame on either Cadieux or Turpel-Lafond for the resulting mess that became the child welfare file. But suffice it to say that a relationship that started as strained would then morph over the years to acrimonious, before devolving further into outright warfare by 2017, the likes of which child welfare advocates have never seen. The undercurrent to the entire mess appears to have been Clark herself.

Ironically, it was during the earliest years of Clark's premiership, when she was under attack from all critics and facing a mutiny within her own caucus, that she was able to achieve peace within the child welfare system. Perhaps it was because, during that time, with so few allies inside and outside of her party, Clark was more motivated to listen to Turpel-Lafond's needs. More likely, though, was that the premier came in with a genuine willingness to change the system, and then, after two years of acquiescing to Turpel-Lafond's demands, began to grow weary of her never-ending critical reports, as well as the unyielding calls for more money and staff to continue making improvements to the ministry. So, slowly but surely, Clark started to tune out Turpel-Lafond.

After Clark's come-from-behind 2013 election victory, she lumped the independent watchdog in with all the other critics who'd caused her headaches. As part of her evolving style of leadership, she became loath to give an inch on any issue to the Opposition or Turpel-Lafond. The relationship became strained. With each child death, and each report by the representative's office, the government response became less accepting of the criticism and less willing to offer a constructive solution.

The height of the rolling dispute came in 2015 when Turpel-Lafond authored a report called *Paige's Story: Abuse, Indifference and a Young Life Discarded*. The representative outlined one of the most troubling investigations of her career, on the death of a nineteen-year-old girl named Paige from a drug overdose in Vancouver in 2013. The report was a heart-breaking read. Paige was an Aboriginal girl who was functionally blind; flagged by the child welfare system at the age of three months, she had been bounced through forty moves and sixteen different schools by the time she was sixteen. She'd landed in Vancouver's Downtown Eastside, where social workers were too scared to visit the hotel rooms where Paige lived in the frightening world of poverty, prostitution, and drugs. She was taken to hospital seventeen times after being found unconscious or intoxicated. Eventually, she would become the third generation of women in her family to die of an overdose.

The system had utterly failed Paige at every turn: teachers hadn't flagged her for help, social workers hadn't kept her under watch, doctors had let her leave the hospital without assistance, government failed to give her help as she transitioned out of the state's care at nineteen, and nobody was there for her in her last moments, when she died alone in a communal washroom next to Oppenheimer Park.

Turpel-Lafond, now deeply frustrated with the system's inability to change, had penned a scathing eighty-page report on Paige's death. She met with Cadieux and deputy children's minister Mark Sieben in the minister's office at the legislature just days before the report was released, to provide a copy.

Cadieux was livid at what she read. In the report, Turpel-Lafond had referred to "the pervasive system-wide professional indifference to this young Aboriginal girl" and speculated as to "whether this is the face of institutionalized racism and a system that discounts the value of some children's lives in BC." The provocative language was a deliberate choice on Turpel-Lafond's part to spark a dialogue. But for the government, it went too far.

Inside the oak-panelled confines of the minister's office, with Cadieux glaring at Turpel-Lafond and the deputy minister red with fury, there was little room for reconciliation. Cadieux told Turpel-Lafond she was "offended" that she'd accuse social workers of professional indifference. Turpel-Lafond retorted that no one in the ministry had even seen fit to review Paige's death, and it was hard to argue in favour of professional competence in a child death the minister would never have even known about without the report.

"How many other kids are like Paige?" asked Turpel-Lafond. "Let's get into a debate. How many do you think there are?"

Neither the minister nor her deputy had a guess.

"I think there are 150 kids just like Paige today," challenged the representative.

The exchange would be repeated in similar fashion, publicly, once the report became public on May 14, 2015.

"If a parent in BC had treated their child the way the system treated Paige, we may be having a debate over criminal responsibility," Turpel-Lafond told media.

"I find it offensive that individuals could be seen as indifferent when they have chosen to make this their life's work," responded Cadieux.

And so on.

The Paige report irrevocably shattered the working relationship between Turpel-Lafond, Clark, and Cadieux. The watchdog and the minister would not hold a meeting again for the rest of their respective times in office, though they did appear briefly together at a press conference to encourage more adoptions of foster children (a cause they shared). On October 1, 2015, Turpel-Lafond and her senior staff met with deputy minister Sieben privately at her office. He allegedly said that "the government would treat her as a 'member of the opposition,'" and that the government "had developed a strategy to personally target" her, according to court documents Turpel-Lafond would later file as part of a pension dispute with the government.

Then there is the story of Alex Gervais. In mid-September 2015, the eighteen-year-old Métis teen, who'd lived a life of abuse and neglect that most British Columbians could never imagine, smashed through the fourth-storey window of the Abbotsford Super 8 hotel where he'd been placed by the province, and jumped to his death. His story would unfold in subsequent months as an example of the many gaps that existed in the child welfare system. Cadieux faced renewed calls to resign, and Clark to overhaul the ministry. Neither happened.

Like Paige, Gervais been bounced through seventeen placements and twenty-three social workers during his short life, after being abused by his biological parents, who were mentally ill. His final caregiver was paid $8,000 a month by a delegated Aboriginal agency to watch out for him, but the agency employee kept in touch by text message and failed to pass on Gervais's messages that he was "extremely depressed and suicidal." After forty-nine days in the hotel, high on cocaine, following a fight with his girlfriend about his drug use, Gervais took his own life.

The fallout from the Gervais report made the government look foolish. Cadieux didn't know how many other kids were being housed in hotels, and, after assurances within her ministry that there were none, was surprised to find that, in fact, there were more. Clark publicly blamed the Aboriginal agency, warning "there would be consequences" for its mistakes. Grand Chief Doug Kelly, who'd helped create the agency years ago, accused the premier of not having all the facts and said she "essentially slapped the agency across the face with a closed first." The Paige and Gervais stories raised louder alarm bells that perhaps the children's ministry was ignoring its most troublesome kids until they reached the age of nineteen, when they would simply age out of the system and no longer be the ministry's problem.

Clearly the child welfare system needed more money, more staff, and more resources. But the Clark government didn't want to be seen to be capitulating to Turpel-Lafond's demands. So, as public pressure grew, it asked Bob Plecas, a respected retired civil servant who had helped design the modern children's ministry in 1996, to conduct his own review of the child welfare system. It was contentious from the start, given that Plecas's daughter worked as an assistant deputy minister in Clark's office.

Plecas spent several months working on his report, which was delivered in December 2015. What stood out in it was the part where Plecas recommended the government phase out Turpel-Lafond's office within two years and start internally investigating its own problems. Plecas argued the constant criticism generated by the representative's office was actually destabilizing the ministry, and things would be better if the ministry policed itself.

It was a stunning suggestion. Turpel-Lafond had single-handedly brought to light many of the ministry's most serious mistakes over her ten-year term, and she'd fought government so fiercely that several times she had to take the ministry to court (and win) to get information. And now Plecas was suggesting her office should be removed?

The idea did not go over well. Half a dozen First Nation chiefs flew from Vancouver to Victoria to stand behind Turpel-Lafond in a show of support for what they called a "smear job." Even Cadieux was unable to defend the idea, though she probably wanted to.

To make the bizarre, messy story complete, four days after his report came out, Plecas would retract his recommendation to phase out Turpel-Lafond's office within two years, admitting in a letter to Cadieux that he'd been "too ambitious" and the issue had overwhelmed the rest of his review. The children's ministry quietly sat on the letter for almost five months, until Turpel-Lafond got a copy and made it public, much to government's embarrassment.

By then, though, the much-maligned Plecas report had accomplished its primary purpose, which was to give the government justification for pumping new money into the system without allowing Turpel-Lafond even a hint of victory. In the February 2016 budget, the government added $217 million in new funding over three years. It was something. But it was, embarrassingly, too late. All the money in the world couldn't repair the reputation the government had developed for not caring for children in care.

Beset by scandal and underfunded, with its primary leaders not speaking to one another, the provincial child care system was the very definition of dysfunctional. Turpel-Lafond finished her term embroiled in a lawsuit with government over her pension benefits. Cadieux tried, repeatedly, to get out of the job, but Clark wouldn't let her. She asked the premier at least three times to be transferred to a new ministry. Something. Anything. But each time Clark talked Cadieux down.

The premier was convinced that the children's ministry needed stability. And she told Cadieux that if she shuffled her, Cadieux would spend the rest of her career being known as the minister who had failed in the children's file and had to be removed from the job. Cadieux was a good administrator, and the ministry needed her, argued Clark. So Cadieux would have to suffer in the job for four years, ten months and thirteen days. It was, by far, the longest tenure of any children's minister in BC history.

WHILE THE HANDLING of children in care was devastating, the struggle to deal with Metro Vancouver transit was baffling. A late addition to the party's 2013 election platform was a pledge that a re-elected Liberal government would require a referendum in Metro Vancouver to get approval for any new revenue sources for transit, such as bridge tolls, road pricing, or increased taxes.

"In order for these solutions to have legitimacy and taxpayer agreement, they need to be tested by the electorate who, ultimately, will be paying for them," read the Liberal platform.

The pledge was popular in certain circles, especially among voters who didn't use transit. But internally it was not without controversy. Dan Doyle, Clark's chief of staff, had been a thirty-six-year employee in the Ministry of Transportation and its former deputy minister. He knew transit policy better than anyone. And when he saw the late addition to the party platform, he had one word for it: stupid. Doyle started telling anyone who would listen, including Clark, that the idea wouldn't work. It will just make the Metro Vancouver transportation system more dysfunctional, he argued.

This view was prescient. At the time, though, the referendum was great short-term politics. It made the public debate less about service and more about the political infighting among local mayors, councils, and regional boards that made the decisions.

Clark argued that people should have a say in how they pay for their transit. It was a populist principle. The local mayors hated the idea with a passion, partly because they knew how tough it would be to persuade residents to vote to increase their taxes. But they also remembered the long history of provincial governments finding artful ways to say no to authorizing new revenue sources for them to use for transit (like a vehicle levy).

"The hypocrisy of this policy platform is unbelievable," was the view of Port Coquitlam mayor Greg Moore at the time. "It just doesn't work any way you look at it."

Richmond mayor Malcolm Brodie called it an "abdication of leadership," while Coquitlam mayor Richard Stewart dubbed it "political posturing."

After Clark won re-election in 2013, her government was tied to the referendum pledge. The mayors locked horns with Transportation Minister Todd Stone. In Stone, they saw a Kamloops-area minister who didn't appear to understand Metro Vancouver congestion. The mayors didn't appreciate taking orders from a guy who lived in the Interior. They bickered for months about the question and timing.

Stone faced internal difficulties on the file. He felt whipsawed by Clark and her senior advisors, like deputy chief of staff Michele Cadario, who Stone felt would tell him one thing one day and then change direction later. One example was Stone proceeding down the path of a new governance model for TransLink, in the process burning up his limited political capital as a minister, only to have the premier's office change its mind and force him to curtail the scope of his proposal.

The premier's office, meanwhile, was largely unimpressed with Stone's performance on the file. He seemed to make more messes than he solved, by putting his foot in his mouth with the mayors and then requiring a great deal of help to clean up the resulting mess.

The mixed internal signals were frustrating, though it may also have had something to do with structural problems within the premier's office that were identified in an outside consultant's report in 2015 and led to changes in personnel, titles, and responsibilities. Regardless, it didn't help that in September 2013, amid the confusion, Clark unilaterally decided to dump $3.5 billion in provincial money into a new bridge to replace the aging Massey Tunnel that links Richmond and Delta. Mayors wondered why this money didn't need to go to a referendum. And why the province couldn't put the same kind of cash into the mayors' pet projects in Vancouver, for a Broadway subway line, or in Surrey, for light rapid transit, rather than into replacing a provincially owned, provincially run tunnel. They began a fight about the bridge that would continue for four years.

As the months ticked by, it was also clear a significant number of people voting in the referendum would be using it to vent their frustration about TransLink, the provincially created agency that oversees transit operations. One survey in early 2015 indicated that 76 per cent of voters didn't have confidence in TransLink's ability to implement projects properly, and the agency was the subject of a number of stories about lavish salaries for its executives, questionable spending, bungled projects like the Compass Card system, repeated breakdowns, and poor service. As the referendum neared, TransLink would force out CEO Ian Jarvis to "restore public confidence" ahead of the vote. The mayors ultimately proposed a 0.5 per cent sales tax increase to fund a ten-year transportation expansion plan, generating $250 million a year and costing an average homeowner $128 a year in extra taxes. By the time the referendum (now dubbed officially a plebiscite) results were revealed on July 2, it was a foregone conclusion: the No side picked up 61.7 per cent of the vote.

The vote led to internal frustrations on the file. Two cabinet ministers—TransLink Minister Peter Fassbender and Health Minister Terry Lake—urged Clark not to proceed with a second transit referendum and to try to gracefully make peace with the Metro Vancouver mayors. But Clark, who viewed the local governments as largely New Democrat–friendly, continued to fight about transit with the mayors. Instead of offering an olive branch, or a solution, Clark seemed intent on lecturing them for years on the inadequacy of their planning.

Heading into the 2017 election, Metro Vancouver drivers would get in their cars and experience traffic like they had never seen before. Transit users found a system that was unreliable and didn't get to enough places. And even though the Liberals committed to funding 40 per cent of new transit projects in the lead-up to the campaign, the history of the dispute ensured they got little credit for the new promise. Transit was a dangerous issue for the government to let drift going into an election, and it affected the outcome of many battleground ridings in the Lower Mainland.

After the election, former deputy premier and Clark leadership rival Kevin Falcon, who had also been the transportation minister who forced through the Canada Line SkyTrain expansion, added his conclusion on the Liberal management of the Metro Vancouver transit file.

"Nobody in government is perfect," he told *The Vancouver Sun*. "But I think it's a mistake to say we're going to force a referendum before we make any major transportation decisions. At the end of the day, the public hates that kind of politics. What they want to see is leadership in action."

Clark didn't agree. She thought the problem on transit wasn't the referendum but rather that people didn't think the Liberals were paying enough attention to transit.

SOME OF THE controversies that began to stack up against the Clark government were of the chickens-come-home-to-roost variety. That included a stunning moment at the Supreme Court of Canada, in Ottawa, where the BC government's long-running battle with the province's teachers' union would come to a head on November 10, 2016.

The opulent wood-panelled courtroom, with its deep red carpet and imposing raised bench for the nine judges, was filled with lawyers and observers that day, many of whom wanted to hear the case's closing arguments before an expected adjournment that would lead to months of deliberation. Around twenty people from the BC Teachers' Federation were also present, including current and former members of the executive, who had spent years fighting the province. They watched as the BC government's lawyer, Karen Horsman, had her argument dissected by the justices in a series of aggressive questions, while legal counsel from the BC Teachers' Federation sat nearby and smiled.

The judges took a short recess, but needed barely any time to deliver their decision. After less than twenty minutes, they issued a rare two-sentence verbal ruling from the bench. It overturned a 2015 BC Court of Appeal ruling that had been in the government's favour, and reinstated an earlier BC Supreme Court decision in favour of the teachers.

"The appeal is allowed," said Chief Justice Beverley McLachlin. "Thank you very much."

The teachers had won. It was supposed to take months to get to a decision. Instead it took minutes. BCTF president Glen Hansman was sitting in the courtroom, still not sure what had happened. He grabbed the legal counsel and asked him to explain what it all meant. Then he rattled off a quick email to vice-presidents Teri Mooring and Clint Johnston with a subject heading that read, "WE WON." The vice-presidents, who were also expecting months before the top court would rule, sent back emails asking, basically, what did we win? Tickets to a show or something? No, replied Hansman, we won the whole court case.

The long and tortured legal battle had taken more than a decade to resolve. It dated back to 2002, when the BC Liberal government legislated teachers back to work and stripped teachers of their right to bargain class size levels and specialist teacher composition. Gordon Campbell had been the premier at the time. But the education minister who'd introduced and passed the contentious bill in the legislature had been none other than a young Christy Clark.

In 2011, BC Supreme Court Justice Susan Griffin would strike down Clark's 2002 bill as unconstitutional. By now, Clark was premier. She had the power to call off the dogs. Instead, she opted to launch round two, passing another bill in 2012 to try to fix the original 2002 attack on teacher bargaining. But Clark's second salvo was also struck down by the same judge, Justice Griffin, in 2014. Clark remained unrepentant. The government appealed, and in 2015 won a BC Court of Appeal decision. It was now the BCTF's turn to appeal. So it sought leave to appeal to the highest court in the land. And that court, in Ottawa on that 2016 morning in November, sided with the teachers. There were no more appeals to make, by either side.

The Opposition NDP wasted no time connecting thirteen years of wasted taxpayer money and legal fights with one person: Premier Clark. A generation of students had missed out on smaller classrooms and better supports because of Clark's stubborn fight with teachers, which had now proven to be completely illegal, charged the NDP. It was an easy narrative to stick on a government that had seen the longest teachers' strike in BC history in 2014, and had previously been accused of trying to provoke a strike among teachers so it could have an excuse to legislate them back to work.

With its court options exhausted, there was nowhere to go for the Liberals but to capitulate to the BCTF's demands. The government began tossing money at the problem to try to staunch the bleeding as the 2017 election approached. It inked a $50 million interim deal to hire a thousand new teachers and then dumped another $740 million over three years into the system in its pre-election February 2017 budget.

Clark's Liberal government had suffered a humiliating loss at the Supreme Court of Canada. Its legal case had been shredded multiple times as unconstitutional. It had wasted years, and millions of dollars, on a mean-spirited attempt to try to break the teachers' union. It took a certain amount of chutzpah to describe a thirteen-year failed legal fight as a "chance" to invest in kids, and it was the kind of spin-doctoring that seemed a step too far, even for the Liberals. The tone infuriated teachers and tainted the funding. And the public didn't buy it. It was just another reason for the public to distrust the current government.

The NDP seized the narrative by adding to the mix complaints about the proliferation of portables in Surrey, the overcrowding of schools across the province, the recent closure of several rural schools due to low enrolment, the slow pace of seismic upgrades to protect kids from earthquakes, and the deferred maintenance of certain facilities that had leached lead into the water, created leaky roofs, and left classrooms in substandard conditions.

The Liberals hoped that education, while an issue, wouldn't sting them too badly among voters. After all, the party had managed to win three consecutive majority governments since picking its court fight with teachers.

The NDP was hoping differently. Voters might not make their decision entirely on the basis of their education, but they could fit it into a larger narrative that Clark was mean-spirited, petty, and only offering up money now because she'd been forced to by the court.

"I don't think she can un-ring this bell," said NDP leader John Horgan, heading into the election. "I just don't think pouring some money into it just before the election is going to work this time."

SOME CRISES WERE the slow-boil kind, in which the temperature of the water increased at such a steady pace over a period of months that, one day, the government would look down with surprise at the severity of its burns.

The *Globe and Mail* newspaper was on a roll with a series of stories involving "cash-for-access" events held by Ontario's governing Liberal party, Premier Kathleen Wynne, and her cabinet ministers. The basic criticism was that when wealthy donors bought expensive tickets to party fundraisers, they were, in essence, buying special access to opportunities to lobby the premier and her cabinet, using their money to get the ear of the most influential political power players at Queen's Park so they could ask them for favours and rule changes that would benefit their interests.

Globe columnist Gary Mason turned his sights on the issue, penning almost twenty columns on the BC Liberals' political fundraising from March 2016 through the 2017 election. Mason, a veteran reporter and columnist, knows how to write with devastating effectiveness. His

critiques were scathing. And they were complemented by *Globe* political reporter Justine Hunter's digging. Mason started by exposing a
$10,000-per-plate fundraiser for Clark at the home of Simon Fraser
University chancellor Anne Giardini, and moved on to analyzing the
party's donor list of corporate bigwigs, comparing BC's lack of transpar-
ency with that of other provinces, and revealing a $50,000 stipend the
party was paying the premier on top of her $195,468 salary as MLA and
premier. For ten solid months, Mason absolutely whaled on the Liberals. Single-handedly, he created a political crisis for the government.

The Liberals for some time just ignored the criticism. Internally, it
was felt that the Ontario-based newspaper was trying to score cheap
political points by taking its successful assault on the Wynne government fundraising tactics and transplanting it to BC. Odd as it sounds,
among Clark's inner circle there was an element of not wanting to let
the easterners tell BC what to do. And they felt that even when Wynne
capitulated to the *Globe*'s demands to halt such fundraising, the paper
simply found another topic on which to hammer her, so what was the
point of changing?

The premier felt that not that many people in BC read the *Globe
and Mail* anyway. And the issue had been, in her mind, invented out
of nowhere, for no cause other than to give the paper a vanity project. There'd been no evidence a crime was committed, no evidence
any money that had come into the Liberal party had influenced its
decision making.

As defensive strategies go, the Liberal response was a blunder.
Mason's reporting continued unabated and caught the attention of the
New York Times, which sent reporter Dan Levin out to investigate. His
story landed on January 13, 2017, with the headline "British Columbia:
The 'Wild West' of Canadian Political Cash."

At first, the Liberals again did nothing to respond. They felt Levin
was a left-wing activist journalist, who'd already treated them unfairly
in a December story he'd done about the Site C dam project. But the

New York Times story generated a flurry of reactionary coverage, which ate up days of political coverage in the province. By now, members of Clark's cabinet were starting to get worried. Many, including Transportation Minister Stone and Health Minister Lake in particular, began saying the government and party needed to respond. Shady government fundraisers, big donors, the premier's stipend—it all just looked bad. The response from Clark and her senior advisors was, "Well, no one is talking about this at the door." Which might have been true at the time. But months later, it would become inextricably linked to the issue of Clark's character and integrity, which, by then, was all anybody was talking about at the doorstep.

Clark also felt the criticism of the stipend had a sexist edge to it. The party stipend for leaders had existed for many years, dating back to Gordon Wilson in 1991, and nobody had questioned it then. She disclosed it on her annual MLA conflict forms (though not the amount). And now, she, a single mother who used the money in part to pay for home care for her son, was being criticized for something men had already received for years. At least, that's how the premier viewed it.

Regardless, after the *New York Times* story, it was clear something would have to change. Clark looked at how many media stories were focused on political fundraising and realized it was eating into the precious pre-election months she needed to get her party's early message out to voters. She agreed to abandon the stipend to make the whole thing go away. She announced the decision in response to a question planted by her staff at an unrelated event on January 20, 2017. The party had also agreed to post its donor list online every two weeks. In March, it did the absolute least it could do to contain a brewing crisis by announcing an independent panel on political financing, to provide recommendations after the May provincial election.

The political fundraising/stipend story was like manna from heaven for the New Democrats for much of 2016. Top critic David Eby would feast on Mason's stories, retooling them for other media and advancing the cause with conflict challenges and formal complaints that would, in turn, give Mason and the media more to write about.

Clark maintains to this day that the fundraising file was much ado about nothing. All parties take money from donors, as the BC NDP proved by doing it at the same time (and brazenly during the party's earliest days in government too). Yet her government was too slow to recognize the political risk of letting the problem fester through months of stories.

The NDP was able to use the issue to devastating effect in the 2017 election campaign, fashioning ads that showed Clark on a throne showered with dollar bills from her donors while a voiceover said she was in the job only for her personal gain and not for voters. In short, the Liberals' opponents used fundraising to assassinate the premier's character.

BY THE TIME the Liberals were ready to unveil their last, pre-election, budget in February 2017, their theme was clear: it's time to share the benefits of a steady economy by returning some of the money back to people.

How that money would be returned proved problematic. When Clark asked her cabinet for ideas, they returned a list of spending ideas totalling more than $3 billion.

Internally, one of the ideas the government would debate was whether to raise the welfare rate. The rate sat at $610 a month. It hadn't been raised by the Liberals in ten years, and the party was under pressure internally and externally to justify how a decade-long freeze to social assistance was anything more than petty, cruel punishment of the poor.

Some ministers, including powerful finance minister Mike de Jong, urged a modest one-hundred-dollar increase to the monthly welfare rate. If the theme of the budget is sharing economic benefits, should the message not be sent that the government is sharing them with the most vulnerable too, he asked. But there were arguments against—mainly that one hundred dollars wouldn't be enough to make a real impact on the lives of the poor and that very few of those people were going to vote Liberal anyway. The premier, in particular, was unenthusiastic about raising the welfare rate. Philosophically, she'd long believed that if government was going to spend money on social assistance, it should do it by creating jobs that could lift people out of poverty rather than giving them payments to stay poor. This translated to critics as, basically, don't be lazy, get a job.

Ultimately, after much debate, cabinet shot down the welfare option in favour of spending money on one of Clark's pet peeves, Medical Services Plan premiums. Clark had publicly pledged to get rid of MSP fees, though her government had hiked the rates on the premiums almost every year under her premiership. The medical surcharge cost an adult with a mid-range income seventy-five dollars a month, though in many cases the fees were paid by a person's employer.

The problem with eliminating MSP fees was that they accounted for $2.5 billion in revenue. So Clark proposed a half measure: announce a cut in the rates of 50 per cent before the election, with a promise to get rid of them entirely at some point in the future when the economy could afford it.

The MSP cut was the centrepiece of the February 21, 2017, provincial budget, and the springboard by which the Liberals hoped to start their early election campaigning. But party strategists didn't particularly like the tax cut. Liberal election campaign director Laura Miller was less than thrilled with the idea of an MSP reduction being the marquee tax cut on which to build an election campaign. To her, it looked like the campaign would be spending a lot of time talking about a tax people didn't like, and in the process reminding voters Premier Clark had actually raised the rates repeatedly.

The Liberal party had done research and polling on the issue, and determined that people would be fine to just see MSP rolled into the income tax system, with those making more paying more, and that overall they would rather have some other kind of tax relief or increased spending on government services. Despite that research, the premier had spent almost a year, in 2016, signalling she was working to kill MSP premiums for people who earned less than $120,000 a year.

The premier's decision also frustrated then–health minister Lake. He'd quietly proposed an alternative plan, which he'd spent months researching on his own. Lake's idea would raise taxes on higher-income British Columbians, while also adding a 1 per cent payroll tax on companies with more than forty employees. That would generate enough revenue to eliminate MSP fees entirely. It would continue to put a burden on employers to pay the tax. And it wouldn't lead to hidden tax hikes on middle-income British Columbians, as might have occurred if government just folded the MSP costs into the general income tax system.

But Clark wanted something that looked better and was more appealing for the middle class than a complicated tax shuffle. As well, there were the regular complaints within the Liberal party that any tax increase on corporations could cause them to flee BC for a more welcoming economic climate.

Lake made the pitch directly to Clark and de Jong. But they never put it on the larger cabinet agenda. It could have eliminated the MSP problem while keeping enough money available to do things like raising the welfare rate.

"An ongoing freeze on temporary assistance rates, I think, people viewed as being inconsistent with our assertions about the strength of the economy," de Jong would say after the election. "If that is so, then surely you can share a little bit more of that. And in retrospect, we probably should have."

The irony of all the internal wrestling the Liberals did on MSP rates was two-fold.

First, the provincial treasury would end the year with a massive surplus, more than double what the party had expected before the election.

De Jong insists he didn't know that before the election, when the Liberals could have used the extra money to fund all the promises, and more, that the party had rejected internally in the February budget. It could have sprinkled significant cash on problem files, like the welfare rate and other hot-button issues, to drum up votes. De Jong's critics suspect the usually cautious finance minister must have known, deep down, that he'd lowballed the figures and there was more money than he portrayed publicly.

Second, for all the fretting the Liberals did internally on how to pay for their MSP cut, they'd run into a New Democrat Party in the election that did virtually no thinking about the same issue. The NDP promised to eliminate MSP rates within four years, with no idea how to pay for it other than to strike some kind of tax panel that would investigate alternatives. Internally, the NDP casually planned to roll MSP costs into income tax, though the party was loath to admit it publicly at the time. The Liberals were aghast at what they thought was imprudent fiscal management from the NDP.

AS THE LIBERAL government began unveiling its February 2017 pre-election budget, it opened the treasury purse strings in an attempt to generate a flood of positive headlines for the Liberal government, including for its MSP reductions. But any positive press was overshadowed by a controversial story entirely of Clark's making.

In early February 2017, it looked like someone from a legislature computer was trying to gain inappropriate access to the BC Liberal website. *Province* columnist Mike Smyth wrote about how an internal spreadsheet was widely available on an obscure page of the party website. The party thought it had been hacked and, behind the scenes, briefed Clark, who was furious.

Clark was coincidentally scheduled to do a Facebook Live event with *Vancouver Sun* columnist Vaughn Palmer on February 7. Campaign director Miller and press secretary Stephen Smart warned Clark earlier that day she couldn't mention the hacking allegations, because the party didn't have enough information. But when the interview went live, Clark veered off message.

"The NDP has said it's going to be the ugliest, dirtiest campaign that we've ever had," Clark told Palmer. "We saw them try to hack into our website the other day. Hacking into websites is illegal."

The NDP was irate. It had not, in fact, hacked the Liberal website. The NDP threatened to sue.

"Whenever she gets into trouble she starts to make things up, and I believe that speaks to her character more effectively than I ever could," said Horgan, during an impromptu media call from his vehicle, which was sliding down a hill in a snowstorm in Victoria. "It was a complete fabrication. She just made it up." His call with reporters was at times interrupted with shouting when the NDP leader was worried his press secretary Sheena McConnell was going to drive the car into a ditch.

Miller texted the premier the next day, urging her to walk it back. But Clark instead doubled-down during an event in Victoria that was supposed to showcase her party's Vancouver Island election platform.

"It's a criminal act," she said. "Whether or not they admit to doing it, I don't know."

On day three, Delta South MLA Vicki Huntington, who was an Independent member, revealed herself as the source of Smyth's original column, noting one of her staff had exploited a security hole in the Liberal website. That left the NDP innocent.

Clark had nowhere to go but retreat. She phoned Horgan to apologize. The call went to voicemail, and Clark was forced to record her apology on a machine.

The entire controversy lasted days, but it served to overshadow tens of millions of dollars' worth of feel-good announcements by the Clark government, aimed at drumming up positive coverage on key files like public education, in the week before the crucial pre-election throne speech. All anybody was talking about was the hacking controversy. And it was another embarrassing mark on Clark's credibility, reinforcing in the minds of her critics that she was too quick to judge.

FUNDRAISING, HOUSING, EDUCATION, Metro Vancouver transit, and child welfare were the biggest structural cracks emerging in the Clark government as its mandate wrapped up in 2017. But small issues had also collected over the years, which added weight to the anchor that was dragging the party's reputation down.

There were the wrongful firings of eight health researchers in 2012, which resulted in the suicide of one of the men, Roderick MacIsaac. The scandal of government's top civil servants having allowed such an injustice to occur would simmer for years. An Ombudsperson's investigation released days before the writ dropped and the election campaign began in 2017 found the government was wrong to fire the researchers and ordered compensation for them and MacIsaac's family.

There was the so-called triple-delete scandal, in which a twenty-eight-year-old assistant to Transportation Minister Todd Stone was accused of grabbing another employee's computer keyboard and permanently deleting emails about the Highway of Tears between Prince George and Prince Rupert so they couldn't be released via Freedom of Information request. The process of scrubbing the emails (by deleting them three times from various computer folders) exposed a larger culture of shoddy record-keeping and hyper-partisan young staffers who'd do anything to protect their political masters.

Clark also faced questions about her personal judgement for giving long-time friend and Richmond-area MLA Linda Reid the job of Speaker of the legislature. Reid would make a mess of the file, becoming embroiled in a series of spending scandals over a first-class African safari she took with her husband, a $48,000 touch-screen computer terminal for her throne in the legislature, and a $733 rack to hold free muffins for MLAS in a snack room.

The spending reflected poorly on Clark, because it came during a time in which the rest of government was dealing with austerity measures, and because it was so clearly the result of a patronage appointment of an unqualified friend. But Reid wouldn't listen to reason. It got so bad that Clark sent chief of staff Dan Doyle to Reid's office for weekly meetings that culminated in a threat to fire her. If she didn't show better judgement, the Liberals would not support her in a vote of non-confidence in her Speakership in the House, Doyle told her. Reid, eventually, got herself in check.

It was the little scandals, like these, that added up.

There was one problem file that was paradoxically both the smallest and largest Clark's administration would face. It was a dispute over a relatively small quarry that sat on top of a hill above Shawnigan Lake on Vancouver Island, where a local company had a provincial permit to store contaminated soil. The Ministry of Environment had granted the permit in 2013, allowing Cobble Hill Holdings to take and store up to 100,000 tonnes of contaminated soil a year at the quarry. The situation infuriated local residents, who alleged runoff from the contaminated site was spilling into Shawnigan Lake, where many locals got their drinking water.

The dispute ground along for years in various stages of court action, appeals, and permit challenges. Politically, it was such a minor local issue that the Clark government paid virtually no attention to it. Locals interpreted that as a dismissive and disrespectful attitude to local constituents by Environment Minister Mary Polak. It was an NDP-held riding in the Cowichan Valley, and the Liberals didn't seem to want to exert much energy to make the problem go away. Plus, it was tied up in the statutory decision-making part of the ministry, where staff have control over permits and politicians aren't supposed to interfere.

The NDP was slow off the mark on the issue. Local MLA Bill Routley had already checked out for his impending retirement, and neighbouring MLA John Horgan was busy leading the party.

Into the political vacuum stepped Green leader Andrew Weaver. He might appear at first an unlikely ally, given he represents an Oak Bay riding some distance away. But quite a few of his constituents were upper-class and wealthy, with second properties at Shawnigan Lake. And Weaver saw an issue he could get behind to help drum up Green support in another riding as well. Among the most vocal activists was Sonia Furstenau, a local regional director who led the anti-contaminated soil movement. She was impressed with Weaver as a leader and a politician. She'd join the Greens as their candidate in the 2017 election.

The Shawnigan Lake controversy became one of the largest, most important, events in the fall of the BC Liberals. Not because of what it was, but because of whom it motivated. From Liberal arrogance grew a candidate in Furstenau that would not only win the riding but also, because of the unprecedented results of the election, hold a surprising amount of power in determining who would form the next government. She had a burning grudge against the Liberals, from a mess that was entirely of the government's own making. Like many of the controversies that began to dog the Clark administration in the lead-up to the 2017 campaign, it would have far-reaching and unintended consequences. Little did anyone know that, in the months to come, during an unprecedented series of events, Furstenau would be the deciding factor in whether the Clark government survived or fell.

CHAPTER 8
THE MAN WHO DID NOT WANT TO BE PREMIER

When BC New Democrats went looking for a leader to replace Adrian Dix, there was one man who definitely didn't want the job. John Joseph Horgan, the fifty-four-year-old MLA from the sleepy Greater Victoria suburb of Langford, took one look at the demoralized troops still smarting from their stunning 2013 election loss, imagined the kind of infighting he'd have to withstand, and concluded, basically, no freaking way.

Reporters at the legislature pulled Horgan out of the Speaker's corridor hallway on October 16, 2013, expecting to quiz a front-runner in the race about the details of his inevitable and impending leadership campaign. Instead, Horgan surprised them all by admitting he was going to pass on becoming leader and potentially the next premier of the province.

"The prospect of the constraints of message boxes and having to check with other people—I'm going to say stupid things and I'm OK with that. But as leader you're under so much scrutiny I believe that would constrain my ability to add to the debate about where we need to go as a party," said the blunt, outspoken MLA.

Horgan had already run for leader once in 2011, when he, Dix, and Mike Farnworth—all friends who'd grown up in politics together—ran a spirited and amicable race that Horgan described as "unbridled fun." Dix had won. Horgan had placed third. Since then, though, "fun" was not a word you'd use to describe any part of being in the perpetually losing BC New Democratic Party.

"I didn't see that [fun] in the future," Horgan said. "I saw difficulty, I saw acrimony, I saw divisiveness, and it seems to be the best course of action when you're faced with that is be grateful for the time you had and be ready to help whoever steps forward."

So with that, Horgan was out. Thanks but no thanks, he said, content to serve out his last term as an MLA before retiring after a full career as a government staffer and politician.

But BC politics is a bizarre and wacky business, where nothing is as it seems for long. Forty-four months later, Horgan would become BC's thirty-sixth premier under stunning and extraordinary circumstances.

HORGAN WAS ONLY eighteen months old when his father, Pat, died of a brain aneurysm. He'd never know his dad, who had immigrated to Canada from Ireland, but he saw first-hand how tough it was for his mother, Alice, to survive as a single stay-at-home parent with four kids. The Horgans were not a well-off family, and for many years they survived largely on the charity and goodwill of neighbours, friends, and their church in Saanich, BC. Food hampers had a regular presence in the house on major holidays, like Christmas.

"People would step up to help me and that was a great help for my mom," Horgan recalled. "She was always grateful and again she instilled in me, 'People have helped us, you should help them.' That's just how I've rolled ever since I remember."

Young Horgan also rolled with the wrong crowd. As a teenager, he was into smoking, playing pool, skipping class, and flunking science, math, typing, and French. Horgan has widely credited his high school basketball coach, Jack Lusk, for righting his trajectory before something worse happened.

Lusk "grabbed me by the scruff of the neck in Grade 10 and said you are going nowhere, friend, you should try this instead," said

Horgan. "Were it not for Jack Lusk, I could be dead, that would be no surprise."

Lusk doesn't remember singling him out for any special reason, but he does remember a polite young leader. So was born "Jumpin' John Horgan" the basketball player, who left his troubles on the hardwood and travelled to play varsity basketball at Trent University in Ontario. There he'd meet his wife, Ellie—his "bestie," as he calls her—and, after a stint in Australia for a master's degree, he'd find himself in Ottawa immersed in the glamorous world of federal politics, working in the mailroom opening mundane constituency correspondence for his local MP, Jim Manly.

Horgan and his wife returned to BC, where he worked for NDP premier Mike Harcourt. Harcourt tasked him with keeping a close eye on ambitious cabinet minister Glen Clark. In those days, the NDP's greatest enemy was itself. Harcourt would be forced out, and Glen Clark would later become premier. Clark would keep Horgan around on his staff. The big Irishman would go on to become a political fixer for NDP premiers, working to solve problems as a senior staffer, advise on communications, and manage priority issues. He developed a keen interest in energy policy, and later was tapped to become Premier Dan Miller's chief of staff.

When the NDP were swept out of office by the Liberals in 2001, that appeared to be it for Horgan's career. Others suggested he get into politics, but Horgan would tell them he didn't think he was tough enough for the job. Indeed, he had thin skin. As a player in the rough-and-tumble game of lacrosse, he earned the nickname Asphalt Gopher for his tendency, when hit, to drop to the ground and help incur a penalty against the opposing team.

One day, Horgan found himself in his Langford home ranting to no one in particular while the TV news played a story about how the Liberal government was building new BC Ferries ships overseas. A friend of one of his two teenage sons interjected to ask, "What are you going to do about it?"

Horgan paused. He didn't know. But he'd been challenged to step up. So he decided to run for the NDP in his riding of Malahat-Juan de Fuca. He won easily in 2005.

As an MLA, Horgan earned kudos for his fiery ability to hurl questions at Liberal cabinet ministers, his quick wit, and his continued mastery of energy issues. In 2008, he was diagnosed with bladder cancer, a life-changing event he described as like getting hit by a baseball bat. But he went through treatment and recovered.

Horgan's old basketball coach, Lusk, re-emerged as one of his constituents. Lusk called on his former player to come hear from his neighbours about problems they were having with logging companies in their area. Horgan went out, listened to their concerns, got involved, and sorted out the issue.

"He came along and listened to our stories," Mr. Lusk, now in his seventies, told the *Globe and Mail*. "I was impressed with the way that he had grown up from the [kid] whose pants I had to kick in order to get him to show up."

EARLY IN HORGAN'S career as an MLA, a local news magazine ran a cover photo of him holding a lacrosse stick with the caption "the enforcer." Horgan's old lacrosse manager popped into his MLA office, tossed the magazine on his desk and said, "Horgan, you were a lover—you were never a fighter."

It was an early sign of the difficulty the public would have in shoehorning John Horgan into an easily definable box. From the outside, he looked like a big, blustery, hard-edged opposition critic. Scratch the surface a little, as the media often did, and you saw an easily frustrated, quick-tempered, sometimes insecure political leader. Digging deeper, to his core, friends saw a genuine, plain-spoken, generous man, who was easily moved to tears, who loved science fiction, who enjoyed restoring antique furniture because he was colour-blind and appreciated seeing the grain of wood, and who was absolutely, completely, and utterly devoted to his wife and family.

It's hard for any politician to showcase the totality of their personality to the public, and it became especially so for Horgan. He was quickly labelled as a hothead for his clashes with the legislative press gallery. After the NDP's 2009 loss, he blamed the "mainstream media" and in particular the Canwest Global newspaper and TV chain for going out of its way, he felt, to prevent the NDP's positive messages from reaching voters.

"We don't get our message out because, in my opinion, the dominant media player doesn't listen to what we have to say," he told *The Tyee* website.

Horgan's war with some elements of the media led to confrontational coverage that would take considerable effort on his part in later years to overcome.

By 2013, after having run in three elections only to watch his party fail to reach the promised land of government, Horgan had had enough. He spoke widely about retiring at the end of his term. And he was unimpressed with Dix's decision to run a positive campaign that refused to allow attack ads against Christy Clark.

"You get full marks for that," he said in one interview after the election. "But you don't get to form government."

The 2013 election defeat "made me retch," Horgan said at the time. "I felt sick to my stomach."

But someone had to be the leader.

Horgan had not been interested in replacing Dix. He did, conceptually at least, sketch out what a Horgan leadership bid would have looked like. In particular, it zeroed in on the idea that the NDP, under Dix, had failed to present people in rural BC with a plan and support for the mining, forestry, and oil and gas jobs that helped them raise families and afford to live. Horgan found himself clearly aligned with the "brown" side of the NDP coalition, which supported natural resource jobs, and not the "green" environmental movement.

"We have lost our way to speak to people in resource-based communities; we have become dependent on particular points of view largely focused in the Lower Mainland," he said in 2014. "If we are going to win we need to speak not just in a pandering way, but in a positive way to people in resource-based communities."

That would have been "the foundation of the campaign" he never ran, Horgan told the media. "There is a chasm between the Coast and the Kootenays that is not represented by the NDP."

Horgan was also aware that if he did run, he'd likely be considered an automatic front-runner who would crowd out potentially younger leadership hopefuls.

But he wasn't the only one thinking about taking another shot at the leadership.

THE 2013 ELECTION made it clear to Mike Farnworth that the party needed a rethink. He was a veteran and one of only a handful of MLAs who'd been around long enough to have the experience of serving in cabinet in the 1990s NDP governments. As Farnworth started talking with party members, many told him that he was the best choice for the NDP to win the 2017 election. He put together his team and got ready to launch. But before the big moment, he invited a young MLA for a tour of his home riding in Port Coquitlam.

David Eby had met Farnworth only a handful of times. The newly elected MLA from Vancouver-Point Grey was the up-and-coming star for the NDP at the time. At six foot eight he stood above the crowd, but it was his reputation as a giant-killer, by virtue of his win over incumbent MLA Christy Clark, that gave him the reputation as a potential leader.

The two politicians drove around the riding, while Farnworth pointed out his childhood home and the land where a former mental hospital, Riverview, once stood, which had been in the news for years. Once the tour was over the two men sat in a parked car and admitted to each other they were going to run for the leadership and become competitors. It wasn't awkward. It wasn't uncomfortable. But it was the last time the pair would chat for a while.

Eby had been encouraged to think about a leadership bid since his 2013 election-night upset. The former head of the BC Civil Liberties Association already had a high public profile. Like Farnworth, he had people pushing him to run. One of those was Vancouver lawyer Bill Duvall. Just a few weeks after Dix announced his plans to quit as leader, Eby found himself in Duvall's office discussing his leadership campaign.

By this point, Eby's supporters were assembling as a team, strategizing, drafting a communications plan, developing volunteer recruitment strategies, and crafting a website. Eby had even gone as far as to have a photo shoot so there would be new, high-quality shots of him for the press. The thirty-seven-year-old also had the support of his fiancée, Cailey Lynch, and his friends and family.

There is no doubt Eby would have launched his campaign. Except for one little thing. He and his fiancée had been trying to have a baby for a while. And just before the campaign launch, they got the news they were hoping for: Lynch was pregnant. The young politician knew what he had to do, so he picked up the phone and called Duvall. He was out.

It was a big blow to the group who saw Eby as the future of the party. Here was a guy who had beaten the premier in her own riding of Vancouver-Point Grey during the election. Many felt he could defeat her, party to party, in the next election as well. His lawyer friend Duvall had some advice.

"I think if you called Horgan and said you would chair his leadership campaign I think he would reconsider," Duvall told Eby.

Eby thought about it. He liked Farnworth, but he thought Horgan was the right choice for the NDP. It was also clear it would take some persuading to get Horgan back in the game. Eby gave him a ring.

"Hey, John, it's Dave calling," said Eby. "Listen, Cailey is pregnant. I am not doing this thing. I am not running for the leadership. I really think you should think about doing this and I think you would be really good at this."

He went on, complimenting Horgan as a house leader. Then the kicker.

"I think you have what it takes to win and I would be glad to be if you want me your campaign chair," said Eby.

Horgan wasn't sure what to make of the offer. He had been receiving calls from a number of MLAs, including others from the younger generation that Horgan was convinced was best to lead the party. That included Nelson-Creston MLA Michelle Mungall, another young New Democrat who'd offered to co-chair his campaign.

The Langford-Juan de Fuca MLA wasn't sure about his commitment to slogging it out in opposition anymore. He'd already served three terms as an MLA. Like many in the NDP, he'd prepped himself mentally for becoming a cabinet minister in the 2013 election that the party was assured it would win. The loss was crushing. He was ready to retire. Now, people like Eby were asking him for an eight-year commitment as the party's next leader. He needed to check with his wife, two sons, and siblings as well.

Eby made his big news public. His fiancée's pregnancy, and the sudden impact it had on the leadership race, became the talk of the NDP.

The day after Eby's announcement, Horgan stopped by his friend Maurine Karagianis's office at the legislature. Karagianis was the caucus whip and the MLA for the Esquimalt riding that neighboured Horgan's. He often came to her for advice. He, Karagianis, and Carole James had spent many an hour batting around the leadership question behind closed doors.

Karagianis wasted no time in her assessment.

"It's got to be you," she said to Horgan.

"No," he replied. "I'm not going to do it. I've already told the press I'm not going to do it."

"John, you are our best hope," said Karagianis. "I think you can actually pull this off."

Horgan kept mulling the issue over. He and James went for a long walk along Victoria's picturesque Dallas Road, where a path winds along the ocean and cuts above clifftops and beaches. James outlined the challenges without sugar-coating her experience: he'd have to deal with all the difficulties of the job and get none of the glory; he'd be isolated; his decisions would upset caucus, friends, and party support-ers; and, eventually, one day, supporters might turn on him to force him out of the job in an inglorious manner. But, she added, he had her complete faith. He'd been a good friend and a loyal supporter, and the two had formed a close bond.

Horgan's major reservations remained that he was too old, and he'd already been labelled by the media as the guy with the temper.

In January 2014, former premier Dan Miller, who'd once employed Horgan in his office, went on Vaughn Palmer's *Voice of BC* television show to add his voice to those who wanted to draft Horgan back into the race.

"I think he'd be the perfect guy," said Miller. "He looks good. He's a stand-up guy. He looks you in the eye. He's a straight-shooter. When I was premier and I was in a jam and had a caucus that was bitterly divided in at least three ways, the guy I brought in to help was John Horgan."

Horgan finally admitted to reconsidering. "There is significant pressure from a whole bunch of people to reassess the call that I made," he told Palmer during the same show.

Horgan was still looking for younger leadership candidates. "That is not really happening," he said. "So I am listening to what people have to say."

As he debated, the race tightened.

Victoria MLA Rob Fleming was wavering on whether he should take a run. The father of two (then aged seven and four) was also one of the younger members of caucus, though it was clear Eby had claimed his mantle as the star up-and-comer in the party. Eby gave Fleming his assessment: Horgan was too far out in front. And so the Fleming campaign folded before it ever publicly launched.

Many others would also bow out, including MPs Nathan Cullen and Peter Julian, Vancouver mayor Gregor Robertson, and Burnaby mayor Derek Corrigan.

That left Farnworth.

Farnworth hadn't officially declared yet. But his campaign manager, Ben West, was getting worried that Horgan was going to pull out in front and beat him on a launch. So the long-time MLA scrambled over an early March weekend and called up *Province* newspaper columnist Mike Smyth.

"I'm running for leadership of the New Democratic Party," he told Smyth on March 2. "I don't believe for a minute Christy Clark is unbeatable. I'm running to be premier—and I intend to win."

Farnworth said Dix's flip-flop on Kinder Morgan, his refusal to go negative, and the party's lack of success in Metro Vancouver's suburbs were 2013 failures he intended to fix as leader.

Horgan was ready to officially enter the race as well, but he forgot one thing: to tell his wife. Ellie knew Horgan was strongly considering it, and it was something the family was ready for. But one morning, while all the pieces were still being put in place, Ellie heard on the radio that her husband was running for the NDP leadership.

"She was a bit unhappy about that," said Horgan in an interview for this book. "But I had committed that I was going to talk to her before anything happened and it came a little bit backwards, I think it was leaked. She is okay with it; she is still hanging out with me."

THE HORGAN CAMPAIGN officially launched two weeks later, with Ellie's blessing, on March 17, 2014. A crowd of almost two hundred people squeezed into the Isabelle Reader Theatre in his home riding. Horgan was joined onstage by Karagianis and James.

As a former leader, James had stayed out of endorsing candidates, but she broke her rule to support Horgan and said she was throwing her full weight behind his candidacy. The remaining dissidents who'd forced her out as leader in 2010 were largely lined up behind Farnworth, showing that the wounds from that rift had yet to fully heal within the party.

Horgan said he'd been surprised at all the younger candidates who'd come to him to ask him to step up, when he'd been waiting for them. He joked publicly, "I'm the younger generation I was looking for."

But early on, things didn't go as Farnworth had predicted. For the next month the supporters did not flock to him as he was hoping. Shortly after his announcement, he received a call from a long-time friend and former MLA. It was someone whose support he desperately needed, yet she told him, regrettably, she was going to back Horgan. Farnworth mulled over his best-case scenario among remaining supporters, did the math, and picked up the phone to call Horgan to tell him he was out.

The leadership race had now come down to one man—the guy who originally didn't want the job. There was no one left in the NDP who wanted to challenge him. Horgan's entire caucus stood behind him on

April 8, 2014, and cheered at a press conference at the Hotel Grand Pacific in Victoria.

Horgan would quickly outline his positions as leader. "Where we have to go is out to the (Fraser) Valley, into the eastern suburbs and into the Interior," he said of the future election strategy under his leadership. He altered Dix's opposition to the Kinder Morgan pipeline, saying he'd take a "wait and see" position on the project. And he softened the rhetoric on the Site C dam, saying it had "always been a case of when" the project would be built, because the power would be needed eventually.

All three positions are worth noting, because Horgan would take the opposite approach on each by the time he got to his first election campaign in 2017. Despite his strong initial tone, he had great difficulty behind the scenes executing on that earliest vision in the face of the environmental wing within the party. The new leader would spend much of his time trying to protect his left flank with a Green party threatening to siphon away supporters with its pro-environment agenda. Consequently, he would make major compromises on what had been long-held personal positions during his earliest days as leader.

Also, Horgan still wasn't sure he could do the job. Partly it was an extension of his humble and modest personality, along with his tendency to self-deprecating humour, that would lead him to tell close advisors he was still worried the Liberals would savage him over the issue of his temper.

"I can't do this, I can't win," he said during meetings with Karagianis and James. "They are going to rip me into pieces because I'm the angry guy."

His first chief of staff did not appear to help matters. John Heaney was an old friend of Horgan's and a colleague from the 1990s government. A lawyer and former deputy minister, Heaney signed on to be Horgan's top aide. The two Johns were very much alike, both quick to rise to what they saw as injustices being committed by the Liberal government. A charitable way to describe it would be that they fed off each other's anger, energy, and similar temperaments. Less charitable would be to say that Heaney reinforced the worst tendencies in Horgan to be chippy and frustrated. But regardless of the impact Heaney may have had on Horgan, the leader had deep respect for his top advisor.

When Heaney abruptly left to work for Alberta Premier Rachel Notley's NDP government in 2015, the plan was always that he would return. At first he extended his leave to stay longer. Months later, in the middle of August, Horgan and Heaney were set have dinner to discuss his return and the upcoming fall legislative session. Then Horgan noticed Heaney packing up his things in his legislative office.

"You aren't coming back?" Horgan asked.

His long-time friend kind of shrugged. But the meaning was clear. Heaney wasn't coming back. Horgan cancelled their dinner, and Heaney left.

The departure stung. Horgan felt abandoned by his friend. Privately, he wondered why people who'd encouraged him to run would leave him, including his communications director, Maya Russell. But over time, it would prove to be a blessing in disguise for the BC NDP, giving the party the space to bring in the right people.

Horgan was slow to trust advisors, and even slower to listen to advice. He had a small inner circle, composed mainly of people he'd worked with in the 1990s or, in some cases, their children. Heaney's departure at first left his office all but rudderless. It also left the NDP without a point person to organize what was needed in the leader's office with an election campaign on the horizon.

AS HORGAN WAS struggling to establish name recognition, one of his colleagues was stealing the headlines. Eby may not have run for leader, but he had become the NDP's voice on many of the party's key files and criticisms of the Liberal government. Time and time again the young MLA would dig up information on loopholes in Vancouver real estate, exposing questionable foreign investors or hammering away at Premier Clark about her $50,000-a-year stipend and cash-for-access political fundraisers.

On April 26, 2016, Vaughn Palmer published a column in *The Vancouver Sun* that said out loud what everyone was thinking. "No wonder that when speculation turns to who might be the next leader of the BC NDP, Eby tends to figure prominently in the list of possibilities," read the last sentence of the column.

The issue wasn't that Eby wouldn't make a good leader—it was that the job wasn't open. Eby didn't solicit the story. He didn't want the story. But there it was and it was awkward.

Eby had already talked to Horgan about the substandard communications division within the NDP. The caucus was so careful not to say anything that might contradict the leader that its MLAs weren't getting out to speak on issues in the media until it was too late and the headlines had passed. He told Horgan the issues his office had him speaking about weren't getting any news, and it was no wonder nobody knew who the leader was. Eby advocated for a much more aggressive communications strategy, and called on Horgan to join him on the front lines of the housing file, where Eby was scoring major points at the government's expense. Instead, Eby was later called into the leader's office by a senior member of Horgan's staff and told to back off on major files like housing affordability, the premier's stipend, and cash-for-access fundraisers, because they were crowding out Horgan's press coverage. Eby disagreed completely, but toned it down. It meant he passed on crucial media coverage and in turn hurt the party's chance to win the election.

By the fall of 2016, the tension between Horgan and Eby was real. In November *Vancouver Magazine* published a list of the year's most powerful people. Clark was number one, Eby number four and Horgan number sixteen. The magazine noted Horgan was "overshadowed by NDP front-bencher David Eby."

By this point, there were many voices in Eby's ear telling him he should be leader—not in 2017, after Horgan lost, but now.

"I have a two-year-old kid at home, I have a lot going on," he would tell whoever would listen. "I would love to be a cabinet minister in a Horgan government. But I do not want to be touring the province right now, especially during a campaign."

The rumblings about a possible takeover were getting back to the leader's office. And once again Eby was booked in for a meeting. This time directly with Horgan. The tension was high. The rumours were swirling. Horgan had heard that not only did Eby want his job, but that he had put together a shadow leadership team. Both rumours disturbed him.

"It's not true," Eby said. "I want you to be premier. I want you to succeed."

Eby told the leader he didn't think it was wise to tone down his attacks on housing and fraud in Metro Vancouver, and he again asked Horgan to be there alongside him, taking the lead on the file. Their relationship had broken down from where it was just a few years earlier. But both recognized they needed each other for the NDP to win. Party morale was low, and the overwhelming sentiment in caucus was that they were all about to lose.

A year before the election, Horgan was openly talking about whether he should quit. Talk continued to persist that Horgan wasn't the right guy to win the 2017 election. The leader still had lingering doubts about himself. He wasn't there because of an undeniable craving to be premier; he was there to defeat what he saw as a bad government. Horgan made it clear to party president Craig Keating, executive director Raj Sihota, and potential candidates outside the caucus that if they thought someone could do a better job than he could, he would step aside.

"I talked to them and said if you think you can do better, I am okay with that," said Horgan in an interview for this book. "I canvassed widely. It's not that I didn't believe I was up for the job but I didn't want some excuses. I didn't want anyone to have excuses."

No one made the pitch they were better than Horgan. But it was clear the NDP needed some help from outside. It would soon arrive.

COMMUNICATIONS EXPERT MARIE Della Mattia had been working with the NDP caucus, helping to conduct media training, craft messaging, and focus the party's energies in 2015. The party had struggled to get Horgan any consistent positive media coverage. His communications director, Maya Russell, left shortly after Heaney departed in the fall of 2015, leaving Horgan without key senior staff. Horgan again turned to the past to find trusted help, in the form of former NDP premier Mike Harcourt's press secretary, Brent Humphrey. Humphrey was travelling around North America in a Winnebago with his wife when the call from the leader came. What made Humphrey appealing to Horgan was their long friendship. That meant that when Humphrey told Horgan what to do, the often-stubborn NDP leader would take it seriously.

Despite Humphrey's positive influence, Della Mattia still saw an anxious party leader, wracked with self-doubt, and a disorganized leader's office. She felt the growing sense of frustration. Horgan had been without a permanent chief of staff for several months when, one night soon after Heaney's departure in the fall of 2015, Della Mattia decided to offer a name over dinner at the JOEY restaurant at the Bentall Centre in Vancouver. She suggested Horgan speak to a man named Bob Dewar, whom she'd worked with in Manitoba as a client of her firm, NOW Communications.

Dewar's New Democrat pedigree preceded Horgan's and ran long. He was former chief of staff to Manitoba NDP premier Gary Doer, the brother of former NDP MP Paul Dewar, and the director of the Manitoba Government and General Employees' Union. He'd been in the trenches on numerous NDP campaigns, provincially, federally, and even once in BC in 1986. But he and Horgan had no history. Which was out of the comfort zone for Horgan, who'd made a point of stacking the early versions of his staff with colleagues he trusted from the old 1990s BC NDP governments. The leader had a frustratingly small circle of people he'd actually listen to.

For months, Della Mattia and others pushed Horgan to make the call. But the leader was hesitant. Mainly, he felt Dewar, at sixty-four, was too old and perhaps represented the past generation of New Democrats, not a new vision. His staff kept pushing, and finally Horgan relented. He called Dewar for the first time in February 2016.

"I'd like you to come out here and work for me and help with the campaign," Horgan told him.

But Dewar had questions. The first, and most important, was "Why do you want to be premier?"

Horgan told him his life story, about his father's early death, his single stay-at-home mother, his challenging youth, and even his basketball coach. He wanted to be in politics to help others, the same way people had helped him growing up. Dewar had been in the game for a long time, and he had a good bullshit detector. But if Horgan's speech was insincere, it didn't set off any of his alarm bells. They agreed to meet in Vancouver the next month.

Dewar and Horgan owed each other nothing. In Horgan, Dewar would see a leader with, as he put it, "the royal jelly" that he liked immediately. And in Dewar, Horgan saw an answer to the question he'd been asking internally: Did he have the right team to lead him to victory in 2017?

Horgan wanted to know if Dewar, unlike Heaney, would stick with him.

"My commitment to you is to work with you until you become premier," said Dewar.

Dewar signed on to the BC NDP as an outsider. It was an important point. He hadn't been a part of the NDP's epic last-minute collapse in 2013. Nor had he been there for the 2009 campaign, when the NDP's ill-fated "axe the tax" campaign against the Liberal carbon tax blew up in their faces and cost them the support of BC's environmental movement. He carried no baggage in BC.

Tall, with greying hair, Dewar had a subdued tone but an infectious laugh that frequently crept into his comments. He was (compared with Horgan) relatively soft-spoken. But underneath was a steely resolve and, occasionally, a temper. He'd been asked to come in and run the BC NDP's election campaign, and he was going to do it his way, much to the chagrin of a group of veteran New Democrats who'd been involved in several previous losses and expected key positions again in campaign HQ.

Dewar had one request for Horgan. "When I do stuff, you have to back me up," he told the leader. Horgan agreed.

Dewar pushed aside the losing staff from the previous elections and brought in new staff from Ottawa, Manitoba, and elsewhere where necessary. There was still a core group from BC's organized labour movement, but they skewed younger, with less baggage than the old crew who'd lost in 2001, 2005, 2009, and 2013. This new crew would quickly find its feet behind the scenes and give Horgan the support he needed as the election grew nearer. Finally, after many months, there was a foundation being built on which the leader could stand. Horgan would soon prove that he was willing to listen and learn on the fly, during the most stressful period of his life.

The John Horgan who at first didn't want to be leader of the NDP, who resisted every effort to recruit him to become the next premier, who a year before the election thought about quitting, would emerge during the 2017 election campaign as a changed man. And despite being worried that he wasn't up to the task, he'd do what no one else within the NDP had been able to do in the past sixteen years: topple the BC Liberals.

CHAPTER 9
FOR WHOM THE BRIDGE TOLLS

NDP campaign director Bob Dewar picked up his copy of *The Province* newspaper on his way to campaign headquarters, scanned the front page, stopped, and then swore. On the cover of the April 9 edition was a headline: "Liberals pledge cap on bridge tolls."

The BC Liberals were first out of the gate on what would become one of the most important issues of the 2017 BC election campaign—providing relief for the pocketbooks of Metro Vancouver voters, and in particular the suburban ridings south of the Fraser River, like Surrey. The party's promise to cap tolls on the Port Mann and Golden Ears bridges at $500 could save daily commuters more than $1,000 a year.

Dewar absorbed the news and cursed again. With only one month to voting day, he knew he had to make a risky move. As he entered the campaign office, several staffers came up to ask him worried questions about the Liberal announcement.

"What are we going to do?" one person asked.

Dewar turned and said, simply, "We're going to get rid of the tolls."

Campaign policy advisor Jon Robinson entered the director's office as Dewar looked up from his desk.

"Find out how to pay for it," Dewar ordered. "Find out how to do it. But we're doing it."

And so one of the most important moments in the entire election campaign for BC New Democrats—scrapping bridge tolls for Metro Vancouver drivers—was actually a policy made up on the fly in a spur-of-the-moment reaction to their Liberal political opponents. Fewer than five hours later, NDP Leader John Horgan would announce the party's position to thunderous applause at a rally in Surrey. From crisis to policy pivot in three hundred minutes.

Both the Liberals and the NDP had identified a key to winning the entire election: picking up the many ridings south of the Fraser River, such as vote-rich Surrey, where they'd need to give ordinary voters some type of financial relief on the tolls they faced to drive over the Port Mann and Golden Ears bridges every day. Surrey residents felt it was unfair that they got dinged in the wallet every time they wanted to get downtown to watch a Canucks game, visit Stanley Park, or attend a concert.

Unbeknown to each other, both the Liberals and the NDP had settled on exactly the same policy to run on in the 2017 campaign: an annual cap on tolls. The Liberals had debated the amount, between $750 and $500 a year, and whether it could be a tax credit or hard cap, before Clark herself stepped in with a firm decision on a $500 cap.

Completely eliminating bridge tolls had never been the NDP's internal position. The cap they'd settled on internally was a 50 per cent cut to the toll rate, which, for daily users, would have been a less generous offer than what the Liberals were offering. The party had concluded, much like the Liberals, that the costs would be too high to scrap the tolls outright. Both were also concerned that if the tolls that kept the bridges financially solvent were eliminated, the bridges would no longer be considered self-supporting entities, and it would mean absorbing billions in bridge debt back into the books of the provincial government, potentially imperilling its AAA credit rating.

For Dewar, the bridge toll issue was bigger than just Surrey votes. A key theme of the NDP campaign was affordability—giving voters a break in their pocketbooks from years of increased costs that had added up under Liberal rule. He wasn't going to let his opponents outflank him on such a key issue before the race had even begun.

After Dewar's decision, the NDP's platform committee of MLA Carole James and Vancouver city councillor Geoff Meggs scrambled to make the numbers work. When they thought they had it figured out—a loose plan to empty the $500 million Liberal prosperity fund to at least pay for at least the first three years of scrapped bridge tolls—they gave the green light.

When Horgan took the stage in front of the large crowd in Surrey to kick off his campaign, he made the stunning announcement that as premier he'd get rid of bridge tolls in Metro Vancouver entirely.

"We're going to give Lower Mainland commuters a break," Horgan said to cheering and raucous supporters. "Eliminating the tolls on the Port Mann and Golden Ears crossings is one way that we will put money back in commuters' pockets and get people moving again."

The announcement put the Liberals on their heels. It turned the media spotlight to the NDP at an early stage, and it established the fact that the NDP was serious about being bold in the election campaign. Nobody realized the entire policy had been scrapped and rewritten in one morning. Internally, the quick thinking of Dewar had also sent a message to veteran BC New Democrats, many of whom were used to the slow, plodding, cumbersome pace of platform development within the party. This campaign would be unafraid to take risks.

The NDP was out of the gates quickly and would never look back in Metro Vancouver. The toll policy appeared to drive up NDP polling numbers not just in Surrey in subsequent days, but also in Maple Ridge and other communities where voters were stuck in bridge-related traffic.

The grumbling began in earnest within the Liberals. Why couldn't we have done this, asked several frustrated Lower Mainland MLAs, who as early as 2015 had internally been driving the bridge toll question in the hope it would result in goodwill among Surrey voters in particular.

Lieutenant-Governor Judith Guichon and Premier Christy Clark meet on April 11, 2017, as Clark requests the dissolution of the legislature to kick off the 2017 election campaign. Fewer than three months later, the pair would be back together again, when Clark argued that she should stay in power. PROVINCE OF BC

But the answer from powerful finance minister Mike de Jong was always the same: We can't afford it. There's just not enough money.

The premier also never heard any of her MLAs advocating for a total elimination of the tolls until after the NDP did it. Instead, the argument to her always centred on a cap or a reduction.

The irony for the Liberals was that there was enough money—in both that current 2016/17 fiscal year and the 2017/18 year that started April 1. It wouldn't be until weeks after the May 9 election that updated financial forecasts showed BC would double its surplus to $2.7 billion because of better-than-expected economic growth in the province. The party could have scrapped bridge tolls twice over and still have had millions to spare.

De Jong insists he didn't know. But that seems unlikely. The government knew the current fiscal year was tracking way over surplus, but it preferred to do nothing and let all that money automatically go into debt reduction. The forecasts for the next year contained more than $1 billion in surpluses, unallocated spending, contingencies, and forecast allowances that—with a little faith in the improving economy—would have easily allowed the government to justify more pre-election spending, more programs, and more big-ticket promises to voters.

It was ultimately Clark who kiboshed a more aggressive move on tolls. She wanted to run on the credibility of the government's fiscal credentials, and felt any move to stretch spending beyond conservative budget projections would have undermined the party's fiscal credibility.

The NDP's early bridge toll gamble would pay off in spades for the party in the election. And the Liberals would later deeply regret getting outfoxed so decisively by the NDP on such an important campaign issue. Bridge tolls were just one of the items that Lower Mainland Liberals felt weren't resonating strongly enough with campaign brass. The Clark government's power base in the Interior and north was failing to take seriously the growing pressure from Metro Vancouver voters on affordability and cost of living.

Some Metro Vancouver Liberals had clearly heard the rumblings that health care, education, new schools, housing prices, utility bills, bridge tolls, and other issues were piling up into an avalanche of anger. Others, especially veterans Mike de Jong and Rich Coleman, were adamant that any change on housing would hurt the economy and ruin the equity people had built up in their properties. Also, the more dominant cabinet ministers hailed from Prince George, Kamloops, and the Peace region, and weren't as sympathetic to the plight of the urban voter.

Bridge tolling was a good example of the urban-rural divide within the Clark cabinet. Interior MLAs, like Transportation Minister Todd Stone from the Kamloops area, argued that the Coquihalla Highway to the Interior was tolled for twenty-two years until it paid for itself in

2008. It wasn't fair for Metro Vancouver residents to expect the rest of the province to help pay for their bridges just because they didn't like the tolls. Stone would eventually support the toll cap, but begrudgingly. He'd wanted to bring in a new tolling policy for all Metro Vancouver bridges since his first year as minister, but had run into a wall of unwillingness from Clark's senior staff to wade into the file. (Part of that unwillingness was a belief in the premier's office that Stone had made a mess of the Metro Vancouver transit file and would make a mess of the tolling policy too.)

The official twenty-eight-day campaign period still had not started, yet the NDP had an advantage on a key issue, in a key area. Dewar's strategy was simple: steal ten to twelve seats in Metro Vancouver's suburbs and win the election. The NDP knew if they were going to wrestle power from the Liberals, they would have to do so there. Surrey was the most valuable of those areas, with nine ridings out of the eighty-seven up for grabs—more than the entire northern half of the province. In 2013, the Liberals had won close races with well-known candidates Peter Fassbender and Amrik Virk.

The BC Liberals had a different election strategy. The party dusted off its come-from-behind successful 2013 campaign and repurposed its core messages about growing the economy and creating jobs. Sprinkle in some fear-mongering that the NDP would shut down major job-producing infrastructure projects like the Site C dam and George Massey bridge replacement, and the core of the Liberal campaign was complete.

The details of the Liberal re-election bid were officially unveiled on April 10 in Vancouver. But as reporters scanned the document, they saw there was something missing: a big, bold vision for the future. The 2013 election had grandiose promises for LNG, a catchy "debt-free BC" slogan, and promises of thousands of jobs and trillions in revenue. Though virtually none of that had come true in the intervening four years, it had at least been something to strive for.

One big aspirational idea had been debated two days before the campaign started—strategist Mark Marissen had proposed the Liberals run on the pledge to allow only emissions-free (mostly electric) vehicles on BC roads by 2035. Marissen felt it could appeal to Vancouverites and give them a reason to get behind the Site C dam project because they could see one potential benefit of all the new clean power. The idea, while intriguing, came far too late and was nixed by campaign HQ. MLAs and candidates would have been hard pressed to unite behind an idea they'd never heard of until literally just before the campaign began.

The muted tone of the platform was odd, because it's not as if the Liberals suffered from a lack of ideas. Cabinet ministers Mike Bernier and Naomi Yamamoto had travelled the province to gather information for party platform development for almost two years. But it seemed the final document was a product of Clark and her core group of insiders, rather than a reflection of the membership or MLAs. The Liberals' 2017 campaign had no free bridge tolls. No freezes on BC Hydro or ICBC rate hikes. No big pledge on housing affordability. Where once there was a bold vision of LNG, now there was just a pledge to maintain the status quo.

"British Columbia is just getting on a roll," Clark declared. "Let's stay strong."

The promises that were unveiled were underwhelming. Clark's party planned to continue a freeze on all personal income taxes for the next four years, maintain a carbon tax freeze until 2021, cut the tax rate for small businesses to 2 per cent, and eliminate PST on electricity for businesses. The message seemed to be, "We don't need big promises because the economy is doing well. Let's stick together and keep on going."

Complacency, too, had begun to set in among the Liberals. They had so much money, were so well organized, and had survived such long odds in 2013 that some felt predestined to win. "Most pundits and the public probably think we will win, which in many ways is a lot more dangerous than the position we were in before," noted retiring cabinet minister Bill Bennett as the election started. McDonald had tried to rattle cages on this issue, earlier in 2017 giving a presentation titled "Reasons We Could Lose" to the party's provincial council.

The party had received so many accolades about its 2013 campaign that repurposing its main theme of job creation seemed a no-brainer. That message was a core belief of Clark's, and it still resonated in rural BC, where voters working in the natural resource industry worried about their next family-supporting job. But in urban Metro Vancouver people already had a job. And life was still unaffordable. Getting told the Liberals would help create jobs meant less than nothing to them.

There were early signs of this problem in the Liberal campaign. At one party focus group, swing-voter moms complained loudly about affordability. Then they got into their Lexus SUVs and other expensive vehicles and drove home to their houses. It didn't make their concerns any less real. But the Liberals were slow to pick up on whether actual affordability, or just the growing affluence of the region and the resulting societal pressures, were the source of voter discontent.

Despite their tepid platform, the Liberals did have one major early advantage over their NDP rivals: Christy Clark. Arguably one of the best campaigners in BC's history, Clark was a formidable threat on the hustings. Whether it was her seemingly unlimited energy, upbeat personality, unwavering smile, or quick-thinking ability to ad-lib and make small-talk with virtually anyone she met, there was no baby unkissed, no selfie untaken, and no rotary club pancake unflipped when Clark was on her game. Clark would need to deploy all of her skills just to keep the party afloat in the media cycle in the first few days of the campaign.

The NDP dominated coverage with bridge tolls and a promise for ten-dollar-a-day child care to ease the burden on cash-strapped parents. Clark tried to portray herself as the prudent money manager and Horgan as the risky big spender.

"He's already run out of money and that's all going to come in the form of higher taxes," Clark told reporters in her first campaign appearance outside Government House on April 11, the day the writ was dropped and the election formally began.

While the two front-runners battled, Green party leader Andrew Weaver was set to embark on the party's first provincial bus tour. The bus had Weaver so excited that in the lead-up to the campaign he invited reporters into his office and told them his new ride was ready but he couldn't show it off until the official launch. Then, predictably, he revealed his own secret by turning his computer screen toward the reporters to reveal the Green-wrapped tour bus with Weaver's face on the side. It was the kind of enthusiasm that his staff constantly had to keep in check.

Weaver was the only incumbent, but behind the scenes the party was confident they would add one, if not two, extra MLAs during the election. Weaver was obsessed with poll results that would come out from Mainstreet polling every week. As soon as they arrived, he would quickly scan the emails looking to see how his party was doing.

The big news came the first night of the campaign—the Greens were tied for the lead with the NDP on Vancouver Island, according to the Mainstreet poll. At 19 per cent province-wide, the Greens were also looking at a potentially major breakthrough. All of this had Weaver excited, and his expectations in the war room changed from just a few seats to a significant increase that would make the Greens an official party. No matter how many times his campaign team told him to be realistic, the climate scientist was dreaming big.

What Weaver was most excited about was his party's platform. The Green Party had put together a plan that wasn't just about climate change and the environment. It also had Weaver giddy. He had spent months collaborating with mostly former public servants who had worked across the country and retired in Victoria. The boldest part of the plan was in education, where the former academic suggested a

Green Party government would extend the province's education system to include preschool for three- and four-year-old children.

But for the promises to become reality, Weaver had to win. Even though the polls on Vancouver Island were trending in the right direction, it was hard for the public to believe a Green sweep was coming. You couldn't tell Weaver that, though. He was convinced that a breakthrough like Alberta NDP premier Rachel Notley's and Prime Minister Justin Trudeau's was going to come for the Greens. It was this deep confidence in himself and his party that had attracted people to his side.

The two heavyweights started the campaign ignoring the new guy on the block. The NDP saw another opportunity to throw the Liberals off their game early in the campaign. The party started an aggressive advertising buy in the first week, blanketing the TV and radio airwaves with attack ads. The Liberals were caught by surprise again. They'd expected an NDP media blitz at the campaign midpoint, after the TV leaders debate, when most of the public actually starts paying attention to the election. But the NDP went big, early.

One Dewar strategy for the NDP was to buy short, fifteen-second ads and try to get them bookended during the start and end of commercial breaks, recognizing that most people now watch TV recorded on PVRs. The bookend strategy meant viewers would catch a few seconds of one ad, before trying to fast-forward through the commercials, and then catch a few seconds of the other ad just before their show restarted. Enough, at least, to leave an impression.

NDP polling told the party that Clark was already massively unpopular heading into the election. In one internal NDP poll, more than 55 per cent of respondents disliked her. Clark tried to deploy the same charisma on the campaign trail that had worked to flip public opinion to her side in 2013. But any gains were overwhelmed by a steady assassination of her character early on through the NDP ad blitz.

The NDP ads were well produced. An early critical spot showed Christy Clark on a golden throne, showered with stacks of cash from "shady donations" made by corporate donors. They mentioned her party stipend with the insinuation she was "bought and paid for" by party supporters and was only in politics to personally profit. "Christy Clark: She took millions in donations from wealthy real estate developers, and turned a blind eye for years while housing prices went through the roof," said another ad.

Clark didn't realize until far too late how effective the NDP ads had become. But in retrospect, she could have known, because personal friends who were not immersed in politics started to contact her to ask what the hell was going on with the vicious personal attack ads crowding their TV shows, and why she wasn't responding.

Attacking Clark's credibility wouldn't work without providing an alternative. To do that, the NDP had to give its leader, Horgan, a prime-time makeover. Horgan was outfitted with new, more stylish clothes, with the help of press secretary Sheena McConnell (whose father had worked with Horgan in the 1990s). He had eye surgery and ditched his glasses. At one point, Horgan tried to change his image too much—shaving off his trademark beard and forcing Dewar to instruct him to grow it back because there wasn't enough money to reshoot all the signs and advertisements with his new clean-shaven visage.

First, there were internal matters to address. Horgan was frustrated with his inconsistent travel schedule, whether his time was being used properly, confusion over last-minute events, and the quality of his briefing materials. There was a disconnect between the leader's office, the legislative caucus, and the party in Vancouver.

Also, Horgan had a tendency to engage in, as his staff put it, "punditing." He liked politics, and he liked talking about it. The strategy. The excitement. The game. He looked at the political scene much like the staffer he'd been in the 1990s. But it wasn't his job to talk about politics anymore. As leader, he needed to be talking about people.

The messaging the NDP was using needed to change as well. Less borderline-sexist language. Fewer references to politics. More direct talk about voters. Don't reference how "an NDP government would," because voters think of the actual NDP government of the 1990s, and their thoughts go negative. Always keep talking about people, Dewar would say. The change proved a challenge. Some MLAs wanted to go flat out and call Clark a "corrupt" premier. They thought it would help highlight the premier's moral shortcomings.

Dewar killed it quickly. "The public believes you are all corrupt," he'd tell MLAs. "So you run on that in a campaign and you are sliming yourself as well."

Instead, it's about choices, Dewar would tell them. The Liberals made choices in the way they ran their government, some good, some bad. They made deliberate choices to cut the education system, for example. Focus on that.

Then there was the matter of Horgan's temperament. He did not like to be criticized or challenged in public, and he viewed the media with, at best, disdain. This led to almost two years of combative encounters with the legislative press gallery, who pushed Horgan on his policies and were pushed back on by a frustrated, anxious Opposition leader. Horgan would begin his media sessions with the line, "I'm happy to take any questions you might have," and then he would glower. He'd reject the premise of enquiries.

There were two instances that helped turn Horgan around. The first came eight months before the election, in September 2016, when Horgan wandered into a scrum at the legislature and on the fly moved his party's position away from opposition to the Kinder Morgan pipeline.

"I find it difficult to see how making Vancouver an export terminal for oil is in the interest of BC," Horgan told reporters in the hallway. "But I can be persuaded."

Dewar was sitting in his office, working on something else, when Ravi Kahlon, then the party's director of stakeholder relations, ran in.

"Have we changed our position on Kinder Morgan?" he asked.

"No," said a puzzled Dewar. "What are you talking about?"

"Well I just heard we did," said Kahlon, who'd already got a call from the Alberta NDP government.

Dewar called Horgan in for a meeting. "You are a leader," he said. "You are a politician. When you speak, everything is on the record. And when you start going on like this, about that, it's going to be reported. Because that's what people do."

Horgan, as he often did back then, reverted to blaming the media. They were unfair and out to get him, he said.

"No," said Dewar. "It's your fault. You cannot talk like that. You cannot do the punditry stuff."

The media, concluded Dewar, "are not your friends."

Another breakthrough moment occurred during a trip up Vancouver Island in March, just two months before the election. Communications guru Marie Della Mattia had picked Horgan up from his Langford home and the two had driven to Campbell River, where Horgan celebrated International Women's Day by visiting a transition shelter for women who were victims of abuse. Later that day, he had a town hall meeting in Courtenay. There were dozens of people in attendance, far more than Horgan had expected.

Horgan started with a short speech, without notes. And then he took questions. Town halls can be a notoriously difficult environment for politicians—the topics and grievances are so varied they'll likely be bounced between every topic imaginable and, inevitably, there's a curmudgeon or crank who wants to pick a fight. A large man eventually stood up near the back of the room, planted his feet, and let loose a long grievance about how his child was now in a modified 4.5-day school week. He was clearly upset. Not at Horgan exactly, but at the government and the system. Yet Horgan reacted as he tended to do at that time, becoming defensive at the first sign of aggression. He answered it as if he were already the premier, feeling responsible for a system he didn't create. The man was clearly unhappy with the answer.

Della Mattia couldn't sleep that night. She'd been working to help the NDP caucus on communications for several months and had sold her stake in her business, NOW Communications, to work full-time on Team Horgan. She is affable, friendly, non-threatening and, it seems, always on the verge of laughing.

Della Mattia was a good influence on Horgan. And he trusted her. So she drafted a long list of notes critiquing his town hall performance. First thing in the morning, she hit the local Tim Hortons and grabbed breakfast for Horgan in the hope it would counteract the fact that he can be an unpleasant early riser. Despite the coffee, Horgan took one look at her long notes and was visibly displeased at the idea of a critique.

"You did okay last night," she told him. "But you could have done better."

At first, Horgan wasn't necessarily keen to listen. But with decades of communications experience, and work on seven victorious NDP campaigns in four provinces, Della Mattia persisted. She made a simple but essential point that would transform Horgan's demeanour: questions aren't attacks. Every question, no matter the person, topic, or level of aggression, is an opportunity to redirect the issue to a point you actually want to make.

"You need to see the questioning as an opportunity, not a threat," she told him.

That night, they had another town hall in Nanaimo. By all accounts, he shone. There were still critical and angry questions—one in particular on how any politician could be trusted to honour a referendum on proportional representation when Prime Minister Trudeau had just reneged on a similar campaign promise—but Horgan didn't rise to the bait.

The issue wasn't solved overnight, but as the election campaign went on Horgan was markedly different in the way he answered pesky questions from reporters, in particular. When he'd slip up and get frustrated, Dewar and Della Mattia would say that their leader had reverted back to "the old John." But by the end of the election, Horgan was almost unflappable when it came to aggressive questioning. It was an impressive transformation, during one of the most pressure-filled moments of Horgan's life.

As Horgan conquered his weaknesses, Dewar began sharpening the campaign strategy.

Dewar and Della Mattia had the same vision for the election campaign. They developed a kind of tag-team approach to dealing with their leader, reinforcing his best qualities, honing his speaking skills, polishing his public persona. Dewar set the campaign strategy, and Della Mattia kept repeating the messaging into Horgan's ear. Together, they were the Horgan whisperers.

The idea of a people-driven campaign was set early by Dewar, and it was not up for debate. It was an election built on highlighting the choices the BC Liberals had made during sixteen years of power and the people who'd been hurt. Their questions were: Who is representing whom in this province? Who is benefiting under the Liberals? What are the consequences for people because of those choices?

A key moment, when the focus began to gel, was at the end of October 2016, when the NDP caucus of MLAS met in Vernon for a retreat and planning session. At one end of the conference room where the NDP was meeting, Della Mattia had tacked pictures of eight or nine people to the wall.

"We are going to meet each one of these people and understand who they are and where they are coming from and why they make the choices they're going to make," she said to the MLAS.

The pictures were of real people, but their stories were composites. Della Mattia began telling their stories. "Elouise" from Kamloops, for example, was a middle-aged pharmacist in a hospital, with a daughter at university, her aging parents living in Trail, and a husband who was unemployed. How does she relate to politics, and what will she base her choices on come election day, Della Mattia asked the room. Elouise isn't interested in politics and the manoeuvring of parties. She wants to know about health-care funding, Medical Services Plan premiums, home care for her parents, education and job prospects for her daughter, and so on.

MLAs later said it was a moment when the basic messaging of the pending campaign became clear. One MLA asked why there were more pictures of women on the wall than men. The answer was because women are more likely to be undecided about whom they're going to vote for and more likely to switch allegiances during a campaign. The NDP badly needed to appeal to them.

The people-centred strategy, though, would later be described by some outside observers as a sort of class warfare. As it evolved in the actual election campaign, it spawned ads such as one in which Horgan is shown walking down a sidewalk in Vancouver's Shaughnessy neighbourhood with large mansions behind him.

"Christy Clark gave the richest 2 per cent a billion-dollar tax break. Meanwhile the rest of us are paying $1,000 a more each year," he said to the camera. "Think about it. She's taking from you and giving to them [he gestures with his thumb toward one of the gated mansions behind him] and she calls that a strong economy."

The ad concluded with, "I'm John Horgan. The people at the top have had their premier. It's time you have one who works for you." It became the undertone of all the NDP's campaign messaging.

Research done by Della Mattia and the party showed that people generally agreed with the Liberal assertion that the economy was doing well in the province. Where they broke with the Liberals was on whether the good economy was actually making their lives any better. The province's GDP was the envy of Canada. But the NDP realized there was a disconnect between that and the family whose adult kids were still living in the basement, stuck with a low-paying job, student debt, and an out-of-control housing market, and with the cost of living for everything from groceries to insurance rising rapidly around them. BC's economy was booming, but its middle-class citizens were drowning, the NDP concluded.

Outside of its attack ads on Clark's character, the bulk of the NDP election advertising focused on Horgan meeting a rotating cast of unique characters, like Margerie, a ninety-three-year-old senior who had her housekeeping and laundry cut back by the Liberal government; or a pregnant Indo-Canadian couple who couldn't afford a new house but might be able to live a bit more comfortably with cheaper daycare.

Former NDP leader James and Vancouver councillor Meggs were put in charge of co-chairing the NDP's election platform. They held meetings with MLAs, took submissions from interest groups, and spent the better part of a year on the plan. Here, too, Dewar insisted on an emphasis on people. For example, the New Democrats had run in every recent election with a plan for "community health centres" that bring together nurses and doctors and other practitioners. It was largely a bureaucratic exercise that had never excited the public. But at Dewar's suggestion, that idea was renamed "urgent care centres" in an attempt to play on people's frustration at wait times in hospital emergency rooms and the inability to get a family doctor. A real problem, with a real solution.

The platform committee was keen to avoid the mistakes of 2013, where so much detail was dumped on every policy plank that not even the candidates could remember what the party had promised. So it focused on three themes: affordability, improved services that matter to people, and sustainable jobs now and into the future. The entire platform was shoehorned into those three frames. Still, the NDP faced the same weakness it usually did in an election: public misgivings about how they'd pay for all their promises. The party knew it was a weakness and worried the Liberals might gain traction with their attacks.

Instead, the Liberals overreached and stumbled. One week into the election campaign, on April 19, Finance Minister Mike de Jong held a press conference in downtown Vancouver. The entire affair was designed to mimic the serious, professional tone of his frequent government budget updates. He epitomized the sober, responsible fiscal management the Liberals hoped to use to hammer their opponents. De Jong walked journalists through a slideshow that outlined a $6.46 billion spending hole in the NDP platform.

"The question is, what taxes are going to be increased in order to accommodate that, or is the NDP simply lying when they say they're going to balance the budget?" de Jong said to reporters. "People," he added, seriously, "deserve to have the facts."

But it was the Liberals who had their facts all wrong. They'd deliberately skewed the NDP platform to present a misleading and inflated gap. For example, the NDP had promised it would "stop ICBC increases." The Liberals then torqued that to mean almost $2 billion in spending (based on an outrageously high estimated 42 per cent auto insurance rate hike that the Liberals themselves had earlier argued was a worst-case scenario that was improbable).

As the half-truths and over-exaggerations spilled out of de Jong's mouth, his credibility faltered. *Province* columnist Mike Smyth took the minister to task with a spate of aggressive questioning about his sloppy accounting that left the normally unflappable de Jong flustered. He lacked the numbers to back up his claims, in part because the numbers had been crunched by senior Clark staffers like Neil Sweeney and not by him. De Jong was just regurgitating the figures. His credibility as one of the party's most effective weapons nose-dived. He went from the respected, trustworthy finance minister to just a guy Horgan accused of using "fabricated" numbers.

The NDP breathed a sigh of relief. Because on some matters, it was legitimately vulnerable. The party had promised to eliminate Medical Services Plan premiums within four years, with no explanation of how to pay for it. And the much-vaunted ten-dollar-a-day childcare plan also didn't have a clear funding model. The Liberals kept trying to hammer the NDP on the big-spending validity of its platform. But the governing party had shot itself in the foot. The self-inflicted damage took away its advantage on a key issue.

Outside of Metro Vancouver, the Liberal campaign was firing on all cylinders. Big crowds. Happy campaign events. And positive internal poll numbers showing the party would not only hold its ridings in the Interior and north, but maybe pick up some new seats on the north coast and in the southeast as well. However, in Metro Vancouver, it was a different story. Clark and her campaign team felt it on the ground in ridings like Maple Ridge, where even ordinary one-on-one interviews between Clark and a community reporter from the local paper turned into aggressive Q&As.

The NDP focus on the Lower Mainland paid off early. Internal polling showed the NDP was doing well in the suburbs every day, pushing back and overwhelming their opponents even in Liberal-held ridings. So the party doubled-down, devoting almost all of Horgan's time to touring the Metro Vancouver region. In retrospect, the strategy was a double-edged sword, offering potentially major gains in urban BC at the expense of essentially giving up in rural BC.

The Liberals capitalized on the NDP's lack of travel to the Interior, hammering Horgan for his failure to travel north of the fiftieth parallel. But the NDP felt that with the media centred in the Lower Mainland, and with the money saved by not travelling, they stood a better chance if they stayed in the suburban ridings. Most of the voters in the province had yet to really lay eyes on "John from Langford," as he often called himself.

And so the April 20, 2017, radio debate was Horgan's first big chance to get inside the living rooms of the electorate and introduce himself. His staff had spent considerable time preparing him for the event. By this point, he had most of the campaign speaking points down cold, and he knew how to prosecute the Liberals on their record from months spent doing just that in question period at the legislature. But his senior advisors knew, no matter what he said, it would be his personality and demeanour that would make the crucial first impression on voters. On that score, the NDP campaign team was nervous. Virtually everyone predicted that Clark would try to push Horgan's buttons and make him explode in frustration and anger. They'd seen it before, at the legislature, frequently.

One of the worst occasions had been in the previous May, when Horgan and Clark had clashed during the annual estimates debate for the budget of the premier's office. It's a marquee event on the political calendar, because it's the only time of the year that has dedicated hours of direct back-and-forth sparring between the premier and leader of the opposition on the files and controversies of the day. But the debate had been a disaster for Horgan. For every question he asked, Clark had found a way to mock him, his party, and his positions, as well as grandstand at his expense. She used a classic technique developed just for him: refusing to ever look directly at him, burying her head in her notes, addressing only the Speaker, and rejecting the premise of almost all his questions by simply sticking to talking points about the accomplishments of her government. It drove Horgan mad. At times he physically turned his chair away from Clark while she was speaking and just stared at the back wall of the chamber.

"This is going to be the longest three hours of my life," he seethed audibly in the House.

Going into the estimates debate, Horgan was already frustrated. It had been rescheduled to accommodate Clark, and if the questioning went on for too long Horgan would have to miss a fundraising dinner in Vancouver. So after those three hours, Horgan threw in the towel, adjourned debate, and got up and simply left. Having questions go unanswered and spun by Clark for political gain wasn't something Horgan thought was worth sticking around for. The NDP had the time set aside to spend another day quizzing the premier if it wanted to, and Clark was obliged to sit and take the grilling. But the New Democrats passed.

Horgan wasn't the only one who was mad. Green Leader Andrew Weaver was furious. He had expected to use the second day to ask his own questions of the premier. Quitting early drove Weaver to accuse Horgan of being afraid of Clark and not up to the task of holding her accountable as a government in waiting. It also stuck in his mind as a clear example of the NDP purposefully trying to damage his own chances, not just in the legislature but in the upcoming 2017 election as well.

Clark's people skills are a well-documented hallmark of her political success. She could talk to almost anyone and charm them, regardless of their occupation or background. It was a by-product of a much more fundamental ability to size people up. She had a knack for quickly zeroing in on a person's strengths and weaknesses. It made her an effective campaigner. And a feared opponent. She viewed Horgan as weak, and she spent considerable time in the legislature studying how to push his buttons.

All of this was on the mind of top NDP officials like Della Mattia as they prepped Horgan for the radio debate. Staff employed a friend of Della Mattia's to play Clark in mock sessions, and that person mimicked the premier by reciting some of the lines she'd used in the past.

The advice Horgan had been given was simple but effective: don't make sarcastic comments, don't be glib, wait for the right moment to engage, moderate your instincts to jump into the debate on every topic, don't talk over your opponents, keep your body facing the camera or moderator, and don't turn to physically confront the other leaders. Above all, his top advisors said, don't talk to Clark directly. Talk to the audience or the moderator. Anyone but her.

"I have to get my head around the fact this is not about a genuine discussion between her and I," he said in a front-page *Vancouver Sun* story that ran on the day of the debate. The story outlined in detail all the things Horgan had been told to do. Bob Dewar was mad when he saw the paper. He reminded Horgan to stop punditing. The story would serve, hours later, as a kind of written scorecard for all the advice Horgan ignored, forgot, or chose to simply throw out the window during the actual event.

Horgan was agitated before the debate even began. The NDP arrived at the debate site when they were asked to. But because Liberal leader Clark was late, Horgan was told to wait in his bus. For thirty minutes he stewed, feeling like a caged animal. He was anxious for his big moment, and grumpy, as he can be, in the early morning. Finally, Horgan was told he could go in, only to be greeted by screaming Liberals who had broken the rules and hung around to greet the opponent even though they had been asked to move along after Clark's late arrival.

Then there was the last-minute fact that the so-called radio debate was actually going to be broadcast on television and in an online web stream from the City Vancouver TV studios. That changed the dynamic significantly, putting much more emphasis on the mannerisms and appearances of the leaders than their campaigns had expected.

By the time the debate actually started, Horgan's staff knew he was torqued up. It manifested itself quickly, when Horgan began accusing moderator Bill Good of being unfair in his time allocation. Horgan had kicked the debate off annoyed with Good. The long-time broadcaster once shared an office with Clark at CKNW and, before the broadcast, the two old friends had chatted, ignoring the other two participants. Horgan's frustration would grow during the debate.

Then, in one of the defining moments of the campaign, Clark put her hand on Horgan's arm and said, "Calm down, John."

Horgan quickly looked down, then glared at the premier and spat out, "Don't touch me again, please. Thank you very much."

Minutes later, when she was taking too long with her answers, Horgan put on a glib smile, leaned sideways, and said, "If you want to keep just doing your thing, I'll watch you for a while—I know you like that."

The line landed with a thud. Horgan later clarified: he was trying to reference how much he thought Clark enjoyed photo ops and being the centre of public attention. But Liberals were seizing the moment on social media, describing it as creepy.

When the debate wrapped up, it was clear most of the attention, news clips, and public debate over the event was not going to focus on the policy issues and platform promises that had also been discussed at length. Instead, everyone would focus on Horgan's temper. Horgan left the studio set and walked back to the holding room where staffers Marie Della Mattia, Kate Van Meer-Mass, and Sheena McConnell were waiting for him.

"How'd I do?" he asked half-expectantly as he entered the room. But only grim faces stared back at him. "I fucked up," said Horgan, answering his own question.

The three staffers quickly called campaign director Bob Dewar, who was put on speakerphone in the room to try to figure out a plan. The media were waiting back in the studio for post-debate interviews with the leaders. They discussed how to make lemon out of lemonade and pivot the image of angry John Horgan with a temper problem into one of angry John Horgan, the passionate fighter of injustice on behalf of all the little people being harmed by the out-of-touch Liberal regime. Realistically, they didn't have many other options.

In the Liberal waiting room, Clark walked in and exclaimed, "Can you believe that?!" Her staff laughed, and she joined in. They insist Clark hadn't planned to touch his arm, though she had planned to find some way to throw him off his game and make him explode. They felt it had been such a bad debate moment for Horgan that it would overwhelm any other points made during the discussion. Clark's communications guru, Ben Chin, put his arms around the boss and said, "That was unbelievable."

Later, staff asked Horgan to watch parts of the radio debate to see what it looked like. He refused. He didn't want to see it again. In his mind it was done and he was moving forward. That moment overwhelmed what had otherwise been a pretty good debate for the NDP.

The bottom line was he'd blown it. There were some in the party who wanted Della Mattia and Dewar to chew Horgan out for his lack of self-control. But the Horgan whisperers knew their leader wouldn't respond to a lecture. Horgan tried, lamely, to argue that if a man had touched a woman's arm like that, the man would have been vilified.

"No, that's not the point," said Dewar, gently. "You are missing the point, my friend. We know that you can do better."

Horgan did internalize his mistake, that night, alone in his hotel room.

"That was the lowest point, when I went back to the hotel after that it was a gut check time," Horgan said in an interview for this book. "I have let a whole lot of people down by being overly passionate, overly responsive to prodding. For Christy and crew it was a set-up, an absolute set-up. And I fell for it. It was like, don't take the bait, don't take the bait. That became the joke on the bus."

It had not been a particularly good debate for Clark either, despite her success in goading Horgan into embarrassing himself. Clark had mainly hidden behind the armour she'd created in the form of her blazing smile and perky demeanour. But she struggled. She came with a large binder of briefing materials and at times appeared somewhat lost in her notes. It was remarkably off-key for a leader whose political success had depended on her instincts and free-wheeling ability to turn a phrase. And it was the clearest sign so far that inside the Liberal campaign they were still trying to find the right message for their leader to say. Clark had been suffering from a miserable cold through most of the campaign. The result was that one of the best campaigners in BC political history was now having to rely on briefing notes to keep up.

In the wake of the debate, much attention was paid to "Hulk Horgan" and his temper. The Liberals kept the heat on by increasing appearances of its so-called Truth Truck. The idea in Liberal HQ was to send a moving truck emblazoned with anti-Horgan signs to virtually every event in the Lower Mainland in the hope that it would get a rise out of the NDP leader. The Liberals also hoped to punch through media coverage and get some attention on their attack points about Horgan, even if it was just in passing in a story about the truck.

The idea largely backfired. The Liberals faced a round of negative media coverage for their "US-style" negative campaigning. On one occasion, the truck, which the NDP had dubbed the "Troll Truck," slowly cruised behind a Horgan press conference at a children's playground, looking like some kind of pedophile's vehicle. Then when the NDP switched that campaign event to inside a candidate's house because there was no approval to be on public school property, the Liberals drove the truck slowly around residential streets, much to the astonishment of neighbours. Regardless, the stunt uniformly fell flat. Horgan refused to rise to the bait.

Instead, the Horgan who would develop during the campaign was remarkably upbeat and serene. He had daily superstitious rituals, such as always patting the shoulder of tour bus driver Rob, a former Victoria Shamrocks lacrosse player, as he left the bus. One time Rob left first to go for a break and Horgan hunted him down in the crowd to pat his shoulder before starting the event. Another ritual involved Horgan touching a feather that hung from the front of the bus; it had been given to him by a First Nations Elder on the South Island during the campaign to help guide his journey. At one point, the feather went missing after the nightly cleaning crew accidentally swept it up, and the Horgan campaign scrambled to find it before the boss was upset. (It was eventually found in the lost-and-found bin at the bus depot.)

Meanwhile, much of the hardest campaigning of the election focused on what became known as Battleground Surrey. The city, nestled between the Fraser River and the US border, was the site of nine ridings, one of them newly created for the 2017 election.

The Liberal candidates in Surrey were under siege by angry voters. The backlash centred on the issues of ride-sharing, bridge tolls, transit options, housing prices, Port of Vancouver trucking licences, the proliferation of portables at local schools, and gang violence. In each case, the Liberal government had tried, and failed, to get a handle on the issues. And in each case the party's platform promises had fallen well short of voter expectations.

None of the Surrey MLAS was feeling more heat than Peter Fassbender, then minister responsible for TransLink. The sixty-nine-year-old, quick-talking former advertising salesman was a veteran of the local political scene, having served for a decade at the City of Langley, including three terms as mayor. He knew local voters, he had the gift of the gab, and he wasn't afraid to take risks in politics or in his regular life. In his younger years he'd logged so many hours jumping out of planes as a skydiver that he became president of the BC association representing sport parachuters.

Fassbender was also the architect of the government's unpopular strategy to allow ride-hailing companies like Uber, Lyft, and others to operate in the province. It was an especially precarious file for Fassbender, who was running in a city were hundreds of mainly Indo-Canadian taxi drivers were going to be negatively affected. Behind the scenes within government, Uber had been a contentious item for many months. There were those who had felt the timing was wrong to announce a position on Uber just before an election. That included the premier herself, who wasn't in favour of taking a position before the election because she felt there'd be little upside from most voters and vicious backlash from the taxi industry. Clark was convinced that any movement toward green-lighting the service could backfire and infuriate the taxi industry, where thousands of drivers would watch the investment they'd put into once-valuable taxi licences and vehicles vanish once virtually everyone with a smartphone app could sign up with Uber. Some in cabinet wanted to put the entire issue off until after the election. Others argued it could help drum up votes in Vancouver.

Back in 2013, Transportation Minister Todd Stone, a former tech-company CEO who was in favour of ride-sharing, had suggested government approve Uber then, and use the next three years before the election to iron out the fallout from taxi drivers. The premier wasn't interested. But then Clark's chief party pollster and former principal secretary, Dimitri Pantazopoulos, was hired by Uber to lobby government on its behalf. And suddenly ministers like Stone found themselves being told one day to get moving on Uber and on the next to cool the file, depending on how recently Pantazopoulos had been lobbying.

The Liberal party, including director Laura Miller, liked the Uber file too. She came from Toronto, where Uber was already on the road. The party tested it out in 2016 by-elections. The Liberals lost, like most incumbents in by-elections, but Uber performed well and seemed popular. Even so, there was little concrete movement within government on the file.

To get a sense of how messy the development of Uber was within government, consider this: Stone remembers the premier standing in front of the taxi industry six months before the election and promising she'd tell them the Uber plan before the election. Fassbender remembers doing that himself, not Clark. Clark doesn't remember doing it at all. The premier didn't want Uber. Her party did. Her cabinet was split. Former heavyweights like Kevin Falcon were pushing approval behind the scenes. It was not a clear-cut file.

Regardless, as the election loomed, Fassbender pushed for a policy. He was convinced the government needed to provide the taxi drivers with certainty, and it was a matter of honour for him personally to be honest with his constituents. The premier's office paid little attention to Stone—he wasn't going to wear any backlash from Uber in Kamloops. But when Fassbender, whose riding was home to hundreds of taxi drivers, mainly Indo-Canadians, stressed that the government needed to move, the premier relented and Uber moved forward.

Fassbender especially liked the "level playing field" approach that became the government's eventual position. The Liberals would eliminate the special driver's licences required by traditional taxi drivers and eliminate the geographic restrictions that prevent cabbies who took a fare from the suburbs to downtown Vancouver from then picking up a downtown customer to drive back.

What the plan didn't do was take into consideration the current value of taxi licences, which some drivers had paid up to $1 million to obtain. And a proposal to allow only existing cab drivers to drive Uber vehicles during a "transition" period had been nixed. The plan did come with a kind of asterisk at the end that said it wasn't final and could be changed depending on feedback. That escape hatch was lost in the media coverage, and those in the taxi industry still found the whole thing a predictable betrayal.

Fassbender had to face the music. At a meeting with taxi companies in late April at a banquet hall in Newton, he was roasted. The NDP sent both Harry Baines and Fassbender's opponent, Jagrup Brar, who lambasted the Liberals and whipped up the crowd.

"At least we've put out a position that you can respond to," Fassbender told the crowd, adding he felt the NDP plan—which was a vague commitment to work on expanding existing taxi licence availability before Uber came out—wasn't much of a plan at all.

Meanwhile, Brar was spending much of his time campaigning outside local schools, passing out literature to parents and highlighting the NDP promise to eliminate portables from all Surrey schools. It was an ambitious and potentially expensive platform plank. Fassbender tried countering with the argument that it was too expensive. Besides, he argued, kids who take classes in portables still get a quality education. This too fell flat.

Three other factors loomed large in the riding. A dispute with truckers—many also of South Asian descent—at the Port of Vancouver had failed to fully be resolved, and Fassbender found himself disagreeing with his own party to promise the mobility of trucking licences that his government and Ottawa had failed to provide.

Fassbender's fate was also affected by shifting alliances within the complicated world of Indo-Canadian politics. Some felt betrayed when Surrey businessman Satnam Johal was told by the Liberals he could organize in Surrey-Panorama, only to have that reversed and the candidacy given to Puneet Sandhar, a lawyer who was connected to local MP Sukh Dhaliwal. There were ramifications, in the form of previously supportive Liberal kingmakers aligning with Brar and the NDP. Fassbender felt others he'd thought would be supportive, like veteran Liberal power broker Prem Vinning, ended up working against him.

In the end, despite his talkative personality and local political pedigree, Fassbender couldn't overcome voter dislike of the Liberals in Surrey. He, Sandhar, and neighbouring cabinet minister Amrik Virk in Surrey-Guildford would fall to defeat on election night. The loss was all the more difficult because Clark had offered to save Fassbender months earlier. His riding of Surrey-Fleetwood had been redistributed in 2017. Taken out of the riding were neighbourhoods that had typically voted Liberal, to be replaced with ones that had historically supported the NDP. Clark asked if he wanted to move to a safer riding that would allow him to potentially cruise to re-election. But the veteran politician refused to bail. He felt it would send the wrong message to the party to skip out on a tough fight. Like the veteran skydiver that he is, he took one last leap into the great unknown of BC politics. This time, his chute didn't open.

CHAPTER 10
"LINDA, NICE TO MEET YOU"

Linda Higgins had a ritual. Whenever her husband, Paul, had a cardiologist's appointment in North Vancouver, they'd leave their Gibsons home, drive onto the Langdale ferry, and spend the day on the Lower Mainland.

April 27, 2017, was an especially busy day. Not only did Paul need to see the cardiologist about his heart condition, but he also had a CT scan set for Burnaby Hospital later in the afternoon. Between appointments, they had time for lunch at Krua Thai on North Vancouver's Lonsdale Avenue. Afterwards, when Paul went to pay the bill, Linda left the restaurant to pick up something to eat from the fruit and vegetable store across the street for later in the afternoon, after their next medical appointment.

And that's when she saw it. Amid an unusually busy flurry of foot traffic and men in suits was the BC Liberal Party bus, emblazoned on the side with a picture of Christy Clark and the catchphrase, "Strong BC, Bright Future." Higgins, who was no fan of the Liberals or Clark, made a spur-of-the-moment decision. She was going to tell Clark she wasn't voting for her. Paul came out of the restaurant.

"Just wait here," Higgins told him.

As she was crossing the street, her brother, Allen, called from Ontario.

One of the lasting images of the 2017 provincial election campaign: Linda Higgins confronting Liberal leader Christy Clark on April 27, 2017, at a campaign stop in a North Vancouver grocery store, while Liberal candidates stare her down. USED WITH PERMISSION OF IAN BAILEY/*THE GLOBE AND MAIL*

"What are you up to?" he asked casually.

"I'm in North Van and I am going to tell Christy Clark I am not going to vote for her," said Higgins.

There was a pause. "Really?" asked Allen.

Higgins stayed on the phone with her brother and walked across the street. Once she was in the market, the first thing she noticed was the cameras. Everywhere Clark goes during an election campaign, at least two videographers and a still photographer follow her. Then she saw Clark, chatting with an older woman. Higgins decided to just stay where she was, near a fruit stand, and wait. It wasn't as crowded inside as it had seemed from the outside. As Higgins continued her cell phone conversation with her brother, one of Clark's handlers approached and informed her that the premier would soon be walking by. Moments later, Higgins saw Clark coming.

"Hold on a sec, Allen," said Higgins, putting the phone to her side.

The Liberal leader walked up and the two women stuck out their hands for a handshake.

"Hi, Christy," said Higgins.

"Hi," replied the premier.

"Linda."

"Linda, nice to meet you," said Clark.

"I'd never vote for you," Higgins began, "because—"

But Clark quickly cut her off. "You don't have to. That is why we live in a democracy," said Clark as she turned and starting walking away.

"Thank goodness," Higgins added as Clark retreated. "Let's hope you don't get elected in."

The conversation lasted only eight seconds. Clark, alongside candidates Jane Thornthwaite and Naomi Yamamoto, moved on to meet more people. As Higgins was walking away, she heard one of them say, "There is always one in the crowd."

With the encounter over, Linda said goodbye to her brother and walked back across the street to meet her husband. She and Paul drove off to the Burnaby hospital, chatting along the way about the interaction. Higgins felt good. She was glad she had taken advantage of her chance to speak to the premier. What Higgins didn't realize was that the story was starting to grow. By the late afternoon, thousands of people had seen a video of the interaction and #IamLinda was trending on Twitter. Once at home that evening, Higgins settled in to watch some television. The phone rang. It was her nephew Cody.

"Auntie Linda, you're trending on Twitter," he said.

Higgins had no idea what that meant. She didn't have Twitter. She didn't even know what a hashtag was.

Then Nicholas Simons called. The NDP MLA and candidate for Powell River-Sunshine Coast had known Higgins for years. They had worked together more than a decade earlier as income assistance workers. Simons had seen the trending encounter, too, and wanted to know if his old colleague might like some advice about what could be a pending media storm.

The pair met the next morning, April 28, 2017, at The Gumboot restaurant in Roberts Creek. Higgins was curious about what was going to happen next with the video.

"You are probably going to get a lot of phone calls," said Simons, who gave Higgins one of his orange "Pick Nick" campaign buttons and took a photo of them together.

Simons left and posted a picture of the two of them on social media. Simons was trying to get a boost from the growing media storm. Instead, the Liberals said the picture was the proof they needed that Higgins was put up to the task by the NDP. Just before 11 a.m., BC Liberal campaign manager Laura Miller went to Twitter.

"As @ChristyClarkBC says, we live in a democracy. Which is why #BCNDP is free to send their members to disrupt #TeamBC2017 events. #bcelxn17," read Miller's tweet.

The insinuation was clear: Higgins was a plant, sent to the event by the NDP to deliberately cause a disruption. The accusation was then supported and pushed by many members of the BC Liberal team. The leading theorist within the Liberal party that Linda was a plant was Clark herself. She'd seen Linda talking on the phone and had assumed she was being put up to the encounter and prompted by someone on how to embarrass her publicly. Clark had the political skills to engage and likely disarm the situation. She'd done it countless times before on the hustings with far more vocal critics than Higgins, who was a relatively mild-mannered retiree. Instead, Clark had made a split-second decision: abort rather than engage.

As expected, Higgins began to receive media calls. She not only denied being an NDP plant but joked with reporters about what she would have done differently if she had been paid to disrupt the premier.

"If I was a plant, I would have done my hair and put on some makeup," she said.

But despite mounting evidence, the Liberals kept attacking. The media fact-checking continued. First the CBC told Miller she was wrong about Higgins. Then it was *The Province*'s Mike Smyth, then the *Globe*'s Ian Bailey, and finally the *Globe*'s Gary Mason.

Nearly a week after the short interaction, Clark was forced to acknowledge that Higgins wasn't part of a conspiracy to take her down. The campaign, meanwhile, had been hit with several days of withering media coverage about both the encounter and the subsequent Liberal attempts to smear Higgins as the enemy.

Clark was furious, and remains so to this day. To her, Linda wasn't representative of the kind of interactions she was having on the campaign trail. Which was true. But by then it was a question of character for both Clark and the party, about how they assumed the worst about Higgins and attacked her without evidence.

Clark believed her poll numbers sharply declined after the I Am Linda incident, and there wasn't enough time to bring them back up by election day. At this point in the campaign, she said internal estimates put the Liberals as high as fifty-five winnable seats. That was the figure strategist Don Guy gave her, based on his own overly optimistic interpretation. It was the only polling figure Clark was given at the time, because the war room didn't give her numbers regularly. Clark didn't make it up; it was the only data she had. And it was completely wrong.

In reality, for the entirety of the election campaign the Liberals' best polling never really moved the party much beyond a tie with the NDP. The range was usually anywhere from forty-one seats to forty-five. Pollster Dimitri Pantazopoulos never saw figures that approached fifty seats, let alone fifty-five.

For the record, Clark still thinks Linda was a plant.

WHILE THE LINDA story continued to grow, Green Party leader Andrew Weaver's role as kingmaker was getting closer to becoming a reality. With a week left on the campaign trail, the Green Party's internal polls were showing them solidly up in Weaver's Oak Bay riding, as well as in Adam Olsen's Saanich North and the Islands riding. The party was also optimistic in Cowichan Valley. Weaver was starting to understand that he wasn't going to have the massive breakthrough he had dreamed of, but instead had a very realistic chance of playing power broker.

The Liberals and the NDP were close in the polls and the three seats could be used to keep a government afloat. On May 2, during a CBC Facebook Live event, Weaver was asked by one of the viewers what his deal breakers would be for working with the Liberals or the NDP. For the first time, the Green party leader started laying out a blueprint for obtaining his future support. He was asked directly whether there needed to be a ban on union and corporate political donations.

"Without any question. That's a deal breaker. We've got to get this money out of politics," said Weaver.

The Green Party leader also told online viewers that the electoral system needed to change, and he wanted proportional representation. The natural ally on those two things was the NDP. They had similar positions to Weaver's. But the alliance between the two parties was not cozy. Horgan and his team had spent years bashing Weaver, trying to convince voters a vote for the Greens was just making it easier for Clark to win.

The breaking point had been just days earlier, when the Greens were in Kelowna. The last few days had been rough. The NDP sent the media a PDF of old social media posts from when Green candidates were teenagers. The posts were nearly a decade old, one of them a tweet from Ryan Marciniw, the Green Party candidate for Richmond North Centre. In the post he supported fat-shaming by claiming it had led him to slim down. He also retweeted a controversial message about the Holocaust.

Then the attacks on the Greens' climate plan started. Environmental activist Tzeporah Berman criticized renowned environmentalist David Suzuki for supporting the Greens and blasted Weaver for his TV debate appearance.

"I think Andrew hit a low bar in his political career in the debate when he taunted John about getting mad at him—John was cool as a cucumber at the time—and when he tried to make it seem as though union donations to the NDP were equivalent to the millions of dollars Christy has gotten from big corporations," Berman said.

When they heard this, two campaign staff, some volunteers, and Weaver were on the bus. They started talking about how it just couldn't get any worse. Press secretary Jillian Oliver and others started crying. It was the lack of sleep. The long hours. The stress of running a campaign on a fraction of the others' budgets. But it was also the frustration of having an opponent, with the same goal of defeating the premier, attack you. Cowichan Valley Green candidate Sonia Furstenau also found out that the NDP were paying people seventeen dollars an hour to go online and attack her character.

Any friction between the Greens and the NDP was good news for the Liberals. They saw a Weaver kingmaker scenario as plausible too. Clark needed to find a distraction. The Liberal campaign decided the BC Liberal leader needed to re-emphasize that she was the premier and not just a candidate running for the job. To make this official meant suspending campaign events temporarily. It also meant any mentions of Clark in the media that morning had to be of Premier Clark instead of Liberal leader Clark. The Liberals wanted that distinction made, to show that here was the best person to serve the province in a crisis.

Around 7 p.m. on May 5, a phone call and email went out to the reporters following Clark on the campaign trail. The next morning's events would be cancelled and the prepaid tour bus would not be departing from Vancouver as scheduled in the morning. Clark was heading to Cache Creek. The flood-damaged community was mourning the loss of their fire chief, Clayton Cassidy, who had been swept away by the flood waters and was reported missing earlier in the day. Clark was going to attend the scene as premier, to offer support and condolences to the community. Considering the impact of the crisis on the community, Clark also had no choice but to visit. The problem for journalists was that getting into the area was challenging. Clark's team was alluding to having just one media event on the day, and it would take place in Cache Creek for whoever found their own way up there.

For CTV's Bhinder Sajan, this was a major problem. On Friday, CTV Vancouver had run a moving interview with Shelley Sheppard and Chris Saini, the parents of baby Mac Saini. The toddler had died on January 18 in an unlicensed daycare that had run in violation of regulations for years. The family had blamed the death on a system where it was impossible to find care and in which the province had not done enough to open up spaces. CTV wanted to get Clark's reaction to the emotional interview and the criticism of Clark's leadership. But with no tour bus heading there, Sajan had to scramble. By midnight she was in a CTV News vehicle in Vancouver with her videographer, heading to the flooded community. Road closures forced them to detour and double back along the route, and by the time the CTV crew arrived in Cache Creek it was past 9 a.m. Clark would be arriving in a few hours.

Having to respond to the child death story was the last thing Clark's campaign wanted on a day so carefully crafted to provide the impression of Clark acting as premier during a crisis. Yet faced with the camera, Clark was forced to answer the questions of the dead toddler's mother, send condolences to the family, and try to stress all the work the Liberals were doing to improve child care. Compounding the frustrations within Liberal circles was the fact that the Baby Mac story could have been handled much earlier by Clark, before it had become a political issue. In fact, an unlikely ally had even intervened to try to defuse the situation.

Kevin Falcon, Clark's old leadership rival and her former deputy premier, now lived on the North Shore with his wife and young child. He'd been hearing in the community how upset people were about the Baby Mac story, as well as the larger issue of sketchy daycares popping up in the absence of government help. Months earlier, before the campaign had begun, Falcon had asked for a meeting with Clark campaign strategist Mike McDonald to suggest Clark reach out to Baby Mac's parents and sit down with them to hear their concerns. The media would probably be interviewing them during the campaign anyway, and wouldn't it be better to have them tell a story of Clark actually listening as a concerned leader, Falcon suggested. Falcon passed along the family's number to McDonald, who in turn gave it to campaign director Miller. But nothing happened.

Baby Mac's parents came forward on CTV four days before the May 9, 2017, election date. His mother had written a letter to Clark a month earlier that pleaded for action. But it went unanswered. When they saw Clark out on the election trail they felt "dismissed" by her electioneering.

"Our own premier, as we pleaded with her publicly, didn't write us back, not even her office," said Saini. "And we thought that was in very poor taste."

With tears in their eyes, and the cameras rolling, the parents put their support behind the NDP's ten-dollar-a-day daycare plan. One of Clark's campaign staff called Falcon to ask if he still had the number for Baby Mac's parents that he could share. Exasperated, Falcon explained it was too late to call now, because it would just look like Clark was calling to take political advantage of the situation.

Child care had become one of the election's biggest issues, and the Baby Mac story was a body blow that fed into the narrative the NDP had created that the Liberals were too cheap, or out of touch, or uncaring to do anything about it. The Liberals had pumped $20 million into the issue in the February budget, adding 5,000 spots to the 113,000 already licensed. But the continued addition of a few thousand new spaces here and there had done little to lessen the skyrocketing costs and long wait-lists for spaces that ordinary voters faced. The NDP, meanwhile, continued to score points with its ten-dollar-a-day child-care plan. The Liberals had nothing in their platform to counter it, other than to complain about the cost.

Falcon had tried to warn about this as well, telling McDonald before the campaign began that he was hearing from young, highly educated professional women who were reacting favourably to the NDP's ten-dollar-a-day childcare plan because of the high costs and lack of spaces. He urged McDonald to go bold, and suggested taking the ten-dollar-a-day plan and applying it to low- to middle-income families to give them a break. It might also help with Clark's abysmal popularity with women, which Falcon was also hearing about through his connections. Yet the Liberals remained flat-footed on the issue.

The Baby Mac story would continue what some Liberals in the war room referred to darkly as "the week of the dead" in the campaign. After Baby Mac, the NDP released a video in which the sister of fired health researcher Roderick MacIsaac blamed Clark and her government for killing her brother, who had taken his own life after he was unfairly fired by the health ministry in 2012. Then the mother of a fentanyl overdose victim criticized Powell River-Sunshine Coast Liberal candidate Matthew Wilson for bringing his stepbrother, Kasimir Tyabji-Sandana, on the campaign trail, when he was at that point facing charges for allegedly importing fentanyl. And then the former foster father of Alex Gervais, the nineteen-year-old who'd been neglected by the child welfare system and had killed himself, confronted Children's Minister Stephanie Cadieux at a coffee shop on the campaign trail and vented at her for almost forty minutes. It was a run of unrelenting negative press.

Then, inexplicably, in the dying days of the campaign, the HST returned. The dreaded tax, which had brought down Gordon Campbell and paved the way for Clark's premiership, resurfaced when Maple Ridge-Pitt Meadows Liberal MLA Doug Bing said at an all-candidates meeting that it was likely the tax would be revived in the near future. It was a spectacular, tone-deaf misstep. The Liberals had no plans to reintroduce the HST. But it took Clark several days to make that case publicly and correct the record. By then, fears about the return of the HST had been whipped up by the NDP.

The Liberals needed to win forty-four seats to form a majority government. But in the final week of the campaign, McDonald looked at polling data and struggled to see how the party could even get there.

Things were unravelling at party headquarters. Campaign director Laura Miller became distant to some, putting on her headphones and disengaging from those in the war room. Two days before election day, Miller called an impromptu private meeting with senior war-room strategists McDonald and Don Guy in a tiny boardroom off the open communal working space in Liberal HQ. Miller had come to the realization that the party was likely not going to win on May 9. She felt it would most likely be a minority government with three Green MLAs who were polling strongly in their Vancouver Island ridings. Miller wanted the premier to have a detailed memo on the Greens for election night, so that she could turn her mind quickly to understanding the Green position.

McDonald didn't see drafting the Green memo as an admission the campaign was lost two days before it even finished. He'd done similar research in 2013, for a variety of outcomes, and so he dived into analyzing the Green party's approximately 166 election promises to find areas where the Liberals could open a dialogue if they needed to start negotiations. On election night, Miller would give the memo to the premier.

THE FINAL FEW days of the campaign had been a blur for John Horgan. The NDP leader focused on the Lower Mainland.

On election night, Horgan and his team were spending the evening at the Pinnacle Hotel. The NDP booked the 360-degree top-floor meeting room. The space famously had been a rotating restaurant and in its new incarnation could still spin. But the party wanted to make sure it was switched off, lest they spend the entire election night twirling in a circle above Vancouver.

Horgan and campaign director Bob Dewar weren't in the mood for food, instead dining on the raw data flowing in from each riding and every return, analyzing the figures to look for clues as to the election outcome. Around Horgan was his senior staff, as well as ten or so close friends from his home riding of Langford and elsewhere who had come over to spend the evening.

Eventually, though, it became clear the NDP, while close, wasn't going to win.

"Let's get in touch with the Greens and talk to Weaver and see what he's thinking," said Dewar.

Dewar took Horgan down to his room and the two got on the phone with Weaver. They congratulated him on growing his party from one to three seats. The conversation sounded jovial, which was somewhat surprising considering that Weaver was still stewing about what he felt were vicious personal attacks on his credibility and character carried out by the NDP and its surrogates during the campaign. In particular, Weaver had been trolled on Twitter by NDP operatives, as well as by third-party supporters from the BC Teachers' Federation and BC Federation of Labour, whose sole goal appeared to be antagonizing the Green leader at all times of the day and night until he said something stupid in response. Regardless, the election-night call wasn't infused with Weaver's anger over the NDP's tactics. Horgan used the opportunity to slide in two comments meant to damage the Liberals.

"Remember Roderick MacIsaac," he said, in reference to the government health researcher who'd been wrongly fired by the Liberal government in 2012 and publicly accused of being under police investigation, and who'd later committed suicide.

"And remember Rich Coleman," he added.

Horgan mentioned the long-time MLA as a counter to MacIsaac. In his mind, the fired health researcher had been bullied, while Coleman had been the personification of Liberal government bullying.

MEANWHILE, IN A suite at the Fairmont Waterfront, Clark watched the results roll in on television. At first the mood was celebratory, as the Liberals surged ahead in the popular vote and expected seat count. Then things grew sombre as the numbers put the NDP in a commanding lead. Finally, it settled as a two-seat Liberal victory with a third seat—Courtenay-Comox—in doubt.

The Liberal party had ended up with forty-three seats—only one seat shy of the majority required for total control of the legislature. The Liberals had lost five seats. The NDP added six, reaching forty-one. The Greens added two seats, for three. The result raised the prospect of the new Liberal minority being vulnerable to attack if the Liberals' Green and NDP opponents ganged up to defeat them.

There was no visible reaction from Clark to the declaration that she'd somehow lost the Liberal party's grip on majority government after sixteen years in power. She didn't laugh or cry, say those in the room. Instead, she and advisors Don Guy and Ben Chin simply started talking about her acceptance speech. The Liberals had pre-written speeches for a loss, win, or minority situation. As Clark read through her options, she dictated an addition that had not been in the text but that she wanted to say at the podium: "British Columbians did tell us tonight that they want us to do some things differently. They want us to work together, they want us to work across party lines, and they want us to find a way to get along so that we can all work for the province that all of us love so very, very much."

She went down to the ballroom late that evening, climbed onto the stage, and began to speak.

"Tonight we won the popular vote and we have also won the most seats," she told the crowd. "And with absentee ballots still to be counted I am confident they will strengthen our margin of victory. So it's my intention to continue to lead British Columbia's government."

Clark had ended the 2013 election with a forty-nine-seat majority. She'd gone into 2017 with a party war chest overflowing with money, a small army of organizers, the full backing of the wealthy business community, a modest surplus in the provincial budget, and the best-performing economy in Canada. After the election, her majority had vanished, she'd lost six seats, four cabinet ministers had fallen to defeat, and her party had been decimated by an orange wave of NDP support through Vancouver, Burnaby, Surrey, and Maple Ridge.

In another room, a few floors below Clark's suite, campaign strategists Mike McDonald and Michele Cadario were poring over the numbers. Cadario's final sheet had forty-four potential ridings the Liberals could win. Dimitri Pantazopoulos, the much-vaunted party pollster, had been bang-on with his overall numbers.

Internally, the Liberals knew it would be close. But they were surprised at particular losses, such as Suzanne Anton's defeat in Vancouver-Fraserview, and rookie candidate Puneet Sandhar's loss in Surrey-Panorama. In Surrey, where cabinet ministers Peter Fassbender and Amrik Virk lost their seats, the results were far worse than the party had expected. In retrospect, Brad Bennett, a close advisor of Clark's who spent the entire campaign with her on the bus, remembers how lukewarm some of the Surrey events had become, including one of the final rallies, when he noticed a bunch of Indo-Canadian men standing in a corner of the room with their arms crossed, as if they had been forced to be there and couldn't wait to leave.

Cadario had been worried about Courtenay-Comox since the start of the election, and on her sheet she'd marked the party down for a loss in the riding. The all-but-dead BC Conservatives had somehow managed to field a candidate in the riding, Leah McCulloch, and she had picked up 2,201 votes. Had that happened in the last two elections, previous Liberal MLA Don McRae might not have won either.

When Clark returned to the room following her speech, she asked advisor Bennett to lead her unorthodox transition team. It would require an unusual amount of flexibility and out-of-the-box thinking from an outside presence during unprecedented times.

"Why me?" asked Bennett.

Clark borrowed a response that Bennett's father, former premier Bill Bennett, had used to persuade Jimmy Pattison to lead Expo 86. "Well, if not you, then who?" she asked.

Clark gave him full authority to keep some personalities in check on her team and read the riot act if he needed to, to get the transition going.

THE ELECTION NIGHT parties were a study in contrast. The Liberals had technically won the election. But the mood was not celebratory, reflecting the fact that they'd lost their majority. On the NDP side, the group partied like they'd won the election.

The Green Party event in Victoria had a similar feel. The party had tripled its seat count, and if the results held, Andrew Weaver would be the one choosing the winner. The highlight of the evening, though, belonged to Weaver's mother, Ludmilla, when she was asked, live on Global television, what she thought of her son's success.

"He was born with a big head, but there were brains in it," she said.

Over at Elections BC, it was business as usual. There was also a special guest. Lieutenant-Governor Judith Guichon had been at the headquarters in 2013 and was there to watch the results come in again in 2017. But this time the feeling in the building was much different. By the time Guichon left, just before midnight, it was clear a minority government was possible and she could be called upon if the government's confidence was tested.

SO WHAT EXACTLY happened in the 2017 election?

In the immediate aftermath, the question went largely unanswered. Usually, the parties conduct some type of quick post-mortem to figure out what went right—or wrong. Instead, everyone's efforts were focused on the next steps, the recount in certain ridings, and the looming prospect of power-sharing negotiations. Not even the NDP—which technically lost the race—put much effort into sifting through the ashes.

Province-wide, it was the closest election in BC history. The Liberals won more of the popular vote count than the NDP by 1,666 ballots—796,772 to 795,106. When you total up all 1,985,623 ballots cast, the margin of victory was a minuscule 0.08 per cent.

The Liberals were not crushed in the election. Far from it: the party actually made electoral gains outside of Metro Vancouver, including picking up the ridings of Skeena and Columbia River-Revelstoke. They also held on in a tough fight in Fraser-Nicola.

But the province was clearly badly divided between rural BC, which the Liberals now firmly controlled, and urban BC, where the NDP had become the dominant force.

At its core, the campaign was a role reversal for the parties. The Liberals traded in their dream-big platform of 2013, with its grandiose vision and bold promise of LNG, for a tepid stand-pat platform that urged caution, restraint, and fiscal prudence. By contrast, the NDP, which had been so meticulous and prudent in 2013, threw caution to the wind with huge promises for things like ten-dollar-a-day child care and the scrapping of bridge tolls, which were big on aspiration but vague on costing and details. In short, the NDP gave something for voters to aspire to. The Liberals promised just more of the same.

Clark was as impressive on the hustings as she'd ever been. But she had little to actually say, and worse, her party's internal message changed so often that she eventually had to rely on notes, neutralizing her incredible skills as a free-wheeling campaigner who could ad-lib an amazing speech off the top of her head. In 2013, she'd portrayed a softer image, holding events in the homes of supporters and literally sitting at their kitchen table, having coffee, talking about their concerns and offering solutions. But those events never materialized in 2017, in part, perhaps, because the Liberals didn't have any good answers in their election platform to the kind of pocketbook questions Clark might have to field.

Everyday affordability became the dominant issue in Metro Vancouver, where a grab bag of items like housing, transit, bridge tolls, social services, schools, and utility fees affected not just young people, but their parents and grandparents, who were upset at not being able to buy a home or have enough money to live comfortably. The result was that the Liberals lost the middle-class, moderate, middle-of-the-road, soft federal Liberal base of voters that had won Clark the party leadership in 2011 and that she'd re-attracted in 2013. A few bled to the NDP, lured away by the kind of families-first agenda that the Liberals had used in 2013. Others, probably more, parked their votes with the Greens.

Clark's core message of job growth resonated well in rural BC. Yet in Metro Vancouver it fell flat. People there already had jobs. But even with a steady paycheque they were drowning in daily costs, unable to afford to live the middle-class life they felt they deserved. The NDP campaign, with its focus on affordability, rental rebates, and a crackdown on illegalities in the hot housing market, spoke more to them than a Liberal premier wearing a hard hat at a construction site in the Interior.

Internally, some in the Liberal Party blame the Metro Vancouver–area MLAs for not being strong enough voices to champion the needs of their constituencies in government, despite the presence of several senior cabinet ministers. And many of those MLAs, in turn, blame a cabinet where the strongest voices were too often from the Interior and northern BC and had little sympathy for the affordability and housing concerns that were ringing like alarm bells in the Metro Vancouver region. Some key figures thought party HQ, in particular campaign director Laura Miller and senior advisor Don Guy, hadn't seen the right signals coming back from the rallies or on the ground during the campaign, and consequently didn't adjust the ad campaigns accordingly.

The NDP did an excellent job of destroying Clark's credibility in the earliest stages of the campaign. The party broke with conventional wisdom and spent aggressively on TV and radio advertising in the first half of the campaign (when voters supposedly are paying less attention), focused squarely on Clark's reputation as an out-of-touch member of the elite, with not-so-subtle insinuations that she was only out to make herself more wealthy by rewarding her friends, insiders, and anyone else who donated to her party.

Say what you will about Adrian Dix's idea to run a positive campaign in 2013, but the truth is that negative advertising works. People say they don't like it, but then they consciously or subconsciously respond to it. It didn't suppress voter turnout; rather, it helped drive unhappy Liberals to the Greens. Years of Liberal strategy to promote the Greens, thinking it would ultimately hurt the NDP, blew up in the faces of the Liberals, who watched the Greens take a sizable chunk out of their soft supporters, new voters, and undecideds. The Green Party watched its votes triple, from 146,685 in 2013 to 332,387 in 2017, and its share of the total vote double from 8.15 per cent of the popular vote to 16.84 per cent. More importantly, in several ridings—like the two Maple Ridge seats—the NDP and Greens increased their votes substantially, while the Liberals pulled in the same support as in 2013, ultimately losing both seats.

By the time the Liberals got around to countering with their much less effective ads, Clark had appeared in the province-wide TV debate and many voters had already cemented early—negative—opinions about her. Brad Bennett, whose father and grandfather had been legendary premiers and who sat by Clark's side on the leader's bus for the entire twenty-eight-day campaign, tried to raise a red flag earlier, urging Clark to intervene in the Liberal HQ ad strategy. For half the campaign, the war room pumped out ads focused on the NDP's connection to the United Steelworkers, the union's connection to US president Donald Trump, and the donations it had made to the BC NDP. They went too long, were over people's heads, and were wasting time the Liberals could have used to pivot back to their strengths of taxes and the economy, Bennett told her. Clark raised it with campaign director Miller and strategist Guy, but no major shift occurred.

The Liberals were also their own worst enemy. The party's decision to troll Horgan with campaign staff who drove around in a truck emblazoned with anti-NDP imagery was viewed largely as petty and overly aggressive, in the style of the worst of US politics. Their efforts to highlight legitimate holes in the way the NDP would pay for its promises blew up in their faces because of research that either wasn't credible or was flat-out dishonest, depending on your charitability.

Meanwhile, the NDP kept focused on people, with a media campaign that emphasized real voters wrestling with the challenges imposed on them by years of Liberal government—failing seniors care, unaffordable housing, long waits in hospitals, and so on. This was largely the doing of Bob Dewar, an outsider who came to direct the NDP campaign on his own terms, without the baggage of the same crew that had lost previous elections. He was smart and flexible, spearheading the party through its massively successful promise to eliminate bridge tolls within the span of a few hours.

And then there was Horgan himself. When the moment arose, he grabbed it, suppressing the worst aspects of his temperament and becoming more premier-like as the campaign rolled on. It was not an unimpressive change for a man who had, until then, stubbornly refused to take criticism. He deserves full credit for the gut check.

Ultimately, the chickens came home to roost for the Liberals, in the form of voter fatigue over sixteen years of scandal. Child welfare deaths. Education underfunding. Teacher strikes. Health-care waits. Triple-delete email scandals. Cash-for-access allegations. And a never-ending fight with Metro Vancouver mayors over transit expansion that culminated in a tone-deaf mid-campaign reiteration of a referendum for any new local funding sources. Voters, it seemed, had just had enough.

Why, then, did the NDP not actually win on election night?

The party all but conceded the Interior and north to the Liberals, offering little in its platform and barely travelling to the region, taking any hopes off the table in dozens of those ridings. Its platform promises

While the BC Liberals focused their campaign across the province, NDP leader John Horgan spent much of his time in Metro Vancouver, including at a rock star–style event at the Commodore Ballroom on Granville Street on April 23, 2017. The strategy paid off for the NDP. BC NDP

would have been unpopular there anyway, including a review of the Site C dam and opposition to the Kinder Morgan pipeline, together worth thousands of jobs for local residents, jobs that the NDP were essentially promising to kill.

The NDP was also beset by infighting in some local campaigns and brewing resentment over a gender-equity policy that prevented men from seeking the nomination in ridings where male NDP MLAs were retiring. In Cowichan Valley, on Vancouver Island, the riding all but imploded shortly before the election, after a prospective female candidate accused NDP HQ of not protecting her from sexism, and the riding association president quit over the party's gender-equity mandate. The Greens won this riding from the NDP. In Columbia River-Revelstoke, Invermere mayor Gerry Taft wasn't eligible under the gender-equity rules, unless he had a disability or minority status, so Taft, a white man with a wife and kids, declared bisexual minority status to defeat a local female politician who uses a wheelchair to gain the nomination. The

Liberals won this riding from the NDP. In Skeena, candidate Bruce Bidgood used a hearing impairment to declare minority status, defeating a woman, a First Nations member, and a gay candidate for the nomination. High-profile Liberal Ellis Ross won the riding from the NDP.

Infighting also prevented the NDP from winning back Fraser-Nicola. Horgan wanted local First Nations chief Aaron Sam to be his candidate in the riding. But former MLA Harry Lali, who had lost in 2013, refused Horgan's request to step aside and subsequently out-organized Sam for the nomination. Lali would fail to win, again, in 2017. Had the NDP won those four ridings, it would have had forty-five seats and a majority government.

THE MORNING AFTER the election, Clark went to work. She was still the incumbent premier, solidified with a call from Lieutenant-Governor Judith Guichon. The two had a cordial relationship. Guichon was appointed by Stephen Harper in 2012, a year after Clark took the premier's job. Their jobs were at times very much intertwined, as when Clark stood on the front steps of the legislature to greet Guichon as she arrived to read the government throne speech or provide royal assent for legislation. It was part of the formality that exists in British Columbia's parliamentary system. The call wasn't long and did not include any talk about the decision that Guichon might have to make down the road or what the lieutenant-governor would have to do if the Liberals could not get the confidence of the legislature.

Soon after hanging up, Clark was on the phone with Prime Minister Justin Trudeau. Trudeau opened the call with congratulations: Clark had become the first female first minister in Canadian history to be re-elected. It wasn't the result the Liberals expected, but it would still be in the history books.

The premier then prepared to meet the press. It would have been no surprise if Clark had arrived at the microphone looking tired and defeated. Instead she was upbeat and confident.

"Our party has the most seats and we lead in the popular vote, but there is no doubt that last night's result will go down in the history books. It's a finish we haven't seen in a very long time in British Columbia," said Clark, reading from her prepared remarks. Voters want all three parties to work together across partisan lines, she continued.

But the one party the premier needed now more than ever was the BC Greens. If the election results held up, Weaver would have three seats in the legislature. It was the most a Green party in Canada had ever won at the federal or provincial level. The premier's opening statement was as much a message to the public as it was a direct message to the Green Party leader. It was becoming clear to Clark that for her to remain premier for more than a few months she would need the support of Weaver and his fellow Green MLAs.

"Your voice has been heard," Clark said. "We will work together, all of us, to earn your trust."

Press secretary Stephen Smart then called on Global News reporter Keith Baldrey to ask the first question. "Where did it go wrong for you?" Baldrey started. "Particularly in Surrey, were tolls a big issue you stumbled on?"

But Clark wasn't willing to take the blame. She didn't think there was any blame to go around. "Elections don't go wrong, they go the way they go," she said. "People made their voice heard."

The questions continued. Vaughn Palmer, the most accomplished political columnist in the province, pressed Clark on how much responsibility she should personally take for the loss.

"The Liberal party share of popular vote went down. You lost four cabinet ministers. Is any part of you willing to acknowledge that you underperformed and you as leader are to blame for underperforming this time?" asked Palmer.

Clark stared at him. "I never thought it was going to be anything but a really, really tough election," she said.

Palmer persisted, listing off the Liberal accomplishments on leading the country in economic growth, job numbers, balanced budgets. "Why would it be tough with that record?" he asked.

It was the sort of grilling Clark was often able to shake free of, normally with a partisan attack on her political opponent. But now the premier was shackled by the fact she was trying to strike a tone that said she was willing to work with her opponents, not bash them.

"The voters are never wrong," she said.

FIVE BLOCKS AWAY, John Horgan was preparing for his own press conference. He too had had a late night.

"What a ride," said Horgan. "It was exciting to watch, nerve-wracking to participate in."

Like Clark, Horgan was targeting his message at one person: Weaver. The two leaders had their personal differences, but policy-wise they had a lot in common. CTV's Scott Roberts asked the question that was on everyone's mind: "Will you ask Andrew Weaver to form a coalition government?"

"We both agree that the BC Liberals have failed British Columbians on a range of issues," replied Horgan. "They failed on child care, they failed on the housing crisis. We agree they are not willing to defend our coast against an increase in tanker traffic."

Horgan had done the math. Sixty per cent of voters voted against the government—a vote for change, as he called it. He also knew that forty-one NDP plus three Green was larger by the slimmest margin than forty-three Liberal MLAs.

"The decision is certainly hanging in the balance," Horgan said to the gathered reporters.

But the reality was that Horgan hadn't won the election. The NDP had won the second-highest number of seats in the party's history and received more votes than ever before, and that still wasn't enough to take down the Liberals on election night. Baldrey used a sports

BC Liberal Leader Christy Clark made two stops during the twenty-eight-day campaign period to support Courtenay-Comox candidate Jim Benninger. Benninger would lose on election day by nine votes. After the final count of all ballots, he'd lose by 189 votes. BC LIBERAL PARTY/JOHN LEHMANN

metaphor to ask Horgan about the result. "Why couldn't you get it over the goal line?" he asked.

"The game's not over," replied Horgan.

HORGAN WAS RIGHT. British Columbia has among the most flexible absentee ballot rules anywhere in the world. Elections BC changed the rules before the 2013 election, allowing voters to cast a vote on election day at any polling station in their riding, even if it wasn't their own polling station. And in the 2017 election, more people than ever before voted absentee. That meant that even though election day came and went, there were still 176,000 ballots set to count across the province, about 10 per cent of the total. And those votes wouldn't start being counted until May 23, two weeks after election day.

There was no riding in a brighter spotlight than Courtenay-Comox, where only nine votes separated the candidates, one of the closest results in the province's history. NDP candidate Ronna Rae Leonard had done just enough to beat Liberal candidate Jim Benninger. The fact that the election came down to the riding on Vancouver Island was a big surprise. Courtenay-Comox had been a Liberal staple since the party swept to victory in 2001. And with new electoral boundaries for 2017, the Liberals were expecting an even bigger win. Incumbent Liberal Don McRae hadn't run for re-election, but retired 19 Wing commander Jim Benninger did. He brought with him some community credentials, including nearly twenty years at Canadian Forces Base Comox. Although the Liberals did not do well on Vancouver Island, this was one riding they thought they could stay competitive in.

Because the election was close, an automatic recount of all the votes had been triggered. That meant that if Benninger could get just ten extra votes after the recount and all absentee ballots were counted, the Liberals would have their majority government. The entire election was in limbo, and questions lingered about who was in charge and what sort of power the governing Liberals had without a majority of the seats. The Greens were getting ready for negotiations, but nothing serious could happen until after the recount.

At 9 a.m. on Monday, May 22, about thirty volunteers and staff from the NDP, the Liberals, and the Greens crammed into a room in Courtenay's mall on the main drag. The ballots themselves were set up in the boardroom, but not everyone could fit there. That meant some recounting took place in the small rooms nearby.

By 5 p.m., the recount was done. The NDP lead had grown from nine votes to thirteen. Out of thousands and thousands of ballots and under the closest possible scrutiny, there was a discrepancy of just four votes. But it was far from over. The absentee ballots, the ones that held the balance of the election, were yet to be counted. It was now clear that the results of the entire provincial election would depend on what happened in this Vancouver Island riding.

Before the scrutineers left on Monday, they were told there were going to be three vote-counting stations for the absentee ballots. But when they arrived the next morning, it was a different story. Just one area had been set up to tally the 2,077 ballots that still hadn't been counted. This wasn't sitting right with the lawyers in the room for both the NDP and the Liberals. They approached the local electoral officers with their concerns. But they got a quick response from the election official: if you keep pestering me you will be thrown out.

Counting absentee ballots isn't simple. The first part of the process is to count every single envelope. Then each envelope is opened to make sure there is only one secrecy envelope inside. Once that is done, the ballots are removed and put into a proper ballot box, where they are mixed around before being removed and then counted. In each riding, the absentee ballots are tallied in the same order. The first boxes to be counted are from special polling stations, including hospitals. Those ballots had all been counted by 2 p.m. on Tuesday and had turned the election on its head: Jim Benninger had moved into the lead, ahead of Leonard by three votes, with 1,940 votes still left to be counted. The Liberal majority government was within reach.

By lunchtime on Wednesday, there were still hundreds of absentee votes left to be counted. The province was on edge. But as more votes were counted, Benninger's lead disappeared and Leonard's grew.

Eventually, Glen Sanford, the NDP's deputy director, had seen enough. Sanford didn't just know the riding, he knew the community at play. He'd been with the party for a long time, his mother had once been the region's MLA, and he'd proven himself a key organizer in the province-wide election campaign. Sanford didn't have the profile of key strategists like Bob Dewar or Marie Della Mattia, but he was just as valuable for his skill at handling the press and crafting the party's message for its candidates and caucus. With Ronna Rae Leonard up by 101 votes, Sanford sent a text to Dewar and NDP provincial director Raj

Sihota. In his mind it was over. The lead was too big for the Liberals to come back from.

By the time every vote was counted that day, the result was clear: Leonard's lead had stretched from nine votes on election day to 189 votes after the final count. Sanford sent another text message. This time he included NDP leader John Horgan in addition to Dewar and Sihota. It was the result they were hoping for. With a decisive victory in Courtenay-Comox, a judicial recount was not needed.

The local electoral officer announced the numbers to the waiting scrutineers. The Green party team let out a big cheer. It was a sign for Sanford and others in the room. Negotiations were already underway between the Greens and both the Liberals and the NDP, but it seemed that at least on Vancouver Island, Green supporters had a preferred option.

The possibility that the absentee ballots in one riding could change the entire government had never occurred before.

While the celebration in Courtenay-Comox was just warming up, Horgan was addressing the media in Victoria.

"After the vote between the two major parties was split right down the middle, this was an opportunity to build on a minority situation to demonstrate in my opinion that people can have a government that works for them," he said. "People can get a government that co-operates with like-minded people."

It was a message to the Greens. Horgan needed them. He was about to find out if they would be willing partners.

CHAPTER 11
THE GREENDP

Sonia Furstenau hadn't been eating well. And the stress of the negotiations was getting to her. It had been more than a week since the final results came in from Courtenay-Comox, and negotiations with the Liberals and NDP over who would form the next government were still seemingly far from an end. She missed her kids. She missed her home. And, above all, she hated the BC Liberals.

Furstenau's disdain for the governing Liberals was well known. Both Premier Clark and Environment Minister Mary Polak had failed for years to visit her home community of Shawnigan Lake and explain why permits were given to dump toxic soil in a quarry near the community's drinking water source. The issue had ignited a political fire within Furstenau and driven her to run for provincial office. The idea of now negotiating with Clark, Polak, and the party that had treated her neighbours so terribly was weighing heavily on her mind.

Furstenau had tried eating some sushi earlier in the day but found she couldn't eat much. As she arrived back at her hotel room in Victoria, she could feel the anxiety and pressure on her growing. She couldn't take it anymore. She raced to the bathroom toilet. And vomited.

The Liberals didn't know it at the time, but their chances of securing a deal with the Greens were flushing away. Furstenau would prove to be the deal breaker within the Green caucus, the MLA who simply could not be brought onside to consider any type of deal that would allow the Liberal government to spend one more day in office.

Ironically, her leader, Andrew Weaver, had actually worked well with Premier Clark in the past. They got along. The Liberals had more seats (forty-three compared with forty-one NDP) and offered a stable partner. And the Liberals hadn't launched an online campaign of bullying and harassment against the Greens during the election, like the NDP had. If anything, Weaver was leaning toward a deal with the Liberals.

But Furstenau could not be persuaded by Weaver or anybody else. Her inability to (literally) stomach the thought of helping the Liberal regime had the serious potential to end sixteen years of Liberal rule in BC.

The pressure hadn't always been that high. A few weeks earlier, the Green Party had been on cloud nine: the election was over, and even though absentee votes were still left to be counted, the Greens were preparing for open, honest negotiations with both parties. But as they prepared to negotiate, they realized they were out of their depth. As a relatively new party, which had never enjoyed power, they lacked a certain practical expertise in the realities of governing. So Weaver made a decision that would come as a surprise to his new caucus colleagues. He called on a man named Norman Spector.

Spector had served as the deputy minister for former Social Credit premier Bill Bennett and later as chief of staff for Progressive Conservative prime minister Brian Mulroney. On paper, he didn't appear to be anything close to a Green. But Spector and Weaver had similar social circles. And Spector provided much-needed experience in the trenches of governance, having been at the table when the Canadian government negotiated the North American Free Trade Agreement with Mexico and the United States in 1992.

Spector was also close with many BC Liberals, including Ben Chin, the premier's executive director of communications and issues management. On May 15, before any negotiations were to take place, Chin and Spector had lunch. Joining them were *Vancouver Sun* legislative columnist Vaughn Palmer and Global News legislative reporter Keith Baldrey. The group had a monthly lunch. The conversation quickly turned to the election results and what the Liberals would do next. Baldrey and Palmer floated ideas about what the Liberals would be willing to give up in order to stay in power and get the Greens on board, things like official party status for the Greens, banning union and corporate donations, and even electoral reform. But when Chin weighed in, the list grew. The Liberals were willing to move on a lot of fronts, he said. And the Greens would be foolish to sign with the NDP, where they'd be absorbed, he argued. They'd be much better to sign no deal with any party and issue demands to the Liberals bill by bill, forcing the government to change its entire agenda to satisfy the Greens and giving them key public victories at every stage of the process, argued Chin.

Spector disagreed. The Greens were far more likely to align with the NDP, he argued. Then he excused himself from the lunch.

"I have to go," said Spector. "I have a doctor's appointment."

But Spector wasn't going to his GP for a checkup. He was in fact meeting Dr. Andrew Weaver, PhD. Weaver offered him a spot on the Greens' negotiating team. The next afternoon, May 16, a press release was sent out announcing the hire. The negotiation team would now consist of Weaver, Spector, newly elected Cowichan Valley MLA Furstenau, and Green Party chief of staff Liz Lilly, who was also architect of the party's platform.

The Greens met the press the next day, May 17, 2017, in the Premier's Rose Garden on the legislative grounds. It had been eight days since the provincial election, and there still had not been any formal talks. The Greens were getting hundreds of emails a day pleading with them to support the BC NDP.

"I know you're expecting big news," Weaver said to open the press conference.

"We're here to say we are in negotiations with both the BC Liberals and NDP," he said. "It would irresponsible for us to preclude negotiations with any political party simply because they have not said something in past. We're in discussions with both."

Privately, Weaver wasn't so sure. He had worked very well with the BC Liberals in the previous legislative session and considered himself a fiscal conservative. He was more comfortable with that direction. But there was one issue that reporters kept coming back to: resource development. The Site C dam and the provincial government's thumbs-up to the Trans Mountain pipeline expansion had been hot-button issues in the election.

The Greens were strongly opposed to the $8.8 billion hydroelectric dam near Fort St. John in the province's northeast. Weaver believed the electricity wasn't needed, and that government should instead invest in energy projects like geothermal. He had also campaigned strongly against the Trans Mountain pipeline twinning. The project had been approved by the federal government and had an endorsement from the Clark government. During the campaign, Weaver had said he would do anything he could to stop it from going ahead. The NDP felt the same way.

"Our position on Kinder Morgan and Site C is not too dissimilar from the NDP's position," said Weaver at the press conference. "But it's quite dramatically far away from the Liberal position. So in negotiations you have to put it all on the table and see where things end up."

After the press conference, Weaver and Furstenau walked over to the Harbour Towers Hotel together and met with their Liberal counterparts. Waiting by the hotel elevator when they arrived was Mike Bernier. The Liberal education minister was Weaver's closest friend within government. The pair had started a friendship in 2013 as new MLAs with offices right beside each other and seats close together in the House. For years they had chatted, complained about colleagues, and sparred on policy. It was a friendship the Liberals now hoped to exploit.

Understanding Weaver's policies was one thing. But understanding him as a person was something totally different. As a teenager at Oak Bay High School, he was someone who didn't fit into the typical cliques. He played on both the chess team and the rugby team, straddling a line between two high school worlds. He got into science because he wanted to use tangible proof in his decision making.

Weaver's decisions would lead him to become one of the country's leading climate scientists and contribute to a Nobel Peace Prize. Weaver was part of a 2007 team that included former United States vice-president Al Gore, which was honoured for its efforts to research and disseminate knowledge about man-made climate change. He was a supporter of Gordon Campbell's carbon tax. But he ultimately entered politics because, after Campbell's resignation, he watched the Clark government move away from carbon tax increases and emissions reductions. He grew so concerned that he threw his own hat into the political arena.

Around the legislature, he quickly became a well-known character. Most times, he'd wander the halls in a loud Hawaiian shirt. He could be spotted playing Pokémon GO, collecting hockey cards, and out at paintball with his son. Predictably, he drives an electric car, often the only one parked at the legislature's designated charging station. The fifty-seven-year-old is also a napper. He can sleep almost anywhere. And when stressed, he's known to lie down on the couch in his office on his belly, his head on the arm rest, his arms forward, and fall asleep in what looks like the most uncomfortable position imaginable. Yet between the daily hustle of bills and debates, he's often able to catch quick naps.

Bernier understood all of Weaver's little quirks. And for that reason, he was on the Liberal negotiating team.

The Greens and Bernier entered the conference room. Bernier took Weaver around the room for formal introductions to Finance Minister Mike de Jong, BC Hydro chair and transition head Brad Bennett, and former finance minister and advisor Carole Taylor. One person noticeably absent: Premier Christy Clark. That was by design. The Liberals knew what Furstenau thought of Clark. They also knew the premier's popularity was dismal at the moment and had been one of many problems in the recent election campaign. Putting Clark across from Furstenau would be a recipe for disaster.

The first meeting was a chance for the Liberals and Greens to get to know each other a little bit. Weaver had worked with de Jong before. Bennett was familiar politically to the group. Spector had worked with Bennett's father, Bill (premier from 1975 to 1986), nearly forty years earlier. The pair joked about how Bennett's dad use to have an apartment in the hotel's tower.

The Liberals watched Furstenau closely. She sat with her arms crossed and an unpleasant look on her face, giving everyone the sense she didn't want to be in the room with the governing party at all. The meeting lasted less than ninety minutes. The Liberals were willing to offer the Greens official party status but, beyond that, didn't have much to say.

"Why don't you come back with some more ideas?" Weaver suggested near the end of the meeting.

De Jong had one additional item to float before they broke. He explained that if the Greens and the NDP worked together, they would have forty-four votes to the Liberals' forty-three. The majority party usually provided an MLA to become Speaker.

"The Speaker will have to come from the NDP," de Jong said, outlining the scenario.

But if that happened, it would reduce the Green-NDP alliance to forty-three seats—a direct tie with the Liberals. That would complicate things, de Jong explained, because the current practice was that the Speaker didn't participate in certain debates, including what's called committee of the whole. In those cases the government's deputy speaker would take the Speaker's place. That would mean two Green-NDP MLAS would be tied up, giving the Liberals a one-vote advantage.

So the NDP-Green partnership was destined to fail on the numbers, de Jong concluded.

"It just doesn't work," he said.

And the Liberals made it very plain that the NDP wasn't going to be able to poach one of their members for the chair. So if the New Democrats made that claim, said de Jong, they weren't telling the truth.

The meeting concluded with the feeling that the Liberals were just humouring the Greens until all the votes were counted.

Two days later, the Green negotiators got together again, this time to meet the NDP. The location was the Grand Pacific Hotel, half a block from the legislature. The Greens got there early. Before things got started, Furstenau decided to head out to a nearby Starbucks for coffee. As she went to the bank of elevators on the building's west side, the doors opened. Inside was the NDP negotiating team.

NDP MLA Carole James, campaign manager Bob Dewar, and advisor Marie Della Mattia got off the elevator. But leader John Horgan stayed on. He saw an opportunity, and offered to walk Furstenau across the street to Starbucks. At first, the pair exchanged pleasantries. They knew each other from Vancouver Island politics. There was even a time when Horgan's riding encompassed many of the people that Furstenau now represented. As they waited in line, the tone of their chit-chat grew more serious.

"How could you actually talk to the BC Liberals after what they did to your community?" asked Horgan.

It was the very question Furstenau was grappling with. She was trying to keep an open mind about both parties, but her dislike for the governing Liberals was so strong.

Back at the hotel, the first NDP-Green meeting was unspectacular. The NDP had their policy issues, and because they felt confident about winning Courtenay-Comox and remaining in the driver's seat during talks, they didn't feel a lot of need to budge on their policies. The Greens, meanwhile, were facing extraordinary pressure from some community groups to side with the NDP. Facebook groups and message boards were full of ideas of what the Green Party should do. The Ottawa-based advocacy group Leadnow had organized an online petition, which collected 25,000 signatures from people who wanted the Greens and NDP to work together. Leadnow executive director Lyndsay Poaps (a former Vancouver parks board commissioner) held a showy press conference outside the legislature on May 23, with a dozen empty boxes meant to symbolize the 25,000 signatures.

"A majority of people voted for a party that pledged to block Kinder Morgan and put brakes on Site C, parties that pledged to get big money out of politics and change the electoral system," said Poaps.

James and Furstenau were there to accept the signatures on behalf of the NDP and Greens, respectively. They were swarmed by reporters asking if the alliance between the two parties was already a done deal.

The Liberals were unimpressed by the optics of the event. Bernier even went as far as to call Weaver and complain.

"Sonia is on the front steps with Carole and it looks like you guys have already agreed with the NDP," he said.

Weaver was quick to respond, explaining he'd sent Sonia because it would have been a bad message if he, as leader, attended.

The next day, May 24, the NDP negotiating team waited for Weaver and his team back at the Grand Pacific Hotel. Horgan was distracted. The two weeks of waiting and the stress of not knowing whether he would be premier were taking their toll. The Greens arrived in the negotiating room, and from the start Horgan couldn't stop looking at his phone and flipping through his papers, barely making eye contact with Weaver and the rest of the Green team. Norman Spector spoke out a number of times to grab Horgan's attention.

"You are reading too much Martyn Brown," he said to Horgan.

The reference was a shot at the NDP leader over a recent column by Brown in the *Georgia Straight* entitled "Why John Horgan Is Really in the Driver's Seat," which argued that the NDP held the ace card in negotiations because, ultimately, the electorate would punish the

Greens to the point of non-existence if they decided to prop up the Liberal regime. Spector's shot at Horgan was deliberate. It translated as "Stop being so arrogant."

The two sides were working their way through policy items, but personal distrust was still holding them back. As negotiations were coming to a close for the day, both Dewar and Weaver received text messages. Dewar read his out loud to the room. It was from NDP deputy director Glen Sanford, who was at the recount in Courtenay-Comox and knew the results.

"We won," Dewar told the room. "We got it."

The election was over. The NDP had won the seat. The Greens were the kingmakers. Power was within the NDP's grasp. The group said goodbye, knowing the dynamics had changed.

Weaver and Furstenau left the negotiation room. Weaver had an important call to make. He was still concerned about the way Horgan had acted in the negotiations. Weaver picked up the phone and called Matt Toner, one of the NDP's star recruits for the 2013 election, a tech entrepreneur who ran in the downtown Vancouver riding of Vancouver-False Creek. Toner had jumped ship to the BC Green Party in 2015, but still had NDP contacts. Weaver asked him to call NDP president Craig Keating and get a message sent to Horgan and his team.

"You need to tell them to bring their A-game," Weaver told Toner.

The call wrapped up. Weaver and Furstenau went to meet the media, and the Green Party leader was hit with the obvious first question.

"How does it feel to be the most powerful man in the province?" he was asked.

"We are humbled by the responsibility that British Columbians have bestowed upon us," answered Weaver, sounding tired. "The BC Greens take this very seriously, we take this responsibility very seriously. We are committed to bring stability to this province. And we are committed to ensuring that the decisions we make over the next few days make government work in British Columbia."

His comments caused the BC Liberals to immediately perk up. They felt the one advantage they brought to the table over the NDP was stability. They might lack the policy objectives that the NDP and Greens shared, but the Liberals had the better numbers. A Liberal-Green alliance would have a true majority of forty-six seats in the House and no problems with a Speaker.

The Greens wrapped up the press conference, realizing that the implications of whatever decision the caucus of three made would be enormous. Weaver also wanted to get the deal wrapped up over the next few days. He shot down the idea that the Greens would support Clark on a bill-to-bill basis, saying he preferred an actual deal for a three- to four-year term.

The Liberals were emboldened by Weaver's press conference. They felt it was clear the Green leader favoured them, even if he was struggling to convince the rest of his Green caucus. As they prepped for the next bargaining session, they had to swap Carole Taylor off their team and replace her with Clark's long-time political strategist, Mike McDonald. For two days, McDonald worked with de Jong to build a presentation for the Greens that included how the government could afford to implement Green promises and what promises they would be willing to agree on. The Liberals booked the penthouse at the Harbour Towers, a sign they were taking things seriously.

McDonald's PowerPoint presentation to the Greens included big ideas. As finance minister, de Jong had received an update from his ministry officials that the province's financials were in better shape than expected. That meant the government would be more willing to spend some money. The public wasn't aware of this yet, and it allowed the Liberals to surprise the Greens with cash. McDonald had sought advice from former Ontario NDP premier Bob Rae before the presentation. Rae, who was also the federal Liberal leader, had navigated a minority government situation in that province in

1985, signing a Liberal-NDP accord that supported a Liberal minority government for two years. Rae told McDonald negotiations came down to two things: arithmetic and chemistry. How would the math work on the seat count, and what's the chemistry between the parties and its leaders? McDonald labelled one of his slides "Arithmetic and Chemistry" and made his best pitch to the Greens on both accounts.

Although the presentation was interesting and comprehensive, the Liberals were careful not to give the Greens anything electronic or on paper that might leave the room and leak to the public. But what was still missing was the big energy projects. The Greens knew the Liberals were not willing to budge on the Site C dam, but they felt there were some options when it came to Kinder Morgan's Trans Mountain pipeline twinning. One thing not in the presentation was carbon pricing. That would have to wait.

The meeting didn't go as the Liberals had hoped. Tension hit a high point early in the meeting, when Furstenau interrupted Weaver and finally spoke up with her true thoughts to the Liberal team.

"If you guys hadn't screwed me in Shawnigan Lake this would be easier," she said. "There is no way I could go back to the people in my riding and say I have worked out a deal with Christy Clark and the BC Liberals."

Bernier watched with disappointment. He saw Furstenau as the deal breaker. He sidled up to Weaver in the hallway on a break, asking for a chat.

"Just remember we are serious," he told Weaver. It was a reminder to his friend that even though the two sides were not natural allies, there was room for things to work out.

But the Green leader wasn't so sure. He was blunt with Bernier. Furstenau was not likely to support the Liberals.

"I almost should not have put her on this team because it is hard to find a neutral path through," Weaver said to Bernier.

Furstenau, for her part, felt she was doing everything she could to negotiate in good faith, despite her feelings about the Liberals, and she told Weaver that.

The Greens went back to caucus. They had hit a tipping point. Weaver was intrigued by many of the ideas the Liberals had put forward and was impressed with how thought out the costed plans were. The Green leader was still stung by the way the NDP had treated him and how out of it Horgan had seemed in the last meeting.

"No way in hell I want to sign with the NDP," he told Bernier.

But the leader was just one member. And the Furstenau problem would not go away.

Scrutiny was intense back in Furstenau's Cowichan Valley riding. While the negotiations were underway, Furstenau's campaign manager, Luke Cross, had been having a lot of conversations. Everywhere he went, from Duncan to Shawnigan Lake, people wanted to tell him the Greens should be supporting the NDP. Each day the messages would be passed on to the MLA. But Furstenau couldn't respond. She had signed a non-disclosure agreement that would preclude her from disclosing what was happening around the table. It was that stress that was wearing the MLA down. She felt cut off and isolated, and she couldn't engage with her loved ones or those she trusted most. It was that night that the thought of supporting the Liberals became overwhelming to Furstenau, and she was sick to her stomach.

By Friday morning, it was clear to the NDP that Furstenau was not willing to support the Liberals. It was the turning point in the negotiations. Horgan and his team were more aggressive with reminders of the ideas that brought the Greens and the NDP together. Weaver also saw a substantial change in Horgan's attitude, now seeing a leader who was eager to strike a deal, rather than one who days earlier had seemed uninterested.

Horgan and his team had chatted with Keating following his call with Toner. The message the NDP received wasn't "bring your A-game," like Weaver had intended, but "make things more specific." A lot had been covered by the two sides through the first two negotiation sessions, although nothing was down on paper yet.

That would start to change. Both Dewar and Liz Lilly started jotting down ideas on paper at the meeting. The sides could agree on creating a fair wage commission, moving the fixed election date to the fall, implementing a strategy to reduce post-secondary education costs, and so on. Progress was being made, and everyone stayed at the table to hammer it out.

By the time things wrapped up on Friday, the Greens were comfortable that there was a deal in place that they could support. Furstenau had been away from her two young daughters and two teenage sons for days, so as soon as things wrapped up she headed home to the Cowichan Valley. Adam Olsen and Weaver left the Grand Pacific and went back to their familiar spot at the rose garden. Reporters anxiously raced from their offices for the update, optimistic that there might be a deal in place.

"I wanted to emphasize: this is incredibly complex," Weaver told reporters. "It's not just about picking the BC NDP or picking the BC Liberals. It's about trying to ensure that we have stability, trying to ensure that we're able to get legislation in place."

Weaver told the gathered horde that a deal was very, very close. It was a direct message to the Liberals, who knew the Greens and NDP had met that day.

While Weaver was outside speaking to the press, Horgan was inside the legislature. The burly politician isn't much of a hugger. But it was looking like a night to buck some trends. Horgan's press secretary, Sheena McConnell, was planning to head across the street to meet her boss at the Grand Pacific to help manoeuvre any media who may be waiting to get an update on negotiations. But as she was walking out of the building she ran into Horgan, already back from the day's talks.

Horgan looked at his loyal press secretary.

"We did it," he said.

McConnell was still not sure what he was talking about. Then her boss opened his arms wide and welcomed McConnell in for a big hug.

"We did it," he whispered again in her ear as they hugged.

Nothing was signed yet. But in Horgan's mind, the deal was done. The Green Party was choosing the NDP.

While Horgan was celebrating, the Liberals were wrapping up an emergency, last-minute caucus meeting in Vancouver. The negotiating team was intent on keeping the caucus updated and ensuring that nothing was being promised that would hurt the coalition. There was a profound sense of angst in the caucus room. Some of the right wing of the party could feel that the Greens wanted the party to give up principles to stay in power. Among them, minister Rich Coleman told Clark privately that she shouldn't even be negotiating with the Greens. She should refuse to name a Speaker from the Liberal ranks when the legislature reconvened, forcing a showdown where, in the absence of anyone taking the job, the legislature would reach a deadlock and the lieutenant-governor would be forced to decide whether to call a new election.

THE LIBERALS HAD heard Weaver's press conference on Friday, with his statement that a deal was close. Now the party was scrambling. On Saturday, Brad Bennett called Liz Lilly, saying they wanted to bump the scheduled Monday meeting up to Sunday evening. The Greens agreed.

"We are really close to full a proposal that we think you will be crazy not to take," Bennett told Lilly.

But before the Liberals could get their audience with the Greens, the NDP had a chance to seal the deal. On Sunday morning, the parties got down to business, and more parts of the agreement were hashed out.

Proportional representation was agreed on, with a promise of a referendum. A carbon tax increase starting in 2018 of five dollars per tonne. A review of the Site C dam by the BC Utilities Commission, but not a full cancellation of the project as the Greens had promised in the election.

Then Horgan offered an invitation. He was heading to watch the women's sevens rugby tournament that afternoon in Langford with the city's mayor, Stew Young. Horgan wanted to know if Weaver would join him for the game. The pair had grown closer over the two weeks of negotiations. They were similar in more ways than made them different. Both grew up in the Victoria area—Weaver went to Oak Bay High, Horgan to Reynolds Secondary in Saanich. They both loved sports, including rugby.

The two met at the rugby field and settled into conversation about rugby and Canada's team. One of the top teams in the world, the women had clinched a trip to the tournament finals with a 17–10 victory over Australia. The two insist they didn't talk politics at the game. And they didn't have to. What most people didn't know was that their staff were busy hammering out the deal behind the scenes. While the fans cheered Canada on, Lilly and Dewar were typing up the language of the confidence and supply agreement. The document would be ready for the Green caucus to review the next morning.

Weaver then headed back downtown to meet with the Liberals. The vibe was different. This time the Liberals had stocked the liquor cabinet for the meeting in the penthouse. They had even found a two-floor suite with views of the harbour for Olsen and the Greens' staff to wait in nearby. But before any celebratory drinks could be placed on the table, there were issues to be dealt with, and the Greens and the Liberals were still a long way apart. The Liberals were not willing to move on Kinder Morgan and Site C.

The meeting started with Weaver unloading on the Liberals in a long rant. How could we possibly do a deal with you people when there's no way we can agree on Site C and no way we can agree on Kinder Morgan, he asked the Liberal team. For effect, he regurgitated a line he'd used frequently in the election campaign about the Liberals being too focused on liquefied natural gas and promising a unicorn in each and every backyard. When Weaver had finished, Furstenau piled on, asking why the Greens should believe the Liberals now, after years in which they hadn't promised any of these changes.

Where do we go from here, asked Bennett. Weaver apologized, saying he hadn't meant to take the air out of the room. All sides decided they would meet again the next afternoon.

The Liberals intended to show up Monday with their big gun, Clark, in tow to hash out the final details. The Greens, meanwhile, never intended to meet again at all.

Weaver's outburst made one thing clear: the part of him that had wanted to support the Liberals was gone. He walked out of the negotiating room and into the giant suite where Olsen and some staff were waiting. Head in his hands, Weaver expressed his frustration over the Liberals' insistence that the Site C dam was good for the province's climate policy. Weaver got into politics because he saw Campbell's climate policies being cast aside by Clark. Now he was on the verge of ending Clark's reign.

The group decided that night that they were going to go with the NDP. A phone call was booked for Weaver, Olsen, and Furstenau for the next morning so they could sleep on the agreement and make a final decision.

The Monday morning call was short. The decision had been made. The Greens were good with the deal. The MLAs logged off the call and Weaver went to the University of Victoria. The politician was set to be part of the PhD defence for his last student. She had started with him years before, while he was still balancing a political and academic career. The professor was a long way from looking like a political kingmaker. Wearing his blue and green Hawaiian shirt, he was in his element, detached from the world with his phone off and his attention solely focused on his final student.

While this was unfolding, Weaver's chief of staff, Liz Lilly, grabbed her phone to call the Liberals' Bennett. It was only half an hour before the two sides were set to meet again, and Bennett was taking a final walk around the legislature to clear his mind.

"I hate to be the one to break this news, but we've met and we've come to an agreement with the NDP," Lilly told him. "So there's no point in us meeting."

"That's too bad, Liz," said Bennett, through gritted teeth. He made one final pitch, arguing the numbers were better with the Liberals to get things done over the next three or four years. But it was too late. The Liberals felt sandbagged, as if the Greens hadn't been honest with them from the start. Bennett walked into the premier's west annex, where the rest of the negotiating team was ready to head to the hotel to meet the Greens. They took the news hard.

Chief of staff Mike McDonald had his feet up on his desk. He'd just finished printing a final package to be presented to the Greens, which had required him to stay up until 3:30 that morning cramming to get it done. Included in the deal that they'd never get a chance to present was a new government ministry that would involve BC Hydro and be charged with transforming BC's economy to a clean one, with more electrification and use of the power grid rather than fossil fuels. The Liberals felt it was a good olive branch to offer the Greens on use of Site C's power, even though both sides disagreed as to whether the dam should go forward. The Liberals had also slotted in more than $1 billion on childcare spending over four years, with increases beyond that. An increase in the carbon tax of five dollars per tonne per year to fifty dollars per tonne by 2022 was on the table and had been approved by caucus. In addition, the Liberals were willing to move on banning the grizzly bear trophy hunt. And a host of other ideas had been pulled from the Green platform.

McDonald felt like he'd been kicked in the gut. He and de Jong asked if there was anything they could do to salvage a deal.

"I've got to get Christy on the phone," Bennett told them.

He dialed the premier and told her what happened. "You should phone Weaver again and have a conversation," he told her.

As soon as Weaver had finished his UVic duties, he headed straight back to the legislature. The Green leader knew he had to change into something more formal before announcing his big deal with the NDP, so he was scrambling to get inside and get his suit on before meeting Horgan. With a suit bag in one hand, he powered on his phone. He looked down and noticed Clark had been trying to reach him. Time was running out; a press release was less than thirty minutes away. He didn't call back.

Weaver hustled into the office and spoke to press secretary Jillian Oliver. He exchanged a few text messages with Clark, but it was too late. The decision was made. The deal was done.

Back in Vancouver, Clark stared at the phone in frustration. She knew exactly what she planned to say if he'd answered: "What are you doing? Don't walk your party off to electoral oblivion," had been her intended message.

Clark never got to deliver her last-minute presentation to the Green caucus, nor was she able to get Weaver on the phone to plead with him to call off the NDP deal. It had been a contentious decision for the premier not to attend the negotiations in person. Though a highly divisive figure, she also possessed the interpersonal skills to, more often than not, at least partially defuse her critics face to face. But the negotiating team didn't want to use her until there was a path to a deal. And the path never materialized.

Clark doesn't regret not going. She thought her appearance at the table would have just aggravated Furstenau. Some Green negotiators

After nearly two weeks of intense negotiations, BC Green Party leader Andrew Weaver decided to support NDP leader John Horgan. The two shake hands before meeting the media to announce the partnership on May 30, 2017. BC NDP

believe Clark missed a key opportunity by sitting on the sidelines. Others on the team think her presence wouldn't have made a difference. Either way, it was a gamble.

While Clark was stewing, Horgan and Weaver were walking to the golden gates in front of the BC legislative chamber. Weeks of waiting were about to end. Before they went out to meet the press, Weaver joked with the NDP leader.

"Now I get to pass this boulder off my shoulders and onto yours," he said, in reference to the pressure he felt.

Then the two leaders walked to the microphone set up with the legislative chamber behind them. Dozens of media assembled, broadcasting the moment live across the province.

"In the end, we had to make a difficult decision," Weaver told reporters. "A decision we felt was in the best interest of BC today. And that decision was for the BC Greens to work with the BC NDP to provide a stable minority government over the four-year term of this next session."

The Greens would get their ban on union and corporate donations, a partner willing to stop the Trans Mountain pipeline, a review of the

Site C dam, and a referendum on proportional representation. However, on closer examination of the deal, it was clear that the NDP had given up little to lock down the Greens.

"The three dozen or so policy commitments, though ambitious, largely echoed those in the NDP platform," wrote *Vancouver Sun* columnist Vaughn Palmer. "It was hard to identify any points where the Greens had persuaded the NDP to abandon its position and adopt theirs."

The NDP had realized during negotiations that the Greens, in particular Furstenau, would never do a deal with the Liberals. And so they didn't have to compromise on much of anything to get the agreement.

"Realizing Weaver had nowhere else to go, Horgan and his able chief of staff Bob Dewar saw no need to offer the Greens more than what was already in the NDP platform, nor did they," wrote Palmer.

Weaver made the decision through the negotiations not to enter into a coalition government. That would have meant a cabinet spot for him and probably his colleagues. Instead he wanted to maintain his party's identity as separate from the NDP, though critics would predict that his party will eventually be absorbed by the NDP.

The NDP caucus gleefully rubber-stamped the deal on May 30, 2017, making it official in a second press conference, with all forty-one members happily signing on to the confidence and supply agreement that would create a path for them to move from opposition to government.

The two parties, which the Liberals had now nicknamed the GreeNDP, held a ceremony in the legislature's Hall of Honour, in which Horgan, Weaver, and all the NDP and Green MLAs would sign the agreement.

It was a historic moment. But the document, ultimately, meant nothing. Because one thing still needed to happen: Lieutenant-Governor Judith Guichon had to decide to ask John Horgan to become premier.

CHAPTER 12

THE LIEUTENANT-GOVERNOR
WILL SEE YOU NOW

Premier Christy Clark walked slowly across the cream-coloured carpet of the French drawing room in Government House, and collapsed heavily into a white chair in the corner. She sighed, exhausted, as her staff gathered around her. The normally chipper premier no longer bore the permanent smile that was her trademark.

"I don't think she's going to do it," said Clark.

The premier had just emerged from a meeting with Lieutenant-Governor Judith Guichon. Clark's last hope to stay in power rested on Guichon agreeing to her request to dissolve parliament and call a new election.

The meeting, though lengthy, had not gone well. Clark was exceptionally skilled at reading people, a technique she'd deployed constantly during her lengthy political career. She could tell the moment she walked into the room that Guichon had already made up her mind. The lieutenant-governor appeared both uncomfortable and defensive. The premier nonetheless gave it her best pitch. She started by handing over an envelope containing her resignation letter, a formal step that was required after an alliance of BC NDP and Green MLAs had voted down her Liberal government on a confidence vote just two hours earlier.

"Here's my letter of resignation and here's my advice to you," began Clark. "You should dissolve the legislature, because no party can

Christy Clark, with chief of staff Mike McDonald, press secretary Stephen Smart, and executive director of communications Ben Chin, in the French drawing room at Government House before the most important meeting of Clark's political life, with Lieutenant-Governor Judith Guichon. STEPHEN SMART

govern in there. The only way a party can govern is by perverting the rules of our democracy. And you have a responsibility, as I do, to protect those democratic principles. That's what the lieutenant-governor is appointed to do, is to safeguard democratic process. That's your job. And my advice to you is, in order to be able to do your job, dissolve the legislature or these principles will be violated."

Clark cited several important things, like how an NDP government backed by the Greens would require the non-partisan Speaker to break almost all the tie votes, and how the NDP had strongly hinted publicly that they'd stack legislature committees to give themselves more seats than were reflected in the makeup of the House.

But Clark got nowhere.

She handed the lieutenant-governor a two- or three-page written analysis of the unworkability of the legislature, partially penned by her house leader, lawyer, and twenty-three-year veteran MLA Mike de Jong.

But Guichon simply took it and put it aside without even reading it. At times, it didn't even look like the vice-regal representative was listening. There were no questions during Clark's early statement. She'd finish a particular point and be greeted by a silence that settled between the two of them, each seated on red leather chairs in the lieutenant-governor's private study.

The premier and the lieutenant-governor decided to have a glass of wine—a BC pinot gris. Clark wanted to keep Guichon talking. For almost forty minutes, the premier alternated between small talk with the Nicola Valley rancher whom she'd known personally for years, and pulling her back to the issue at hand. Clark felt she needed to make every effort to persuade Guichon to change her mind. Even though it looked like Guichon had long since decided that an election was off the table, Clark pushed to change the unchangeable. Guichon was uncomfortable with the approach, which Clark recognized and exploited to pressure her further. Occasionally she could briefly draw her into the debate, like when she argued it was the lieutenant-governor's job to safeguard the democratic process, and Guichon would reply that no, that was the official Opposition's job, and the media's.

Clark tried to argue that there was history and precedent in the lieutenant-governor being required to act on her first minister's request for an election. Here too, though, Guichon refused to engage. Clark got the impression that the Nicola Valley rancher hadn't made up her own mind; she'd been told by advisors what to do and was unwilling or unable to defend it when pressed. She was just repeating what she'd been told.

After almost three-quarters of an hour, Clark gave up. It seemed hopeless. Guichon wasn't willing to budge. They concluded the meeting. Guichon wouldn't tell her what her decision was going to be. That was the worst sign of all, because had Guichon accepted her advice on calling an election, Clark would have been told and then gone outside to inform the public.

Clark knew all the signs were bad as she walked back down the red-carpeted hallway of the Government House mansion to the French drawing room, where four of her senior staff were waiting for her.

"I think she'd made up her mind before I got there," Clark told them. "And I think she's going to call on John Horgan."

FOR DAYS BEFORE it all came down to the historic meeting with the lieutenant-governor, the Liberals had been scrambling to find something, anything, to save their government in the wake of the NDP-Green power-sharing deal. Their options were limited.

Perhaps the most obvious solution was for Clark to accept the inevitable and quit. The NDP and Greens had forty-four votes, compared with her forty-three. Her options ranged from limited to none. But veteran house leader Mike de Jong kept advising the premier that if your opponents want to defeat you they should do it in public, on the floor of the House, using the time-honoured traditions of the legislature. Clark, a pragmatic realist, took some time to be brought around to de Jong's idea of spending days in wasted, and ultimately hopeless, debate, only to have to sit feet from her opponents as they publicly gloated over toppling her party. But de Jong and Clark still had a couple of moves left that the premier felt were worth trying.

Clark's enemies expected her to deadlock the House by refusing to appoint a Speaker, in an attempt to force an election. Instead, she surprised them with a show of goodwill, on June 22, 2017, by placing widely respected Forests Minister Steve Thomson in the role—a choice all sides celebrated. But Thomson made it clear that if his government lost a confidence vote, he would quit as Speaker. The NDP and Greens had been trying to persuade several Liberals to essentially defect from their own party and take the Speaker's job (along with the perks and extra $52,940 salary that entailed) in an attempt to jam the governing party. But nobody took the bait—this time, at least. One courtship, of disgruntled Liberal backbencher Darryl Plecas, would eventually yield a defection under different circumstances in the future.

The next move would require the premier to press ahead with plans for her first throne speech since the May 9 election. So the Liberals reconvened the legislature for June 22 to outline the vision for a government almost everyone knew was doomed.

"In June, we believed we needed to test the strength of the NDP-Green pact, which was predicated on the false promise of the NDP attracting a Liberal to serve as Speaker," Clark's chief of staff, Mike McDonald, would later write in an op-ed in *The Vancouver Sun*. "Throughout early and mid-June, Weaver privately expressed his misgivings about his course of action. Some observers suggested that we fold our tent and take defeat with 'dignity.' Hogwash. Our responsibility was to find a way to govern, especially given that we hold the most seats. You don't quit before the whistle is blown."

The Liberal caucus had already approved many new policies as part of the offer they had wanted to make to the Greens during the negotiations. Things like a carbon tax increase had been debated internally and begrudgingly settled.

In addition, caucus MLAS were invited to submit new ideas. They didn't hold back. New ideas began appearing by the boatload, like doubling arts funding (which came from Clark directly) and an ambitious new vision for rapid transit stretching from Squamish to Chilliwack. McDonald and Clark hoped the throne speech would do several things all at once: show the public that the Liberals had learned from their shortcomings in the election, were willing to change, had a plan to change, and wanted to work with the other parties. Tactically, they also hoped they might stress-test the new bromance between Weaver and Horgan, to see if that new alliance would crack once many of their best ideas were being promoted by their enemies.

There was another motivation for some of Clark's advisors, like McDonald: they saw in the throne speech the kind of bold vision that should have been in the party's election platform. They might not have known they had the money back then, but they could have pushed the envelope and they chose not to. It had been a mistake. And this time would be different.

Before the ink was dry on the speech, de Jong offered a warning. It would be difficult, if not impossible, for Clark to stick around as Opposition leader once she'd repurposed most of the NDP's and Greens' best ideas as her own.

"In the poker table that is politics, you've decided to go all in," he told her.

Clark said she understood. Privately, de Jong thought the speech went too far. Some of her senior staff also thought it was a mistake.

"This is too much," executive director of communications Ben Chin told McDonald. "It's almost like a repudiation of the last four years."

Chin, who had planned to leave the office anyway, didn't take his concerns directly to Clark. If she wanted to make this throne speech her legacy, as a kind of departing document, it was entirely her right to make that call.

Clark's trusted advisor, Brad Bennett, also disliked the speech. He called the premier as soon as he heard about it to express his concern that it looked like the Liberals were willing to abandon some of their principles and open up the government coffers to spend everything that everyone had asked for. The conservative side of the coalition, in particular, would be unimpressed, predicted Bennett.

"This is a Hail Mary," Bennett told the premier. "And politically it's not only going to be tough in opposition, but it will be tough on you."

In fact, within the ranks of Clark's insiders and election 2017 campaign crew, most advisors hated the throne speech. But only a few would tell the boss that to her face. Clark and McDonald were still of the mind at this point that there'd be a fall election and the throne speech would be the document that would kick-start their re-election bid.

What Clark eventually unveiled on June 22, 2017, will probably go down as one of the most risky, contentious throne speeches in provincial history. Depending on whom you ask, it was a monstrosity of poor judgement, a desperate Hail Mary pass, or a long-overdue shift by the party to the kind of social spending and centrist policies it should have embraced years earlier.

Most Liberal MLAs didn't know the entirety of the speech until Lieutenant-Governor Judith Guichon started reading it in the House. Enough had been leaked over the previous week that the NDP and the Greens knew that many of their ideas had been borrowed and repurposed for political effect in the speech. But until the words came out of Guichon's mouth, there was no sense of how much was borrowed.

"The May election delivered a divided result," said Guichon. "Your government has listened to that result and brings forward this agenda to gain this house's confidence and, in doing so, the confidence of the people of British Columbia. It is submitted with humility and openness to change."

In total, the speech made forty-five commitments, thirty of which weren't in the previous Liberal budget or its election campaign platform. Some of them were stunning flip-flops. That NDP proposal to ban corporate and union donations that the Liberals had fought so stubbornly for more than six months? Now the Liberals were willing to do it. Scrapping tolls on Metro Vancouver bridges, which the Liberals had insisted was financially reckless? We'll find the money to do it, the government said. A referendum on electoral reform that the Liberals had deemed unnecessary? Now very necessary. The Massey Tunnel replacement bridge, which Clark had pushed forward for years despite the opposition of local Metro Vancouver mayors? Now up for review, with an acknowledgement of all the concerns. The carbon tax, which the Liberals had promised to freeze until 2021? Now it would jump by five dollars a tonne in 2019.

And so on. Promise after promise, flip-flop after flip-flop. More than $1 billion in new funding for child care, in a nod toward both the Green and NDP proposals to make it more affordable. And a hundred-dollar hike to income assistance that the Liberals had chosen not to enact in February was now back on the table.

The next day, *The Province* captured what many felt with its front-page headline: "CLONE SPEECH." The reaction from most media and pundits was cynical. It looked less like the Liberals were changing their stripes and more like they were desperately trying to persuade one MLA from either the Greens or NDP to break ranks and vote with the Liberals.

Internally, that was part of the Liberal strategy. But the other motivation was simpler: if the province was headed for another election, the new throne speech, complete with its massive shift on hot-button issues important to voters, would form the Liberal party's new pitch. Basically, the throne speech would become the election platform. For Clark, it represented where the party had come up short in the eyes of voters during the election.

The NDP and Greens were not long in rejecting the Liberal proposal.

"We've made it very clear that we believe that the BC Liberals need to be put in a time-out," said Weaver.

"You can't change after an election," said Horgan. "You have to change before an election... It is our intention at the earliest opportunity to seek a confidence vote, dismiss the government, and move on to put in place a government that will work for people."

The NDP prepared a poison pill for the throne speech, in the form of an amendment declaring no confidence in the government. But the rules of the legislature would mean it would be a week before the vote could be called. The Liberals used that week to stir up more trouble.

On Monday, June 26, everyone expected the Liberals to table legislation to ban corporate and union donations. Instead, first, the government tried to catch the Greens by surprise with a different tactic.

They tabled a bill with the obtuse and vague title of "Legislative Assembly Management Committee Act, 2017." Almost nobody knew what it meant.

"I wonder if the House might recess long enough to ensure that the bill can be distributed to members before the vote," said de Jong.

What the Liberals were actually proposing was to give the three Green MLAs official party status, along with more funding for their opposition caucus. It was something the Greens had specifically requested. Now the Liberals had put them in the position of having to potentially vote down one of their key requests.

De Jong and Weaver met at the back of the chamber, where they discussed the bill. Weaver went back to his seat beside MLAs Sonia Furstenau and Adam Olsen.

"That was legislation to grant us party status," Weaver whispered. "To me, it's a $25,000 bribe," he added, referencing the pay hike he'd get for passing it.

Weaver asked Olsen and Furstenau to think whether they wanted to vote down $10,000 pay increases for them as well.

"It's thought about," retorted Olsen. "Done."

The Liberals, meanwhile, heckled the Greens from the other side. "Are you going to have to ask your buddy John about how to vote?" one of them shouted, referencing Horgan.

The vote was called. The Greens and NDP aligned to kill it, 44–42.

The Liberal government moved on. Next was the bill to ban corporate and union donations. The Liberals had fought for months against this very idea, as proposed by the NDP, using scare tactics to make it sound like electoral reform would ultimately result in taxpayers footing a multi-million-dollar bill to fund political parties (which it ultimately did). But desperate times required desperate measures. And so now electoral reform was literally on the table of the legislature's clerk.

The Liberals viewed their political donation flip-flop as a no-lose proposition. They were showing the public they'd listened and learned on an important issue. They were pressuring the Greens to break ranks with the NDP to pass a law immediately, rather than wait several months. If it passed, they might be able to use the vote as an argument that they'd obtained the confidence of the House and should be allowed to govern. And if it failed, they had their own comprehensive bill (including specific provisions to prevent unions from donating in-kind resources) that they'd later use in opposition to hammer the NDP if their eventual legislation wasn't quite as detailed.

But Weaver and the Greens had already declared it a non-starter and didn't blink. The bill officially died by a vote of 44–42.

On a day of history-making events, the defeat of the two bills was also notable. It was the first time in sixteen years that the Liberals had failed to pass what they wanted in the House. And it was the first time in BC's history that a government bill had been defeated in what was called "first reading" stage, killing it before it was ever even read in the legislature. Normally, MLAs agree to at least hear the bill before they kill it. Voting this way meant both bills were effectively scrubbed from history. They aren't archived on the legislature website. It was as if they'd never happened. The vote was a strategy suggested by NDP house leader Mike Farnworth. He wanted to send a message to the Liberals: you've already lost the confidence of this House. The weakened Liberals left the legislature that day licking their wounds. But they still intended to cause trouble.

Later in the week, de Jong formally asked new Speaker Steve Thomson for written "clarity" on the rules of the legislature concerning the Speaker. If the NDP formed the government with Green help, they'd have to put one of their forty-four MLAs up as Speaker, leaving every vote deadlocked in a 43–43 tie with the Liberals. That scenario would force the Speaker (who is supposed to be a non-partisan referee) to become just another partisan NDP MLA whipped into voting for his or her party at every turn.

It was an esoteric point for most British Columbians, who have never either heard of or had reason to care about the Speaker of the legislature. The most they probably knew about the Speaker's job was that it came with a weird triangle hat. But it was another plank in a case the Liberals were building to make the NDP government appear unworkable before it had even started.

Behind the scenes, the Liberal party was also seriously prepping for a new election. Michele Cadario was put in charge of organizing a campaign that could start the moment the Liberal government fell. The forty-three Liberal MLAs all committed to running again in a snap election. Cadario and McDonald were set to run the campaign. The party had secured lines of credit, though the plan was to spend considerably less. Signs would be reused, materials recycled. The tour would focus heavily on the Lower Mainland, with volunteers and candidates from secure Liberal ridings coming down to pitch in on the tougher fights to save costs. Clark might travel to the Peace region, Kamloops, and Prince George once, but the bulk of the tour would focus on Surrey, Vancouver, and the Metro Vancouver battleground.

DESPITE ALL THE last-minute machinations, the Liberals ultimately could not avoid the confidence vote in the House.

BC's election night might have been on May 9, but it wouldn't be until fifty-one days later that British Columbians truly understood the results. June 29, 2017, will go down in the history books as one of the most interesting and important days in provincial political history.

It started, oddly enough, like almost any other at the BC legislature. MLAs held an opening morning prayer. Then Donna Barnett started talking about cows. Cattle ranching is big in Barnett's riding of Cariboo-Chilcotin, and the MLA used some of her time debating the throne speech in the early morning to extol the virtues of first-class beef suppliers. It's quite possible that no one was paying attention to Barnett's speech except her. Everyone was readying for the main event later that afternoon. But, in the meantime, the day would be notable for similar mundane discussions, as one of the most historic moments in the chamber's history loomed that afternoon.

"Comparing notes with the Minister of Transportation, we've calculated that between my family and his, there are probably about a half a dozen people watching right now," joked Environment Minister Mary Polak as she started her speech. "I jest. Although I'm certain the ratings for Hansard are going to rise significantly around about 5 p.m. or so today."

Five o'clock was roughly when the eighty-seven MLAS were set to gather to vote on a motion of non-confidence in Clark's Liberal government. You didn't need an advanced degree in mathematics to figure out the numbers. Ever since the Green-NDP power-sharing deal had been signed, it was clear that the two Opposition parties had a combined forty-four votes, compared with forty-three for the Liberals.

But Clark had one last meeting to convene before 5 p.m. Education Minister Mike Bernier walked down to the basement of the legislature and knocked on the door of Green leader Weaver.

"Would you be willing to meet the premier?" asked Bernier.

"I'd be delighted," said Weaver.

The two walked to Clark's west annex office, where the premier was spending her final hours in government with her son, Hamish.

"Andrew, what are you doing?" Clark asked Weaver. "You are driving your party off a cliff."

Clark made one last pitch: you don't have to have an alliance with the BC Liberals. Just be independent. Do what you think is right. Make us vote with your ideas. Vote with the NDP when their ideas are better.

"Actually be somebody rather than a footnote in history," charged Clark.

Weaver wouldn't do it.

"Please understand the decision is not personal," Weaver told her.

When Weaver left, Clark knew it was over, her last attempt to persuade him unsuccessful.

WHILE CLARK WAS adjusting to the reality of her imminent defeat, NDP leader John Horgan was adjusting to a new kind of reality: he could become premier within a matter of hours.

New Democrats had a good feeling about things. Earlier that morning, Horgan's chief of staff, Bob Dewar, had taken a call from Lieutenant-Governor Judith Guichon's private secretary, Jeremy Brownridge. He'd wanted to know what number Guichon could reach Horgan at that evening if she wanted to call on him to come for a meeting. Dewar was left with the very clear impression he'd be getting a call back later that night.

"We're in, baby," Dewar told Horgan.

The boss was more cautious. "Yeah, we'll wait and see," said Horgan.

But they nonetheless shared a smile, both thinking the same thing: the only reason to call him that night would be to ask him to form a government.

THE PUBLIC GALLERIES of the BC legislature are not typically full at 5:40 p.m. on a Thursday. But on this extraordinary day, two hundred people came to have a first-hand view of political history.

On one side of the legislative chamber sat Clark, surrounded by forty-one BC Liberals members. Across from her sat forty-one New Democrats and three Greens. Emotions were still raw from the election, seven weeks earlier, and from a week of bickering and sniping between the benches. Clark rose to give what would be her final speech to the legislature.

At times she was contrite.

"Now, you know, when I've been successful in my life, it has been because I've been a fighter," she said, acknowledging public criticism of her partisan tendencies. "But I know, as I reflect on this election, that British Columbians want something different from me and they want something different from all of the members in this House. That's why we put forward a throne speech with an open mind and deep humility..."

At times she was conciliatory.

"When we go into political combat, we all acknowledge that we sometimes spend so much energy fighting with one another in here that it's hard to listen to what British Columbians want," said Clark. "The throne speech is an answer to that. It's an answer to what voters told us on May 9. It's an acknowledgement—a sincere acknowledgement—that we didn't get it all right. It is an expression of renewed priorities, based on what voters told us, including that they want us to work across party lines with one another."

But the premier couldn't resist taking a swipe or two at Weaver, for rejecting her continued overtures up to, and including, their secret meeting that day.

"We attempted, in good faith, to work with the Greens, but they wouldn't even hear our offer," she said. "The member from Oak Bay came here saying he wanted a more civil debate, more good ideas being adopted from all parties, and instead, he behaved exactly like those he's criticized all these years. This week we kept that door open. The member from Oak Bay knows it stayed open, but he still decided to slam it shut."

"And what have the NDP offered in the last six weeks?" she added. "Grasping for power and vowing to twist the rules of our legislature in order to hang on to it."

Clark closed with a bit of a foreshadowing that she wouldn't be back to address the chamber again.

"If this marks the end of our government, then I stand here in humility and with great gratitude to the people of British Columbia," she said.

During her speech, Clark looked across the aisle for Horgan. But he wasn't there. His staff had made the decision to keep him out of the House, in an almost symbolic gesture of disdain for the Liberal government's last gasp. He wouldn't enter the chamber until just before he had to vote.

Across the aisle, Clark did lock eyes with former NDP cabinet minister Moe Sihota, who was sitting in a chair along the wall reserved for former MLAs. The two were old combatants from the 1990s, when Clark had on more than one occasion managed to cause Sihota, then a cabinet minister, to lose his cool in the chamber under questioning. They had a kind of shared respect that came from being veteran political street-fighters, divisive public figures, and contentious characters of political history. He gave her a look that was the unspoken equivalent of "nice try." Clark saw in her old foe confidence that the NDP was going to form a government.

Clark's speech concluded. There was nothing left to do but vote.

NDP MLA George Chow too arrived just before the vote. The rookie MLA had felt the call of nature during the premier's speech, and had chosen perhaps the most inopportune time to go to the bathroom in modern political history. Just before the doors locked for the vote, Chow rushed back to his seat.

Clark saw the look of satisfaction on the NDP faces and guessed, correctly, they'd somehow been tipped off by the lieutenant-governor's office about her decision.

At first, there was silence. Then Steve Thomson, the Speaker, called an amended version of the province's speech from the throne to a vote. Thomson read aloud to the members:

> Seeing no further speakers, the question is the amendment to the Address in Reply to the Speech from the Throne moved by the Leader of the Official Opposition, seconded by the member for Cowichan Valley, which reads that:

"Be it resolved that the motion 'We, Her Majesty's most dutiful and loyal subjects, the Legislative Assembly of British Columbia in Session assembled, beg leave to thank Your Honour for the gracious Speech which Your Honour has addressed to us at the opening of the present Session,' be amended by adding the following: 'but Her Honour's present government does not have the confidence of this House.'"

In near equal measure, those gathered to the Speaker's left called out yea, followed shortly by the nays to his right. Then they waited, in silence. Clerks counted each member to ensure their vote was cast into provincial record. The forty-one NDP MLAS all voted in favour of the motion. The three Green MLAS did the same. The vote total was read aloud by deputy clerk Kate Ryan-Lloyd: it was 44–42. (Liberal Speaker Thomson did not vote.) The throne speech had officially been amended to include the poison pill of non-confidence.

Now the amended speech had to be adopted by the legislature. A second vote was called, with the same procedures. It passed again, 44–42. The government had officially fallen on a confidence vote for the first time since 1953.

Those watching in the public gallery weren't sure how to react. They had been told by security on the way in that they were not to cheer, clap, stomp, or make any type of noise. Their cell phones had been confiscated before they sat down.

But soon the formalities were over. Thomson stood in the Speaker's chair for the last time to declare, "The House stands adjourned until further notice."

First the NDP cheered, then the Greens, and then, almost in unison, the supporters of both parties who had come to watch from above. Outside the chamber, where about two dozen journalists were waiting, the cheering was so loud it reverberated down the empty hallways and shook the walls.

Liberal MLAs started to empty the chamber in front of the waiting media. But it was Clark everyone was waiting for.

Once all of the members had left, Clark stepped out. It was a walk Clark had done hundreds of times. This one was different. Her head held high, tears in her eyes, she strode out the double doors of the legislative chamber and through a gauntlet of MLAs and staff who'd packed the building's Memorial Rotunda, cheering, clapping, and shouting in support of their leader. It was a moment of solidarity for the beleaguered premier, who, just minutes earlier, had watched sixteen years of Liberal rule crumble in a historic confidence vote in the House. Clark smiled to the assorted crowd of ministers and political aides, as TV networks carried her walk live on the evening news. She soaked it in, the tears forming in her eyes gone once she brushed them away. The whole walk lasted only about a minute and thirty seconds. Clark thanked the last well-wisher near the doorway to the premier's west annex and stepped through to the second-floor breezeway. She and her staff walked inside.

Clark stopped, took a deep breath, and thought, "Alright. Now I have to go make my best argument. This is a historic moment."

THE LIBERALS HAD earlier tried one last trick to influence the lieutenant-governor. Clark's office had quietly proposed bringing Finance Minister Mike de Jong to Government House, where the veteran house leader, who knew the intricacies of legislative procedure better than anyone else, would try to help convince Guichon, with the aid of charts and graphs, that the NDP and Greens could not govern without breaking the unwritten conventions that make the legislature function. But Guichon's staff had shut that idea down quickly. The meeting was meant to be a traditional, private one between only the lieutenant-governor and the premier.

And so, with her options exhausted, Clark prepared to meet her fate at Government House.

"Here we go, guys," she said to her staff, as they walked out the door.

The first thing Clark noticed outside the legislature was the CTV News Chopper 9 helicopter buzzing overhead, broadcasting her departure live. She and her staff quickly piled into the armoured minivan used by the RCMP to transport the premier to events. Press secretary Stephen Smart joked to the Mountie behind the wheel that, with the helicopter following them, this was their OJ moment (in reference to the famous moment in 1994 when helicopters followed OJ Simpson's speeding white Bronco).

Don't screw it up while the province is watching live, Smart said.

They all laughed. But then the minivan unceremoniously bottomed out on the legislature driveway due to the weight of all the staff, scraping and smashing the concrete below. Shortly after, the RCMP officer who was driving almost blew a stop sign. Everyone was nervous, including the cops.

Inside the cramped vehicle, there was momentary small talk before communications boss Ben Chin and chief of staff Mike McDonald steered Clark to the topic of whether the lieutenant-governor would call an election. It's very unlikely that the lieutenant-governor will take that route, they told her, and you have to be prepared to be rejected. Chin and McDonald made a further point—she'd need to give advice to the lieutenant-governor if asked. There's no way around that. If you're asked, and you want an election, you need to recommend it, they said.

For several days, Clark had been artfully trying to appear as if she didn't want another election, when secretly her staff had pinned their entire hopes on such a call. She faced blowback from voters, who had gone to the polls just seven weeks earlier and might take out their frustration at having to do so again on the Liberals.

Constitutional experts were clear: Clark was obliged to give the lieutenant-governor advice if asked. She couldn't sit there mute. She could either recommend an election or recommend that the lieutenant-governor ask Horgan to form a government. But Clark had tried to create an artful "third option." She had told media a day earlier that she'd only give advice if asked and wouldn't volunteer it formally. But if asked, she'd recommend a new election. The ultimate call would be Guichon's, Clark had told the press corps, in an obvious attempt to pin any blowback on the lieutenant-governor.

Reporters accused Clark of trying to push an election without calling for one.

"If she asks me a question, am I supposed to lie?" Clark shot back in her typically combative way with the media. "Or should I just say, 'I'm sorry, your honour, I can't talk about that'?"

The third option was a mixture of bad advice and political smoke and mirrors. Clark knew it was highly unlikely she could get a new election and skate by without looking like she'd called for one.

Even without Clark's third-option antics, Guichon was in a bit of a constitutional quagmire. In all but the rarest of circumstances, the unelected lieutenant-governor is constitutionally obliged to take the advice of the elected premier. But constitutional experts also said the lieutenant-governor had a duty, by convention, to call upon other parties that might be able to form a government because it was so close to the last election. They spoke of a generally accepted six-month window after an election, in which a lieutenant-governor would be more inclined to look for another party to govern than plunge a fatigued electorate back into another vote.

The general consensus among academics appeared to be that if Horgan was to assure her he could command the confidence of the House, then Guichon would be obliged to take him at his word and give him the chance to succeed or fail in the legislature. To dismiss the Green-NDP alliance out of hand, when the two sides had a written framework of governance, could cause the lieutenant-governor to make a decision that would plunge the province into a constitutional crisis.

Still, the lieutenant-governor has extraordinary powers to act in the province's best interest. She could make whatever decision she wanted.

As an unelected representative of the Queen, she was also supposed to take and act on the advice of the premier, unless that advice was not, in her mind, in the best interests of the province.

Press secretary Smart asked the RCMP drivers to drop Clark off at the bottom of the winding driveway that leads to the Government House mansion in the upper-class Rockland neighbourhood of Victoria, where the vice-regal representative was waiting inside. He had suggested that the visuals be of Clark walking alone to meet the lieutenant-governor, without any staff or police, and Clark agreed.

So Clark made the long walk up the driveway, past the small army of assembled journalists, unaccompanied. All the while, she stared straight ahead, ignoring the questions called out to her, as she strolled past the press line under the covered carriageway and up the red carpet–lined stairs to the open double doors. Inside, in front of a massive stone fireplace at the top of the stairs flanked by portraits of Queen Elizabeth II and Prince Philip, she met the lieutenant-governor's private secretary, Jeremy Brownridge, who shook her hand and escorted her down a long wood-panelled hallway to the French drawing room. Several of Clark's staff were already waiting there, having entered through the side door, including Smart and events coordinator Anish Dwivedi. Chin and McDonald would join them shortly.

The French drawing room had been a frequent waiting area for Clark during her visits to Government House as premier. The last time she'd been in the room, eight months earlier, it had been filled with toys as the designated play area for toddler Prince George, during the visit of Prince William and Kate Middleton. Clark settled into one of the many gold- and cream-coloured chairs. Her staff asked for a few minutes and slid closed the drawing room doors. The premier's staff had noticed that the previously friendly Government House staff was now stiff, formal, and nervous as well.

The premier already knew what she wanted to say to Guichon. So this last moment of preparation before she met the lieutenant-governor was mostly an intense one of realization that everything was riding on the next few minutes, combined with the surreal feeling that they were also all part of a historic moment, no matter what happened.

When Clark emerged from the drawing room, Brownridge led her down a corridor beside the French drawing room, past a replica of the throne chair used in the legislature, and into Guichon's private office. Tea was served. Wine would follow. The meeting lasted around forty-five minutes. During much of that time, Clark was making her pitch.

When the meeting ended, Clark went back to the French drawing room to tell her staff it was all over. Government House officials had expected the premier to then leave, but soon heard that she intended to stay until Guichon had made her decision. The two sides appeared confused over the order of their press conferences. Government House wanted Clark to go outside and address the media first. Clark wanted to wait for Guichon's decision and then speak.

Brownridge told Clark's staff that Guichon wouldn't announce any decision with Clark still in the building. Then he left to stand outside with the press corps and assembled crowd on the front steps of the mansion.

Clark, however, still did not leave.

Chin and Smart called Brownridge back in to ask what Clark should say to the reporters waiting outside. That's up to her, Brownridge replied, but she could simply go outside and tell the media what had happened: she'd offered her resignation and recommended dissolution for a new election.

Clark's staff balked at the idea of having the fallen premier use that spotlight moment to publicly announce she'd reneged on her promise not to trigger a new election. Nor did they want her to get into the intricacies of how she was obliged to resign. There was also a feeling that details of the chat might put Guichon in a kind of jam, and Clark didn't want to do that either.

Clark and her staff huddled in that French drawing room for forty minutes. Which means that of the approximately ninety minutes Clark spent inside Government House, only half was actually spent in conversation with Guichon. The rest was an extended session in political damage control.

Clark eventually emerged to make a brief statement.

"Thank you for waiting. The Lieutenant-Governor and I had a very good long conversation, as I think you can guess given the amount of time we were there," she said. "She has now retired to make her decision and I'm going to wait and respect her time to do that. And when she has made that decision, and made that decision public, I will be available to all of you to offer any comment."

She added, "I know that people want to know, and with everyone else in British Columbia, I'll be waiting too."

Clark and her staff then left Government House, feeling Guichon had already made up her mind before they'd even got there.

They were right. The vice-regal representative had largely settled on her decision to call on Horgan to govern before Clark arrived, say those privy to Guichon's deliberations. But there was enough flexibility in her thinking that had Clark played her cards differently, Guichon might have reversed course and been seriously tempted to take the premier up on her election call.

There is a theory that Clark committed a fatal error that night. During her press conference outside Government House, she failed to tell the public that she'd recommended a new election. Had she done so, it would have put significant public pressure on Guichon, and those who were there that night think it's possible Guichon could have fallen in line with Clark's request.

Clark, who'd spent part of her forty-five minutes with the lieutenant-governor trying to persuade her to call an election, doesn't believe there was anything she could have said outside to the media that would have changed Guichon's mind. But there will never be a definite answer.

Guichon had been watching Clark's public comments via live-stream on her computer. As soon as Clark finished, Brownridge came into Guichon's office. The premier had made things easier. Brownridge picked up the phone and called Horgan.

Back at the legislature, huddled around a television inside chief of staff McDonald's office, half a dozen of Clark's senior staff watched the premier leave Government House. The office is a modest room next to the premier's expansive suite, just a short walk down the hallway in the legislature's west annex.

Hamish sat alone in his mom's office, with its view of the legislature's front lawn. It was the best political real estate in BC, but a lonely spot for a teenager to hold a silent vigil for his mother. Eventually, recognizing he was stressed and hungry, staffers went out to get him a pizza.

The prevailing theory was that the lieutenant-governor would now consult with constitutional scholars and begin a detailed study of the issue. Visions of leather-bound ancient texts, full of convention and constitutional rules, were conjured up. It was the wrong read of the situation.

Clark arrived back in her legislature office roughly ten minutes later. During the ride, her normally effervescent mood had been subdued, and she seemed down. She could read the writing on the wall.

Her staff leaned out of McDonald's office to watch her walk in. Clark offered merely a shrug of her shoulders. She went into her office, where someone had added sushi to the menu with the pizza, and ate dinner with her son. Everyone mostly left her alone, though Mike de Jong arrived for a debrief.

IN A DIFFERENT room at the legislature—within throwing distance if you had a good arm—John Horgan and his staff were nervously waiting to see if they'd get a call.

Around ten people were in chief of staff Bob Dewar's office, also watching television coverage of the developments at Government

House. Horgan paced in and out of the room with his lacrosse stick, hurling a soft stress ball against the wall of his adjoining office and catching it, again and again. The longer Clark was inside, the more confused and worried the group became. They thought Guichon had made up her mind, so why would she be speaking with Clark for more than an hour?

It didn't seem likely to them, or to others even in the Liberal camp, that Horgan would be asked up to Government House simply to be quizzed by Guichon on his intentions, or to have the news of a new election broken to him personally. No, once that phone rang, Horgan was as good as premier.

But to add to the New Democrats' confusion, Clark told the media following her meeting that the lieutenant-governor had "retired to make her decision."

Dewar took out his phone and started to compose a text message to Brownridge. He wanted to know what Clark meant when she said Guichon had retired for the evening. As he did, his phone rang in his hand.

"Bob," said Brownridge. "This is your million-dollar call."

"Really?" asked Dewar.

"Yeah. Can you come right over?"

"We'll be right over."

Dewar grabbed his bag.

"Let's go," he said to Horgan.

The man who was about to become premier-designate now wore the weird smile of a man who wasn't sure this was really happening. As he grabbed his belongings and prepared to leave, he started hugging everyone he could see.

Press secretary Sheena McConnell's husband, Liam, brought the car around.

Horgan called Weaver.

"Andrew, I just got the call," he said. "Just letting you know I'm headed to the lieutenant-governor's office."

Weaver congratulated him and expressed confidence that the lieutenant-governor would make the right decision. As they were talking, Horgan emerged from the library entrance of the legislature, where Weaver's ground-floor windows were. The Green leader threw open a window and yelled, "Good luck!" as Horgan rushed by.

It was a long drive for Horgan and crew, even though it was really only ten minutes. They made small talk to cut the tension. Dewar wanted to know why the trip was taking so long. Isn't Government House, like, a block away from the legislature, the Manitoban asked. Not in British Columbia.

Horgan was a bundle of nervous excitement, but his instincts on that long drive led him to believe the lieutenant-governor was in his corner.

"I know she's going to ask me to form a government, I just know it. In my bones I can feel it," he said in an interview for this book.

Horgan, Dewar, and McConnell entered Government House and almost immediately knew it was good news. When Horgan was escorted to see Guichon, Government House officials gave Dewar a copy of a press release they'd prepared announcing Horgan had been asked to form a government. Dewar texted Marie Della Mattia, who was back in his office at the legislature.

"We did it," was the message. It was 8:01 p.m.

Government House wanted the NDP to wait and hand out the paper press release as Horgan exited the building. At 8:08 p.m. Dewar sent out a text anyway, kicking into action the NDP's digital communications team.

Inside the lieutenant-governor's office, Horgan and Guichon had a relatively short chat, compared with the forty-five-minute conversation between Clark and Guichon.

Horgan awkwardly broke the ice.

"So," he said. "This is interesting."

"Yes, it's been quite an experience," said Guichon. "I have two questions for you. Do you have the confidence of the House?"

"I believe I do," responded Horgan.

A photo taken at that moment shows Guichon leaning back casually with her legs crossed in one red-leather chair, while Horgan sits in another, literally on the edge of his seat, leaning forward, his arms resting on his knees, smiling.

"Can you form a government?" asked Guichon.

"Yes," said Horgan.

"Well, best of luck," concluded Guichon.

With that, Guichon's private secretary, Brownridge, excused himself from the room to start preparations for announcing the new government. Guichon and Horgan would make small talk for a few more minutes, during which the lieutenant-governor explained she'd talked to experts and the only recourse when the province had just had an election was to give Horgan a chance.

Horgan emerged from the meeting as premier-designate. He met his staff in the French drawing room, where Brownridge introduced him to Government House staff, saying, "And here's your premier."

Horgan gave them all big bear hugs.

"This is the moment we've been waiting for," said Dewar, after the embrace.

"Wow," replied Horgan, smiling.

Horgan wanted to call his wife, Ellie, but he didn't have his phone. He used McConnell's iPhone, but Ellie, who was at home in Langford, didn't recognize the number and didn't pick up. Horgan had to leave a message.

"Hey Elle, it's me, the premier, calling," Horgan left on the machine. "I'll see ya soon."

The public was waiting to see what would happen next. Networks carried live shots of the front doors, waiting for any movement. The first announcement of a new NDP government came in a fittingly modern form: a tweet from Horgan's account.

"Today British Columbians finally have the change they voted for," it said. "Thank you to everyone who got us here. The hard work starts now."

The tweet was quickly followed by an email to NDP supporters from the new premier-designate, saying Guichon had asked him to form a government. Outside, the small crowd that had gathered on the Government House driveway broke into applause and cheers.

BACK AT THE legislature, Clark's press secretary, Smart, saw the tweet. He dashed to Clark's office, where she was still talking to de Jong about the conversation with the lieutenant-governor.

"Premier, I'm really sorry to be the one to tell you this, but I should read you this tweet that John Horgan put out," Smart said.

As he read out Horgan's message, he watched his boss physically deflating with the words.

"Okay," she said simply.

Smart left, and Clark and de Jong had a moment alone, sitting in the chairs beside the window overlooking the legislature lawn.

"Well, it's over," the fallen premier said.

And then she started talking about resigning. Other staff, like Chin, began trickling into the room.

"I should just do it now and get it out of the way," she said, of quitting.

"Premier, tonight is not the night for you to make such a decision," replied Chin.

De Jong was more direct. "You're not going to resign tonight," he said.

De Jong argued that the evening belonged to Horgan, and after all the work she'd put into her party she should wait for her own moment to announce, in a more dignified way, that she was through. Eventually, Clark agreed.

Later that night, Clark would approach some of the remaining staff, including Smart and Jessica Wolford, with Hamish at her side, and ask bluntly, "Should I resign?" Everyone said no.

The now toppled premier had a flight to catch at the airport, but as she was leaving she saw cameras in the rose garden outside her office and went over to make a brief statement about the decision. In it, she revealed publicly that she'd advised the lieutenant-governor to call an election, and then congratulated Horgan on becoming premier.

Horgan emerged from Government House to address the media.

"It's my honour to stand before you," he said. "I've just spoken with the lieutenant-governor and she's asked me if I have the confidence of the legislature to form a government and I've told her I do."

A crowd of almost two dozen onlookers burst into applause, interrupting his speech with their cheering and hollering.

"I look forward to working harder than I've ever worked before," said the new premier-designate.

Back in Horgan's office, Della Mattia, who'd spent virtually twenty-eight days straight at Horgan's side during the election, transforming him into what the public saw as a premier-in-waiting, sat down in front of the TV, listened to his speech, and cried.

Celebrations broke out in various NDP offices throughout the building, as MLAs and staffers realized they'd finally won power.

Meanwhile, Clark and Hamish left the building for Victoria International Airport, where they ran into minsters Todd Stone and Mary Polak, already at the airport bar having a drink. Clark joined them, commiserating until their commercial flight to Vancouver was ready to depart.

Clark arrived home to her dark and empty house in Vancouver's Dunbar neighbourhood close to midnight. Hamish informed his mother, in the fashion typical of a fifteen-year-old, that he was starving.

So Clark made him toast and sent him to bed. The premier herself felt a relief that weeks of stress were over, one way or another.

Back in Victoria, as the evening wound down, everyone would end up at various bars, in varying moods and degrees of intoxication.

Liberal staff walked across the street from the legislature to an old bar nicknamed "The Swifty" that the Liberals had adopted as their watering hole over the years. Around thirty staffers had gathered. The mood was funereal. It had finally begun to sink in: there would be no miracle comebacks. The Liberal dynasty was over.

Horgan was down the street, holding court at the Garrick's Head Pub, with a growing celebratory crew of New Democrats. As he was leaving Government House, he'd told the media his first move as premier-designate would be to find some food because he was hungry. He wasn't kidding. But at the bar, he was swarmed by staff, well-wishers, and the public. It would be a while before someone ordered him a hamburger—no onions and hold the mayo—and a Diet Coke. By then the new leader of the province was well into a debate with a bar-goer about whether the best Star Trek television series was *Voyager* or *Deep Space Nine* (Horgan is firmly in the *Voyager* camp).

Even Guichon kicked back to relax. She'd made it through one of the most stressful and contentious days in the history of her office. But it was so late now that the building's chef had already gone home for the night. So she and six staffers went for a bite to eat at the Ross Bay Pub, where patrons appeared surprised by the attendance of the woman who'd just made BC history.

ONLY GUICHON KNOWS for sure how she made her final decision. But more has emerged on whom she talked to. It seems likely that Guichon solicited the opinion of the then governor general, David Johnston. Guichon had recently been at a public event in Ottawa, where she met with Johnston—by profession a legal and constitutional expert—and it's widely believed that led to his providing advice on what to do about the BC situation. BC's chief electoral officer, Keith Archer, also gave her advice, centred mainly on the fact that he was logistically able to conduct a new election if that was the decision she chose.

Guichon had the right to ask anyone she wanted. She asked clerk of the legislature Craig James for advice, as well as two former MLAs, Social Credit attorney general Brian Smith and Liberal universities minister Ida Chong. Chong had always been friendly with Guichon during the annual New Year's Day levees at Government House, so she sent a note to Brownridge before the Clark government fell asking for an opportunity to give her opinion and was granted a half-hour audience. Chong advised Guichon that she personally wanted to see a new election, because the close margin meant the opposition would spend its entire time focused on bringing down the government and it would be problematic. She was surprised when the lieutenant-governor made the opposite call.

It's likely that Guichon talked to a constitutional law expert of some kind, but exactly who is unclear. The leading constitutional law expert in the country is Peter W. Hogg, a professor emeritus at the University of Toronto who has long advised governments, vice-regal representatives, and governors general. Guichon's office phoned Hogg one day, but he missed the call. Hogg returned the call. But the lieutenant-governor never phoned back. Hogg, whom other scholars widely point to as the best resource for constitutional matters in Canada, never actually spoke to Guichon, and she never heard his advice.

Had the lieutenant-governor followed through, though, she would have heard from Hogg what several other scholars were saying in the wake of her decision to call upon Horgan: ultimately, constitutionally, the lieutenant-governor made the right decision.

CHAPTER 13
"I'M GOING TO QUIT"

At the end of Victoria's picturesque Ogden Point Breakwater, down a long walkway that stretches eight hundred metres into the Strait of Juan de Fuca, sits a small lighthouse. Beside it, a tiny set of stairs leads down to a rocky landing where your feet can touch the water.

There, on July 17, 2017, a crew of around twenty people toasted the end of their political careers with shot glasses, red cups, and a bottle of Scotch. These were the junior and mid-level members of the once-mighty BC Liberal political offices—the crew who kept the ministers and premier on schedule, the phones answered, the travel booked, and the speeches written. They had managed the meetings and events of some of the most powerful politicians. Now they were all out of jobs.

The staffers gathered for drinks at 4:30 p.m. to celebrate the official time the legislature was deactivating their keycards to make way for the incoming NDP administration, being sworn in the following morning. They toasted themselves for a job well done. And an uncertain future.

Across government, similar scenes of varying size (and alcohol content) were playing out as British Columbia lurched through an awkward transition, the likes of which it hadn't seen in sixteen years. At its core was the principle that the province must always have a premier and a cabinet. And so even when Christy Clark had fallen to defeat in the legislature, and even when John Horgan had emerged from Government House with the lieutenant-governor's request to form a government, Clark was still premier. Technically. Until Horgan could take the oath of office.

The NDP asked for nineteen days to formally prepare their transition into power. Liberal staffers began doing the once unthinkable: packing their offices.

A walk through the legislature at this point in time was a bit like strolling through a university dormitory at the end of semester. There were boxes stacked in hallways, overflowing with papers. Framed paintings and certificates rested against doors and walls on the floor outside ministerial offices. Office chairs, couches, desks, and conference tables began stacking up in the corridors outside both the opposition and government caucuses. There were also bags of shredded documents from both parties.

As the transition date drew nearer, Liberals whose keycards had given them access directly to the premier's suite now found themselves locked out at the side entrance of the building, watching tourists with reservations at the legislature's in-house restaurant hustle past them.

Clark never returned to the legislature after the night the lieutenant-governor rejected her advice. Her staff packed her belongings for her.

CLARK HIRED ONLY a small number of people back to her new Opposition leader's office: Stephen Smart, her press secretary; Jessica Wolford, an up-and-coming organizer who'd cut her teeth now on two provincial election campaigns; and Nick Koolsbergen, a former operative in Prime Minister Stephen Harper's office whom colleagues described as a kind of research ninja who was also shy and suspicious of outsiders. They joined thinking their leader would stick around until at least the spring of 2018, spearheading the party's efforts to drive a wedge between the Greens and NDP to somehow force a snap election.

But Clark had no intention of ever stepping into the legislature as Opposition leader. Internally, she was planning to resign later in the summer, before the legislature was recalled for the NDP's first session. There were two factors influencing Clark's plan. The first was her growing realization that Weaver and the Greens wouldn't bail on their NDP partners any time soon, and therefore no matter what she did a new election was highly unlikely. Clark had underestimated Weaver's willingness to stick with Horgan, despite early disagreements over things like a minimum wage commission and a ban on the grizzly bear trophy hunt. The second was, of all things, the pension plans for her Liberal colleagues.

MLAS enjoy a highly lucrative (some might say gold-plated) pension plan, but it only kicks in after six years of service. Several of the MLAS first elected in 2013 were already fed up with politics and were not planning to run again whenever the next election was called. If Clark had been successful in breaking up the NDP-Green alliance and triggering a new election that fall or spring, those MLAS would have ended their political careers around one year short of pension eligibility. They'd be giving up a base pension of $22,050 annually, for life.

Clark had been in politics for a long time, and she knew you couldn't underestimate how a person's financial self-interest can override all their other concerns. She counted at least four members of the 2013 class who weren't planning to run again and so were at risk of losing their pensions with an early election. She wasn't sure she could count on their support, or manage their concerns, as she tried to trigger a way for voters to head back to the polls early.

If Clark's plan really was to quit that summer, she certainly didn't let anyone in on it, including the new staff she'd hired.

Shortly before Horgan was sworn in, Liberals who had worked in the premier's office over the years were invited to a celebratory goodbye barbecue at Clark's house in Vancouver. For many, it was like a reunion. Present were old faces like Kim Haakstad, Clark's former deputy chief of staff, as well as some of her recent and current crew. The barbecue part of the evening failed to materialize, ditched in favour of sushi and samosas.

The boss, as some staff affectionately called her, made a short speech in her living room. She thanked everyone for their hard work over the years, recited some familiar job growth statistics and accomplishments, and then said what she was most proud of was to have worked with such a great staff. But the most interesting comment came during a short question-and-answer session that followed. Those who were there heard Clark make an explicit promise she'd be there until the following spring to help fight for another election with the first full NDP budget and throne speech next February.

Less than a four weeks later, her political career would be over.

ON JULY 26, 2017, when the Liberals met in Penticton for their first caucus meeting after being dethroned by the NDP-Green alliance, there was more than a small amount of angry grumbling. MLAs who had once ruled the roost as powerful cabinet ministers were starting to face the harsh reality of life on the opposition side.

First, there was the pay cut—a $52,940.92 hit for ex-ministers. But there was also the dawning realization that the ordinary day-to-day political life of once-important senior Liberals was about to get much tougher. Forget a phalanx of government staff available to book travel, answer phones, collate research, and print documents. Ministers who'd spent sixteen years surrounded by aides, assistants, and the vast resources of the civil service would now have to book their own travel, set up their own meetings, and write their own documents. There'd be no more oak-panelled ministerial offices with private bathrooms either.

The most senior Liberals would still be shoehorned into tiny cubicles in the far-from-glamorous Opposition offices at the legislature.

The anger wasn't directed at Clark specifically. Many still believed she had the jam to pull the party back into power. But Clark certainly felt the cooler atmosphere when she walked into the Penticton Lakeside Resort and Conference Centre to address her forty-two Liberal colleagues. She had already received a unanimous vote of support from the Liberal caucus on May 16. This time, though, the situation was different.

The former premier arrived midday Wednesday. She made a presentation to the caucus about restructuring the Opposition offices and getting ready to hold the new NDP government to account. When she finished, the Liberal MLAs got to their feet and delivered a standing ovation—everyone, that is, except one person.

Abbotsford South MLA Darryl Plecas had been slowly stewing since the election. And he continued to vent his frustration by sitting in his chair, not clapping, while all his colleagues rose around him to salute Clark. The former University of the Fraser Valley criminologist had been complaining about his party even before the final votes were counted. He used the acceptance speech in his constituency on May 9 to start to air his grievances.

"Our party should take a lesson from this... this close call here," he said, according to the *Abbotsford News*. "I think we have to speak to a broader group of people. It comes across sometimes that we are a very arrogant group of people. That's not the case, but it sometimes seems like that. I hope this makes us more humble and more respectful of the constituents overall."

A month later, he'd say the Liberals had been too "hell-bent on balanced budgets" and conservative forecasts while crises brewed on mental health, social programs, and housing affordability.

"We still have wanted to do these things—in caucus, we yell and scream about the need to do more—but it's always been up against:

'Yeah, but we will do those things so long as we can afford them,'"
Plecas told *The Vancouver Sun* on June 26.

Now, thirty days later, on July 26, he was fully going rogue.

Plecas wasn't a natural politician. He had never been a BC Liberal
member and had once been courted by the NDP. He'd defeated John
van Dongen, the former Liberal dissident who'd tried to push out Gordon Campbell and then Clark, to capture the riding of Abbotsford
South. Yet he would continue the grand tradition of MLAs from that
riding mutinying against their leader.

"It makes you wonder what's in the water in Abbotsford South," said
Ron Gladiuk, president of the riding association.

Regardless, as his colleagues were mingling at a Wednesday night
reception in the hotel, Plecas was alone in his room. Around 7 p.m.
Mike Bernier got a phone call.

"Bernier, what are you doing?" asked Plecas over the phone.

The Abbotsford South MLA had a bottle of Scotch in his room and
wanted his caucus colleague to stop by. Bernier never did.

At 8 a.m. the next day, Bernier's phone buzzed. It was a text from
Plecas.

"Bernier I didn't see you last night, can we talk?" it read.

Bernier went up to Plecas's room.

"Do you want to run for leader?" Plecas asked.

Bernier played along.

"Sure, at some point," he responded. But Bernier wasn't looking at
the job because the job wasn't open. Clark had control of the caucus
and wasn't sending any signs that she was ready to leave.

"No, now," said Plecas. "I am done."

Plecas was ready to speak out against Clark and was adamant that
she quit the party.

Bernier went downstairs. Clark was walking into the conference room with caucus when Bernier stopped her chief of staff Nick
Koolsbergen with a message: Plecas is going to speak out against your

leadership and is threatening to quit caucus to sit as an independent. Bernier's warning was passed to Clark, who by that point had no choice but to sit and wait for the inevitable. First, the Liberals re-elected MLA Jackie Tegart as caucus chair. Then it was time for MLAS to make statements.

Plecas stood up to make one hell of a statement. It covered a variety of issues, including intensely personal criticisms of Clark's mannerisms, like her insincere perma-smile, which Plecas labelled a smirk. The Liberals had run a terrible election campaign, for four years they'd been an uncaring government, people are tired of Clark, and he felt mistreated and bullied by unspecified staff in the premier's office who wouldn't let him speak freely or express himself.

It wasn't the first time Plecas had raised the latter issue. When he was sitting on the legislature's Select Standing Committee on Children and Youth he once praised the province's children's advocate, and vocal government critic, Mary Ellen Turpel-Lafond. Within minutes of the meeting he received a call from the premier's office.

"Did you just say what I think you did," said the voice on the other end.

"I did. And it's true. She is doing a good job," responded Plecas.

"I don't give a damn whether it is true or not," was the response.

As Plecas was planning his move in Penticton, all these memories came into play. He told his caucus colleagues that he was so sick of Clark's leadership that he was going to put out a press release Friday morning announcing his resignation from the Liberal caucus and plan to sit as an independent if Clark remained leader. Plecas closed his statement with two things: he would never mention that he had stood up to speak out against Clark, and whether she resigned or stayed on that she not say support in caucus was unanimous.

Clark, throughout, kept a blank look on her face and took the criticism. Loyalists shot death-stares at Plecas that, if looks could kill, would have melted him down to his loafers.

Clark rose to her feet and politely thanked Plecas for his thoughts, said she was sad to hear them but perhaps Plecas could stay in the room to have a frank discussion with his colleagues about what he'd said. She'd leave to give them time to talk, recognizing that if they didn't get it out of their system it would just bubble up somewhere else later.

Clark retreated to a small meeting room at the end of the hall.

"Well, this changes things," Clark told her staff as they regrouped around her.

What Plecas had done had irreversibly shattered whatever time-line Clark had been on to leave. To lose even one Liberal MLA in a legislature where the parties were virtually tied would have been a tre-mendous loss of clout for the Liberals and given the NDP enough easy breathing room to govern for years.

For Clark, though, the calculation was slightly different. At first she thought, Either Plecas will leave, or I will leave, but whatever happens the party is going to be down one vote and in a weaker position to fight the NDP.

But her mindset changed as she sat at the end of the hall.

Clark has said that in her heart she had wanted to leave ever since the lieutenant-governor asked Horgan to form a government. People kept talking her out of it, asking her to stay just a little longer to do one more thing, set up one more office, or hire one more staff. But her gut told her: get out now.

Inside the caucus room, the Liberal team was anything but united. There were several other MLAs who stood up to say they agreed with a lot of what Plecas had said but didn't want to say it to Clark's face. Caucus chair Tegart wanted MLAs to stay in the room until they'd made some type of decision. But Bernier faked having to go to the bathroom and snuck out to where Clark was waiting. The two walked outside onto a grassy area, where Clark kicked off her high-heeled shoes to walk barefoot in the grass.

"Am I okay?" she asked Bernier.

Bernier told her what was going on. Despite the undercurrent of goodwill toward their leader, there were some MLAs who wanted Clark gone before things got worse and the caucus split apart, like it had in Gordon Campbell's final months.

Bernier went back inside, and Clark talked to McDonald. They ran through ways to manage the different scenarios. But even as they spoke, Clark's mind was whirling in a different direction. Clark was thinking, This is my moment to leave. As she ran through the scenarios with McDonald, she realized she didn't want to do the job anymore.

The MLAs broke for lunch. Clark ate out on a patio area, and during the break a tearful Rich Coleman, her former deputy premier, came out to give her a hug, followed by Mike de Jong, her former finance minister. Others would join, including Shirley Bond, who took the attack on Clark by Plecas incredibly personally. At one point, as the events unfolded at the caucus retreat, Bond threatened to quit the party herself over how Clark was treated.

Afterwards Clark went back inside to address her caucus. Everyone but Plecas was there.

"Okay, you guys, look," began Clark. "I understand that there are a lot of people in this room that have complaints about the way things went… we're not going to talk about that yet. I want to talk to you about one thing: Do you want me to stay on as your leader or not? That's the only question we should be talking about right now."

The MLAs began standing up to talk. They all expressed support. But Clark noticed many would then digress into subtle complaints about how they'd like things to be different in the future and how they'd like to have more freedom. After several speakers, one Lower Mainland MLA stood up and alternated between saying he wanted her to stay on as leader and agreeing with Plecas that he hadn't had the freedom to be able to say what he wanted under her leadership.

Clark, who'd been listening intently up to this point, exploded in frustration. She'd prided herself on running caucus meetings in which everyone was allowed to vent, in a direct repudiation of the time she'd spent having to bite her tongue under Gordon Campbell. She tried to play referee, forcing her ministers to go out and explain their policies to MLAs and then overseeing the discussion with backbenchers over the merits of the plan. She'd always thought she was fostering open discussion. So the comment infuriated her.

"Are you kidding me?" said Clark. "Seriously? Does anybody remember Donna Barnett, who used to stand up every time in caucus and complain bitterly about everything government was doing? What happened to Donna? She got into cabinet. Pat Pimm, we'd spend hours on Pat's issues with natural gas and First Nations and guide outfitters. What happened to Pat? He got into cabinet... If you aren't speaking up it's because you choose not to speak up."

Other MLAs said they didn't want to be a "negative" Opposition; they wanted to be positive. This bothered Clark most of all. She'd been an effective Opposition critic in the 1990s, and she knew you did it by being highly critical of almost everything government did, not by playing meek, quiet, and conciliatory. More than anything, she'd later say this was the surest sign yet that the Liberals hadn't accepted their new reality. They were no longer government. They had to stop acting like government.

"You know, six years of looking these guys in the eye, I knew it was time for me to go," Clark would later say publicly. "I knew it. You can just tell. And a leader should know when it's her time to leave. I just don't admire people who hang on because they believe they are irreplaceable. Because nobody is irreplaceable."

At the end of the conversation, there was a kind of informal vote on her leadership. Everyone in the room stood up to ask her to stay. But Plecas had already left. Clark would later tell media she had unanimous support for remaining as leader from "everyone in the room," a sly bit of wording that skirted the actual truth of the matter.

"I'm going to spend some time tonight thinking about whether I'll stay or go," she told MLAs. "Thanks for all your feedback. I really appreciate it."

Back in Clark's meeting room, Koolsbergen, Smart, Jess Wolford, Primrose Carson, Mike McDonald, Sharon White, and Emile Scheffel huddled with their boss. They were irate about what had happened, but Clark, the political veteran who'd seen leaders toppled before, was more philosophical.

"This is what happens in politics," she said.

There was a dinner and reception that evening at Painted Rock Winery, where MLAs were supposed to mingle and bond. Clark wasn't there. Neither was Plecas.

Later that night, Chilliwack MLA John Martin came up to Clark's hotel room. He was one of Plecas's closest friends, but also close to Clark.

Martin is an interesting character. Since defecting from the BC Conservatives in 2012, he'd settled in comfortably with the Liberals and the premier. She trusted him. Short, stocky, and balding, with glasses and a greying beard, he looks every bit the criminologist that he is by training. But looks can be deceiving. He's also a musician and martial artist. He had enjoyed early punk rock and has stories of attending some of the wildest early concerts in Vancouver. One of his Shetland sheepdogs was named "The Dude." On weekends, he competes professionally as a master barbecuer.

Martin tried to persuade Clark not to decide her future on the basis of whatever Plecas might do. He's spoken out in caucus before, and that's just who he is and it's always worked out, said Martin. But we need you to stay as leader.

The wide belief among Liberals was that Clark had the loyalty and support to stay if she wanted. The caucus could eject Plecas, settle on their diminished position in the House, and carry on with Clark—for a while, at least.

Clark stayed in her hotel room and went to bed early.

She rose at 5:30 a.m. and called McDonald, whom she considered her most trusted political supporter and one of her oldest friends. The two donned shorts, T-shirts, and baseball caps and headed out for a walk along Okanagan Lake, outside the hotel. The sun was just rising, and the warm glow and fresh Okanagan air caused Clark to pause in thought.

"You know," she told him after a moment, "I'm going to quit."

Pierre Trudeau had his famous walk in the snow when he decided to quit as prime minister in 1984. Clark had a walk beside Okanagan Lake.

The two long-time friends and political operatives started to plot out Clark's departure from politics. At 7:30 a.m. they called over her staff, who arrived on the lakefront walkway to find an emotional Clark.

"I'm going to resign," she told them.

Clark phoned her son, Hamish, who was staying with his dad, her ex-husband Mark Marissen.

"I'm just phoning you because I made a decision and I'm going to quit," she told him.

"Why?" he asked.

"Because I don't want to do this anymore. I think it's time somebody else took this on."

"Well, that's awesome," replied her son.

"Don't tell your dad. I'm going to phone him next."

"Okay," said Hamish.

His questions exhausted, the fifteen-year-old, who is keenly interested in Broadway musicals and theatre, switched to other subjects.

"Hey, did you hear *Great Comet* is closing on Broadway?" he said, referencing the long-running production of *Natasha, Pierre & The Great Comet of 1812*.

Clark laughed. Here she was, standing tearily beside Okanagan Lake with her political career abruptly over, and her son had already moved on to pressing matters in his own life.

"Listen, sweetie, I've got to phone some other people, so maybe let's talk about this later," she said.

Up next was Marissen, her ex-husband, friend, and close advisor.

"I've wanted you to quit since they called on Horgan," Marissen said. "I just didn't want to tell you that because I wanted you to make your own decision."

Clark called her two brothers and some other close associates, then prepped for her caucus meeting.

At 10 a.m., she broke the news to caucus in a speech in which she listed their joint accomplishments over six and a half years: the strongest economy in the country, thousands of jobs, major projects, and balanced budgets. She held it together until glancing at Bond, who was bawling.

"You're not helping," Clark joked, as she too started to cry.

"You guys, it's really important you move on quickly," she concluded. "You move on fast, and get your feet under you."

Then Clark left the Liberal caucus for the last time.

The weekend had not played out as she had expected. She'd always intended to leave far sooner than she'd ever let on publicly, even without the Plecas incident. She had wanted to quit in the summer, but under different circumstances.

The crisis, however, was not over. Bernier jumped up to the microphone to inform caucus that Plecas still planned to send out a media release in fifteen minutes, quitting the party. He offered to try to stop it, and a majority of members asked him to try to get Plecas to stay, if for no other reason than to allow Clark to control the narrative of her departure. Bernier called Plecas, who had no idea Clark had just resigned, and asked him not to leave caucus and for Clark's resignation to be 100 per cent her decision. Plecas promised that as long as the story didn't leak, he'd never talk about it publicly. Bernier and Plecas walked back into the Liberal caucus room together. Plecas called his office and told them to hold off sending the release. He was staying.

It was now up to the caucus to tell the public about Clark's departure, with a press release. Coleman and the MLAs then gathered outside to meet the press. The big former Mountie began to cry again as he described how much he admired Clark's leadership and friendship. Now interim leader, he began outlining what the party would do next to prepare as an opposition.

Coleman had become interim leader without much of a voting process in the room. Several MLAs were upset about the lack of process and surrounded party president Sharon White in the hallway, saying she should do something. White pointed out that the party constitution has no provision for interim leader, and the person is decided by caucus. If you want to change the process for interim leader, she advised, go back in the caucus room and say something. But after an entire weekend complaining they didn't have the freedom to express themselves, the Liberals went back in the room and there was nary a peep of dissent to Coleman's face. The MLAs had their supposed freedom to speak now that Clark was gone. But nobody used it.

Clark, meanwhile, had already skipped town. She was supposed to fly back to Vancouver, but staff were worried there'd be cameras and reporters staking out the airport. So they tried to rent a car, only to discover there were none available. Eventually, Clark's deputy chief of staff, Jessica Wolford, loaned Clark and McDonald her cream-coloured 2008 MINI Cooper. There wasn't much room, but Clark and McDonald squeezed inside and started the drive back to Vancouver from Penticton. They took the scenic route, winding their way through Oliver and Osoyoos. It was the best way to really see the province, Clark had long thought. As they drove, they reminisced about how their journey in BC politics was coming full circle.

It was in 1991 that the two, then just junior political aides, borrowed a van from politician Clive Tanner and took off on BC's Interior highways to try to recruit candidates for then–BC Liberal leader Gordon Wilson's upstart political party. Wilson needed to show he had a full slate of candidates to try to get a spot in the October election debates. Clark and McDonald were tasked with driving north and filling out that slate any way they could. The road trip has since become a slice of BC political legend. Small details, like the fact that the van had one of the first car phones, have been added to the story over the years.

Clark, then twenty-five, and McDonald had used every trick they could to try to persuade people to run for the Liberals. And if that person wouldn't, they'd ask whether he or she had a relative or friend who'd be interested in flying the party flag. Once, after filling yet another riding with a dubious prospect, Clark half-jokingly told McDonald (later recounted in Wilf Hurd's book about the Liberal party), "I sure hope that candidate wasn't phoning from the jailhouse because I just approved his candidacy and I don't know anything about him."

The duo had come a long way since then. Clark had made her mark on history and would forever be remembered as BC's thirty-fifth premier. McDonald was by her side for the most important moments: he ran her leadership bid, directed her 2013 election victory, and served as both her first and last chief of staff. They were ending their political run the way they began it: on a road trip together.

In Princeton, they stopped at the Dairy Queen, in the town's downtown, just a stone's throw from the Similkameen River. They ordered and pulled up to the first drive-thru window. When the female worker opened the window to tell them their total, she found herself face to face with the former premier.

"Oh my god, you're Christy Clark!" she exclaimed.

Other staff started gathering at the window. They all wanted pictures. As the drive-thru lineup of vehicles grew behind them, Clark jumped out of the car and went inside. The fry cooks abandoned their post and the staff lined up for selfies. Customers went unserved as the restaurant ground to a complete halt. You could have mistaken it for a campaign event. But there was nothing left to campaign for.

Eventually, Clark was able to grab her order of chicken strips and a chili dog and extricate herself from the restaurant. Even without an ounce of political power left to her name, Christy Clark still knew how to draw a crowd.

CHAPTER 14
THE RETURN TO POWER

David Eby turned the key and entered his new office on the second floor of the legislature. On the door was a gold plaque engraved with the words "Attorney General." He went inside and turned left. A flat-screen TV hung on the wall, along with a whiteboard, and there was a window with a view of Victoria's inner harbour. It was palatial compared with the hundred-square-foot space he had in opposition.

Eby was ready to settle in when his assistant, Candice, popped her head inside to point out that this wasn't actually his office, and he was supposed to go to the other side of the suite. So Eby walked over to that next room, which was smaller, with three desks in a shared space. Great, the new AG thought, I'll be close to staff, and we can collaborate here.

Then Eby noticed a door—perhaps to a closet or a bathroom. He opened it to find a massive room, with red carpet, red drapes, and a huge wooden desk in the back left corner. His true office. He walked to the desk and noticed there was a note left from predecessor Andrew Wilkinson, the last Liberal attorney general. It was probably a letter, he thought, penned in the fine tradition of politicians who transition out of office, while offering up sage advice and support for their successors. Eby opened it and read:

David,

Enjoy the office and I will try to make your stay here as short as possible.

Andrew

Eby chuckled. Not quite the inspirational words of wisdom he'd been expecting, but he and Wilkinson were lawyers and old sparring partners in the legislature, and he recognized the attempt at humour.

Becoming attorney general was a dream job for the young lawyer. Just two days earlier, he had been flying from his home in Vancouver to Victoria to attend the swearing-in of Premier John Horgan's new cabinet. He got on the Helijet flight not knowing if he was going to be part of the cabinet the next day. When he touched down, a text message had popped up on his phone.

"Call me," read the note from Premier Horgan. Eby called and found out about his new job while standing in the Helijet terminal. But it was only now, standing in the actual office, that the achievement seemed real.

Similar scenes were playing out throughout the building. Finance Minister Carole James, working in her new office, left to use the public washroom down the hall before her staff reminded her she now had her own private bathroom connected to her ministerial suite.

Just next door, Education Minister Rob Fleming was trying to settle in. Part of the challenge with the transition of power is that the NDP did not get to look at many of the offices before picking what ministers would go where. The decision was made to take the old government house leader's office and turn it into Fleming's office. It was on the first floor, with a great view of the front lawn of the legislature. But what Fleming and his staff quickly realized was that the office door was often mistaken for the gift shop across the hall. Tourists kept trying to get in to buy souvenirs, like the little containers of breath fresheners with the legislature logo, called Parlia-Mints.

And there was another problem. The legislature grounds are a busy place in the summer. Community celebrations, concerts, and picnics take place almost every day. So when Fleming invited his new deputy minister to meet him for the first time, he didn't realize it was Thailand Days outside, making it nearly impossible to hear a thing his deputy said during the course of their forty-five-minute meeting.

Down the hall, House Leader and Public Safety Minister Mike Farnworth was also moving in. The office he took over had been Rich Coleman's for years. But you could barely tell anyone had been there. When Farnworth arrived, all the staff had been fired and the only thing in the whole office was a packet of soy sauce in a desk drawer and a poster of defeated premier Christy Clark that the outgoing staff had cheekily tacked to the minister's door.

But there was nowhere that the new reality had sunk in more than in the premier's office. For the NDP, the west annex had been a building they could see from their office windows but never enter.

Press secretary Sheena McConnell and her husband, Liam Iliffe, went into the west annex together for the first time. First they stopped by McConnell's new office. On the wall were head shots of former Clark staffer Ben Chin. On the desk, half-consumed glasses of wine. It was looking to McConnell like a lot of staff had just got up and left as if fleeing from a zombie invasion. Then the pair looked around a bit, found a spiral staircase, and climbed up it. There in front of them was the cabinet room. "Are we really in government?" they both thought. That thought was interrupted by a voice down the hall.

"Hello?" said the voice. In a seemingly empty office, there was still one person working. The holdover was part of the public service and was doing work on the transition of power.

"I am so sorry," said McConnell. "We are just looking." It was her new workspace, but she still felt like an intruder.

The Greens were changing too. The caucus had outgrown Weaver's old offices, which were located in the corner of a hallway in the basement that looked at first like a dead end. The election meant that the old space was not going to be big enough to accommodate Sonia Furstenau and Adam Olsen, plus the additional staff that comes with a three-member party. The NDP threw a bone to their new best friends, the Greens. Weaver and his team were given the much larger suite of offices next door, with a private bathroom for Weaver and space for a receptionist. The rooms had belonged to Liberal public safety minister Mike Morris. Weaver might not have joined Horgan's cabinet, but he now had a minister's office.

Even for the Greens, though, the transition was awkward. Morris's staff continued to work in the space until Horgan was sworn in. An over-eager Weaver was still tempted to show off his new digs, often inviting fellow staff and journalists to come take a look. Each time, Morris's receptionist would greet the Green Party leader and his guests and walk him around. In one tense moment, Weaver popped his head into an office where Morris's legislative assistant worked. She got up from her desk and closed the door in the leader's face. On his next visit, the Green Party leader was less than thrilled to discover that all the furniture in his new office was gone.

"It belongs to the ministry," said the receptionist.

"Can I get it back?" asked Weaver.

"I don't think so. It belongs to the public safety ministry."

When Weaver finally claimed his new space, Morris's legislative assistant was fired. But the helpful receptionist was asked to stay on with the new government.

The "intrusion" had actually started weeks earlier. On June 30, Horgan arrived at the leader of the official Opposition's office as the premier-designate. The NDP had a transition team that included Eugene Kostyra, a Manitoba NDP finance minister from the 1980s. They helped the New Democrats as they went through the documents provided by the previous government. Those documents would be turned into briefing notes and presented to Horgan on a daily basis.

The bureaucracy had produced briefing binders, roughly one per ministry, that contained detailed information about things like the current financial situation, a staff count, and ministerial priorities. Each binder contained what's called the 30-60-90 schedule of key time-sensitive issues stretching over the next three months. The binders were also supposed to contain notes prepared specifically to guide the NDP in implementing the promises contained in the NDP-Green power-sharing accord, as well as the NDP's election platform.

Complaints started to trickle back to Horgan right from the first day. The books were sparse. There were files the NDP government was looking for that just weren't there, such as the report commissioned by the previous government on ICBC. Work that had been done on the liquefied natural gas industry was only two pages long. The Massey replacement bridge project had no specific documents on bids. Horgan and his new deputy, Don Wright, met with Kim Henderson, the outgoing deputy minister to the premier. Horgan wanted more information and asked Henderson to make it happen.

"I ended up getting a big honking book on what we thought were the shortcomings of what these smart people had been wading through," said Horgan in an interview for this book. "That was the first real document I got, a compilation of their work to assess what government had left behind. Which just raised more questions... There was limited information in the first couple of days and then it started coming and I said to someone, I characterized it like, we're getting the owner's manual a page at a time but we don't have the keys yet."

There were around thirty people on the NDP transition team, hunkered down in the old Queen's Printer building, a block south of the legislature. Campaign director Dewar was in charge, working with Vancouver councillor Geoff Meggs (who was named Horgan's chief of staff) as well as Wright, who as Horgan's deputy minister was also head of the civil service. Suzanne Christensen, Horgan's former acting chief of staff, was in charge of recruiting the team members.

Wright was a familiar face at the legislature and to political junkies. In February 2013, he quit his position as president of the BC Institute of Technology and was announced as Adrian Dix's incoming deputy minister. It was an act of hubris by the Dix regime to publicly announce its top civil servant three months before an election, as if it had already won, though at the time the announcement was intended to send a message of stability and trust to the business community. The gamble would not pay off for Wright; the NDP lost in May. He became president of Central 1 Credit Union, and when the Horgan team approached him to become deputy minister again, his first reaction was no. So the team asked him to just help out with the transition at first, which he did until, eventually, he was persuaded to do the job.

Wright tried to send a message to the civil service that the NDP would run a professional, respectful administration. Six deputy ministers were terminated, representing one-third of the top civil servants, but he also began promoting from within and kept several contentious deputies that some New Democrats felt were partisan Liberals.

There was one file that appeared first in every briefing binder: the ongoing fires in British Columbia's Interior. During the limbo period, the government under Clark had declared it a provincial state of emergency. Thousands of people were being displaced from their homes, and fires were putting people's lives and properties at risk. On July 9, 2017, Premier Clark arrived in Kamloops. She was still in charge of provincial decision making, and she announced $100 million in relief support for the fire-ravaged communities.

"There's only one premier at a time," Clark told reporters. "We needed this to happen fast, we couldn't wait until the 18th, so I think it's the right thing to do."

She also spoke to evacuees who had been forced north from areas like 100 Mile House and Ashcroft. It was a short visit.

Later that day, premier-designate Horgan arrived in Kamloops with Sheena McConnell and deputy communications director Jen

Holmwood. Waiting for the premier-designate at the airport was Emergency Management BC deputy minister Robert Turner. There may have been only one premier, but Horgan was getting the executive treatment. When they arrived at the fire response centre for a briefing, there were four staff members from the government's non-partisan communications branch, including Hannah Glover.

Glover had spent the last two years working for the Liberal government, handing out press releases to the media and calling out "last question" when ministers needed to get away from reporters' questions. She was familiar to McConnell, who thought perhaps staff was left over from Clark's morning visit. But then Glover approached McConnell and said she and the team were there to help the premier-designate with anything they needed to do, including scouting out locations in advance.

"Will the premier-designate be doing a scrum?" asked Glover.

For the NDP it was like the twilight zone. Those whom they had always seen as the enemy were now on their side.

WHILE GLOVER AND others were working at the fire, the NDP transition team was trying to figure out who would serve in their government. The Liberals had hired thousands of people over sixteen years, and how many of them remained throughout government was still unclear. The NDP would go on to fire 148 Liberal appointees, paying out $13.6 million in severance. The transition team probably wanted to fire more, but it needed to cap the payouts so it could claim the NDP hadn't spent more in severance than the Liberals did when they transitioned into power in 2001.

Some of the changes were more obvious than others. Staff in the premier's office were let go and so were all the chiefs of staff to the ministers. Horgan's office prepared a short list of Liberal hires that they wanted to keep on. That list included Karen van Marum.

Van Marum was one of the government's most recognizable faces. She was also a breast cancer survivor, having recently helped organize the royal visit while undergoing chemotherapy treatment. Within the bureaucracy, she was widely considered non-partisan, handling mostly communications logistics, like event planning. Unlike most government staff, she had a friendly relationship with Horgan. The premier-designate often asked about her health. And when she was diagnosed with cancer, Horgan, then Opposition leader, gave van Marum a big hug in the legislature hallway.

That's why it came as a surprise to van Marum when she was abruptly fired during the transition. Glover and the handful of communications officers handling the wildfire crisis in the Interior were also fired. An uninformed (or extremely incompetent) mid-level NDP staffer had somehow put them on a list of Liberal enemies to be terminated. The news came as a surprise to the new premier, who blamed the Liberals for the bungled terminations.

"How is Karen doing?" Horgan asked McConnell at one point.

"She was fired," responded McConnell, who had already received several calls from reporters questioning why the NDP would target a non-partisan cancer survivor whom Horgan actually liked.

The new premier was extremely unimpressed with that news, to put it mildly. He directed his office to intervene. Van Marum was rehired, along with Glover, though they didn't get their old jobs back, because the same NDP strategists who'd fired them had already filled the positions with loyal New Democrats.

MEANWHILE, STAFF WERE preparing for the swearing-in, which was going to take place on July 18, 2017, in the main ballroom of Government House. Along with the private event, the new government would throw open the doors of the legislature from 5 to 7 p.m. that evening for a kind of celebratory open house. The original plan had been for

More than two months after the provincial election, John Horgan officially becomes premier of British Columbia. He was sworn in as the thirty-sixth premier of the province by Lieutenant-Governor Judith Guichon, in front of his brand new cabinet. PROVINCE OF BC

Canadian rock band 54-40 to perform at the legislature later that night. But when Horgan saw the $40,000 price tag just to stage the band he decided it wasn't the right thing to do, considering all the support needed to battle the province's fires.

More than six hundred people were invited to the swearing-in, the largest ever held at the lieutenant-governor's residence. Invited to be part of the audience would be the entire NDP caucus, the Green caucus, union leaders, environmental leaders, and politicians of all stripes, ranging from Vancouver mayor Gregor Robertson to former federal Conservative minister James Moore.

Horgan had been working on his speech for weeks. But he had pushed the event to the side of his desk as the fires continued to rage. And before he could get to the speech, he needed to take care of getting his cabinet in place. For weeks he had been scribbling different possible cabinet selections in his notebook. The only person who knew for sure she was going to be with Horgan at the table was Carole James. Horgan and James had met the day the lieutenant-governor asked him to form a government.

"How do you feel about being deputy premier?" Horgan asked.

"I would love to," said James, who had been the provincial director of child care policy for two years during the NDP government in the early 1990s. "Do I get MCFD too?"

"No," Horgan responded, chuckling. "You have to do finance."

The other minister to find out early was Adrian Dix. With his deep understanding of many of the new government's most critical files and his near-photographic memory, the former leader of the party was seen as someone who could be slotted into almost any ministry. But Horgan wanted him for health and broke the news early so he could seek out his advice on the new Ministry of Mental Health and Addictions.

The rest were part of the waiting game. On July 17, 2017, a day before the swearing-in, Horgan sat down at his desk and started making calls. His job was to inform his new cabinet of their new roles. One by one, alphabetically, Horgan was working his way through the list. The last one was Claire Trevena. The North Island MLA had served as the NDP's transportation critic and was now slated to be the transportation minister. Horgan had reminded all of the MLAs to keep their phones on because the call could come anytime. But soon after Trevena left her home on Quadra Island she turned off her phone, even though her husband was the one driving the car. She powered it back on a few hours later, near the top of Malahat, about an hour from Victoria. What she didn't know was that a very frustrated premier-designate had spent more than an hour waiting to connect. Trevena eventually picked up.

"Where have you been?" asked Horgan.

"Just driving down the Island," replied Trevena.

"Well, you are minister of transportation and highways," Horgan said, "so as you are coming over the Malahat you need to find a way to fix it."

While Horgan was making the good calls, chief of staff Meggs was left with the hard ones. It was his job to call the nineteen NDP MLAS who were not picked. Some of those politicians would be getting parliamentary secretary jobs or caucus roles, though some would get nothing at all at this point. Many of the MLAS had sat in opposition for more than a decade and it was especially difficult to break the news to them.

There was none tougher than Leonard Krog, who represented Nanaimo. He and Horgan had matured together as members of the NDP caucus. They were both Island boys. And Krog had done a good job as the attorney general critic for the whole time Horgan was leader. But it was a numbers game, and with a commitment to name a gender-neutral cabinet, there could only be so many men. Krog was beaten out by Eby.

THE NEXT MORNING, Horgan was up bright and early. It was his day. The swearing-in was set for 2 p.m. He got into his Prius early and drove to Government House to practise his speech. The ballroom was ready to go, hundreds of chairs set up on the floor with a program sitting on each seat. To stage right was the podium, to the left a table where Horgan and each minister would sign the oath book.

Sheena McConnell and Kate van Meer-Mass took a seat in the front row, where Horgan's family was going to sit. But Horgan kept thinking about two people who were going to be missing this afternoon: his mother and his brother Pat. His mother had died and his brother was gravely ill, battling cancer. Horgan stood at the podium, looked at the front row, and started to cry. The lieutenant-governor's private secretary, Jeremy Brownridge, placed a box of tissues by the podium.

"You have to move them," Horgan said to van Meer-Mass. He knew he couldn't handle his wife, Ellie, and the rest of the family directly in sight during the speech. Van Meer-Mass made a quick change, and the family was moved to stage left, where Horgan would sit and sign his name to officially be written into history as British Columbia's thirty-sixth premier. After a few more cracks at a tear-free speech, Horgan was told to move down and practise the signature portion of the ceremony. And once again the waterworks, Brownridge dropping another box of tissues for the soon-to-be premier to access.

"I guess the good news is I got it out of my system," said Horgan.

While Horgan was blubbering his way through the rehearsal, the caucus was gathering around the legislature to get ready for the afternoon's event. The plan was for the cabinet to ride on a bus with the premier-designate from the Grand Pacific Hotel to Government House together. But Horgan had a different idea.

"How many seats are on the bus?" Horgan asked. He was told there were forty-one, the same number as members of the NDP caucus.

"Then why wouldn't we put everybody on the bus?" Horgan said. "Let's all come together because we are all in this today."

McConnell and van Meer-Mass drove with Horgan to the Grand Pacific and had lunch. Bob Dewar and Marie Della Mattia were there as well. This was the core group that had spent the most time with the incoming premier during the election campaign. They went through the speaking notes and the afternoon's schedule.

Dressing Horgan is a challenge. He was constantly being reminded he wasn't supposed to wear his Doc Martens with his suit; they looked clunky and lacked style. The premier-elect's colour-blindness also made it difficult for him to match shirts and ties. That meant the fashion part often fell to McConnell. The choice for the swearing-in was exactly the same as for the televised leadership debate: a mid-bright-blue suit, a modern-looking orange and pink tie, and a blue shirt. Horgan changed into the suit in a room at the hotel. Waiting outside the door was McConnell and, for the first time, a member of Horgan's RCMP detail, one of the last-to-appear signs that he was about to run the province.

The group went downstairs to where caucus was waiting. It was the last time they would all meet before Horgan would officially become premier and others would be sworn in to cabinet. The ovation was huge, and Horgan was swallowed up by hugs and cheers. Then they got on the bus.

At Government House, Brownridge and his team were hurrying to get everything ready. More people had shown up than expected, which meant they needed to open up the top balcony so people could watch. All told, more than seven hundred people filled the main ballroom.

Horgan was officially sworn in, and then the cabinet. The loudest cheer was saved for Carole James. Then it was time for Horgan's speech.

First he paid tribute to those affected by the wildfires.

"As we gather, of course, we are mindful of the tens of thousands of British Columbians who have been forced from their homes, and the thousands who are fighting fires, and the many more who have opened their hearts and their homes to those who have been displaced by a natural catastrophe which is increasing in regularity here in our Interior and in our forests," he said.

Then he shifted to his family.

"It is an honour to be your premier," said Horgan, starting to choke up. "I wouldn't be here today were it not for my loving family. My beautiful, spectacular, stellar wife, Ellie. My good son Nate is not with us today, but my gooder son Evan is here. To my brother Pat, my brother Brian, my sister Cathy—here come the tears, I can feel them flowing already—I want to thank you for getting me here today."

Horgan wasn't done with the thank-yous. He looked out at the crowd, searching for Jack Lusk, his old basketball coach. Horgan mentioned the one piece of advice that stood out for him from the many Lusk had provided over the years: "If you show respect today, there will be people to show you respect tomorrow."

Once the speech had wrapped up, the first order of business for the new cabinet and Premier Horgan was what's called the family photo,

Moments after Lieutenant-Governor Judith Guichon vacated the front middle seat for the official cabinet photo, Kody Bell sneaked in to take a picture and ended up occupying the vacant seat. Bell is a constituent of Horgan's and his enthusiasm has been an inspiration for the new premier. PROVINCE OF BC; COURTESY OF KODY BELL

the official photograph of the new cabinet along with Lieutenant-Governor Judith Guichon. When it was done, Guichon got up, leaving an empty chair in the middle of the twenty-two-person cabinet.

But before a picture was taken of the group alone, Horgan saw a familiar face peeking around the corner. Kody Bell is one of those guys who is hard to forget. Horgan first met him around 2007 at a Tim Hortons near his home in Langford, when Bell had approached the MLA. "You won the last election by 1,932 votes," Bell said. He may have a developmental disability, but he's brilliant with facts about Horgan's electoral history. Horgan was impressed. And over the years he has run into Bell dozens of times. So when the list of who should be invited to the swearing in was being made, Bell was there. And when Horgan saw Bell peeking around the corner of the picture room in Government House, he had no idea how the young man had made his way so far into the mansion, but he nonetheless called on him.

"Kody, come on in," said Horgan.

Bell plopped down in the chair that had just been vacated by the lieutenant-governor. The young man became the only British Columbian, other than Guichon, to get a picture with Premier Horgan and his entire cabinet at Government House. Horgan later reflected on how this was one of the happier moments in a day filled with them.

But the day was far from over. Once the cabinet left Government House, they got back on the bus to return to the legislature, where thousands of people were waiting. On arriving at the legislature grounds, they were whisked inside. Horgan spoke briefly to the crowd and then he was swarmed. Hundreds of people wanted to shake his hand and take a picture. Eventually the crowd got so large that the premier couldn't move.

"Sir, we have to get out of here," said a member of the premier's security detail, who was wedged into an uncomfortable spot near the gift shop.

"Great," said Horgan. "It's really hot in here."

They went back outside, and the crowd was just as big. Horgan stood outside for quite a long time, taking selfies and greeting anyone who wanted to meet him. The next stop for the premier was a number of receptions being held in his honour around downtown Victoria. He got into his provided van for the first time as premier, and the RCMP officer behind the wheel started to drive. As they went down the street, Horgan noticed his friends sitting on the patio of the Steamship Grill.

"Hey, my friends are there," he said. "Stop the car."

But before the RCMP officer could put on the brakes, Horgan was out the door, the van still moving. Soon after, the child locks were switched on to stop the exuberant premier from getting out of a moving vehicle before the RCMP detail had secured the scene against any potential threats.

THAT WOULDN'T BE the only time Horgan had a hard time adjusting to life as premier and the issues that come with it.

Horgan went from the leader no one knew to the premier everyone wanted to speak to, almost overnight. There was nowhere Horgan could go where people didn't recognize him, including a wedding in Campbell River, where the house band asked him up on stage to sing and, despite deferring to his son to do the singing, he was still photographed for the local paper with the caption "the premier's got pipes." There was nowhere he could go where his RCMP detail wasn't with him. The new premier was struggling to understand why a guy like him needed to have protection everywhere he went.

Then something happened that made it all click.

Horgan is one of the biggest Victoria Shamrocks fans there is. The lacrosse team is the premier's hometown team, and he can be spotted at most home games at The Q Centre in Colwood, wearing his jersey with "Horgan" stitched on the back. Soon after becoming premier, the Shamrocks made a run to the league championships and a date with the New Westminster Salmonbellies. The premier was in Vancouver for the day and decided to take in a playoff game in New Westminster, which the Shamrocks lost. Once the game was over, Horgan and press secretary Sheena McConnell were making their way to the exit. Six or seven drunk men in their twenties started approaching the premier.

"You fucked up the Shamrocks, just like you fucked up the tolls," one of the group yelled at Horgan.

One of the members of the security detail was walking behind Horgan. The premier had a history of wanting to engage with hecklers, no matter how much they may have had to drink.

"Sorry about saving you money," snapped back the premier.

The conversation continued, the yelling from one side and Horgan responding. Before they made it to the door, the RCMP member turned to the group, put her hand on her gun resting in the hip holster and spoke to the group.

"Show some respect," she said.

They all got to the vehicle, Horgan now realizing the encounter had gone on a little longer than it should have.

"John, you can't do that. You can't goad people," said McConnell. "Especially a group of drunk people. You just can't do that anymore. You have a detail for a reason."

The premier disagreed. If he was going to be in public, he was willing to engage with whatever member of the public came up to him.

But by the next morning, Horgan had changed his mind.

"I understand why you guys are with me all the time and why I shouldn't put myself in those situations," he said to the RCMP officer. For a guy who was a pleaser, understanding that not everyone was going to like him and that he couldn't change their minds was hard.

"The challenge is that I'm the same person but my responsibilities are different," he said in an interview for this book. "So I'm not going to curtail my desires to wade into things, but at the same time the security detail . . . I'm curbing my enthusiasm not because I want to change who I am, just because it's probably better for everybody."

Inside the party, Horgan isn't going to be able to please everyone either, which is no surprise for any leader—especially a leader of the BC New Democrats.

The John Horgan who'd been persuaded to run in 2014 had spoken of a need to appeal to rural BC, to better balance natural resource projects and jobs with the powerful environmental wing of the party and its opposition to things like mines, pipelines, and dams. He'd pledged to find a path forward without breaking apart the party and without giving an inch to the Greens, whom, until very recently, he had all but loathed.

"There is a tension between the constituency in the NDP that constantly wants to pull us into more environmentally focused policies," Horgan said in an interview for this book. "And the whole essence of the NDP in my time is to try to balance those things. How do you keep the working-class roots with environment and new technologies that are going to create new opportunities for employment and wealth? That's the challenge of the NDP. And Andrew [Weaver] was trying to take our component parts apart and that didn't put us in a position where we could be buddies."

Whether Horgan can navigate that tricky path within his own party while managing the Greens will prove the true test of his early premiership. He didn't accomplish it in the 2017 election, when his party all but gave up on rural BC in favour of Metro Vancouver.

Many of Horgan's future battles will be internal. He rose to the occasion in 2017, listening to key advice, finding his centre, polishing his image, controlling his temper, and emerging sounding and acting very much like a man who could be premier. He has it in him to continue, but with the inevitable scandals, infighting, and staff changes that beset any political office, will his gains be permanent?

THOSE WEIGHTY PROBLEMS were distant issues on the night of the swearing-in, when the legislature was packed with New Democrats and Horgan was being mobbed on the front steps. Everyone who decided to hang around that night was in support of his government.

The whole night for Horgan had a sense of finality. It had been the most chaotic three months in British Columbia's political history—from the back-and-forth election to the recount, the Green-NDP alliance, the confidence vote, and now the swearing-in of an NDP premier for the first time since Ujjal Dosanjh was sworn in seventeen years earlier.

"I haven't waited my whole life to become premier," Horgan said in an interview for this book. "I waited a few years to become premier because I never aspired to do the job. But I have to say I was ridiculously serene, because the series of events that started with the calling of the election were really an opportunity for me to not be the person you observed as leader of the opposition but to be myself."

Horgan and Ellie finally made it home around midnight. They got ready for bed and, before the lights were turned off, Horgan's head hit the pillow. He was still wearing the giant grin that came from enjoying one of the best days of his life.

Ellie said one last thing before saying goodnight. "Will that smile still be on your face when you get off that pillow?" she asked.

Tomorrow would be another day, his first full day as premier. The weight of the office would be immense, the pressure, at times, crushing. Yet the next day, the smile persisted.

It's too soon to write the history of Horgan's earliest days as BC's thirty-sixth premier. But the history of BC politics does put an interesting perspective on the new leader. Most of the thirty-five premiers before him failed to last more than one term in office, some significantly less. The list of those whom voters sent back to the government benches in more than two consecutive elections is soberingly short, those titans of history, including Gordon Campbell and W.A.C. Bennett, few and far between.

Horgan knows this. He's a keen student of politics. He served in the trenches of the NDP government in the 1990s, when the party elected, and overthrew, four of its own premiers within ten years. His jubilation at becoming premier will be tempered by the fact that never in the history of the province has an NDP premier won re-election to a second term. They've all been forced to resign or have been overthrown by their party friends, caucus colleagues, and eventually voters.

Horgan didn't win the 2017 election. But he fought hard, reinvented himself on the campaign trail, and won the subsequent battle for power. He emerged, at the end of the day, as British Columbia's premier. Holding on to the job will be a matter of confidence.

EPILOGUE

The first six months of Premier John Horgan's government did not provide much of a breather for those exhausted by the political drama that had gripped British Columbia in 2017.

Thirty minutes before the new government took its seat for the first time in the legislature, on September 8, reporters spotted Liberal MLA Darryl Plecas sitting alone in the chamber. It was unusual, because all Liberals are required to attend a caucus meeting before each morning's legislative session. Why was Plecas skipping his own party's meeting to sit by himself?

Plecas's odd behaviour set off alarm bells. But only a small group of senior New Democrats, including Horgan and veteran MLA Mike Farnworth, knew what was about to occur.

As Plecas sat alone in the House, Farnworth briefed the NDP caucus: Plecas had defected from the Liberals to accept the NDP's offer to become the new Speaker of the legislature. Stunned NDP MLAs burst into applause. It meant the Liberals, already weakened by Christy Clark's resignation, had lost another vote in the House. The new government was safe for its first session of the legislature. And the NDP-Green power-sharing deal, though still in its infancy, was now stronger than ever.

The Liberal caucus, in its own meeting room on the other side of the building, was hearing about the Plecas deal at the same time.

Abbotsford South MLA Darryl Plecas sits alone in the BC legislative chamber on September 8, 2017, just minutes before his surprise defection from the BC Liberal party to accept the NDP's offer of Speaker of the Legislature became publicly known. RICHARD ZUSSMAN

"I hate to break this to you," interim leader Rich Coleman said to his MLAS, "but we've all been duped."

Many of Plecas's colleagues were furious. The guy who'd forced Clark out as leader by threatening to quit the party during a July caucus retreat was basically quitting anyway, two months later. Those who'd fought to convince Plecas to stay after the showdown with Clark wondered openly if this had been his plan all along.

Plecas's defection underscored just how unpredictable British Columbia's political landscape continued to be. The move was the result of weeks of secret negotiations. Shortly after Clark's resignation, Farnworth had reached out by phone, sensing that the disgruntled Liberal could be turned. He took Plecas for lunch and then, over a series of phone calls, locked down the arrangement before Plecas went on holiday in August.

When Plecas returned, he began a cat-and-mouse game with his oblivious Liberal colleagues, avoiding meetings and carefully parsing what little he did say to Coleman. Coleman later publicly accused Plecas of lying to him repeatedly. Plecas insisted he hadn't lied, because he'd never explicitly promised that he wouldn't take the job. It was a tough argument to advance, because as recently as June, Plecas had said to *Province* columnist Mike Smyth, "I would never be Speaker without the blessing of my colleagues in caucus."

Between June and September, though, the world of BC politics had changed. The Speaker's job, which included ruling on procedural disagreements, appealed to Plecas because of his background as a criminologist and federal prison judge. It also came with a $52,941 pay raise.

"When there was an opportunity to be Speaker, I had to choose," Plecas told Smyth in September. "Am I going to do this, which I think is suitable for me and the kind of person that I am? Or am I going to continue having to restrain myself for years? I made the right choice."

However, the choice came with a cost. Some Liberals, including Coleman, refused to speak to Plecas again, while others openly undermined his authority in the House.

THE SPEAKER DECISION gave the NDP some wiggle room during a busy first six months in office. The new government used cabinet powers to raise welfare and disability rates by one hundred dollars a month, ban the grizzly bear trophy hunt (which would later be expanded to including hunting for meat), strike a commission to move toward a fifteen-dollar minimum wage, and launch a legal battle against the Kinder Morgan Trans Mountain pipeline expansion project, through newly won intervener status. The government also honoured its big-ticket Metro Vancouver election promise to scrap tolls on the Port Mann and Golden Ears bridges. Within two weeks, traffic on the Port Mann had jumped more than 20 per cent.

Once the legislature returned, the NDP passed seventeen bills. Some, such as changing the fixed election date from spring to fall, or closing loopholes on rent increases, passed without controversy. Others went less smoothly. Horgan followed through on banning corporate and union donations to political parties, but approved transitional public funding, breaking a promise not to put taxpayers on the hook for election campaigns. The government passed enabling legislation for the 2018 referendum on proportional representation, but caught flak for a low threshold that diminished votes from rural BC.

There were other early controversies for New Democrats. Horgan and Jobs Minister Bruce Ralston were sued after they bungled the firing of former BC Liberal leader Gordon Wilson from his job as the province's liquefied natural gas advocate. Agriculture Minister Lana Popham was accused of intimidation and activism over a letter she wrote threatening to discontinue provincial permits for a coastal fish farm because of concerns over the BC government fish research lab. The resulting uproar forced the fledgling government to take a hard look at itself in the mirror.

"If we're going to be a government that governs for all British Columbians, we have to set aside our activism and start being better administrators," Horgan told Global BC's Keith Baldrey.

Popham, and others, struggled with the transition.

"It was a lot harder than I thought it was going to be," she told the *Times Colonist*'s Amy Smart. "I was used to lighting my hair on fire and then all of a sudden I was in the line of fire."

The NDP administration also wrestled at times with its new Green partners. The Greens successfully demanded that the NDP slow plans for ten-dollar-a-day child care, its 2021 timeline for a fifteen-dollar minimum wage, and a four-hundred-dollar annual renter's rebate. Green leader Andrew Weaver publicly declared the NDP election platform "irrelevant" to their new power-sharing deal.

Money was a particular sticking point for the new administration. While the NDP had inherited one of Canada's strongest provincial economies, the $2.7 billion surplus left unspent by the Liberals had automatically gone toward provincial debt. Finance Minister Carole James raised taxes on corporations and high-income earners in her September budget update, but was still left with a razor-thin surplus. Finding a way to fund all the future promises on child care and housing affordability, without resorting to massive tax hikes, would occupy much of the NDP's early internal deliberations.

FORMER LIBERAL PREMIER Christy Clark kept a low public profile during this time, while the new government debated whether to cancel her signature projects.

Transportation Minister Claire Trevena stopped construction on the planned $3.5 billion ten-lane bridge that was set to replace the aging Massey Tunnel between Richmond and Delta. Clark had announced the bridge after her 2013 election victory, unilaterally pushing it on the region's mayors as her solution for commuter gridlock.

"I don't think the former government had buy-in from the communities," Trevena said as she delivered the deathblow to the Clark bridge in early September.

Yet it was a different Clark megaproject that caused the NDP the biggest headache. BC Hydro was spending almost $2 million per day constructing the Site C dam. Though Horgan had been careful during the election to say only that he would "review" Site C, his party had nonetheless left the clear impression (thanks to public comments by outspoken MLAs like Michelle Mungall and Popham) that it would scrap the dam once elected.

At the very least, many in the NDP expected Site C would fail to pass a government-ordered review by the BC Utilities Commission. Instead, the commission released a 299-page report on November 1 that offered no recommendations on how to proceed. It said government could choose, if it wanted, to get the same amount of power for similar cost by using smaller-scale wind and geothermal projects. But that would mean writing off $4 billion in sunk and remediation costs, with nothing to show for it. Pausing construction and restarting the dam later wasn't financially viable either.

The deck was stacked against Site C within Horgan's twenty-two-person executive council. During their Opposition days, several ministers had called for the dam's abolition. Environmental groups pressed their influence to argue that Site C would unnecessarily harm the Peace River valley's agricultural land. Local First Nations, to whom the NDP had promised reconciliation, claimed Site C violated their treaty rights. Unlike when Clark's Liberals approved the project in 2014, Site C had no champion at the NDP cabinet table. During roughly nine hours of debate, over three cabinet meetings, virtually no one spoke out aggressively in favour of continuing the project based on its own merits.

In the end, Horgan's decision came down to figures put together by the finance ministry's powerful treasury board staff. They calculated that stopping Site C mid-construction would cause a 12 per cent rate hike in hydro bills in 2020 and financially devastate the Crown power corporation. That kind of rate shock would undermine the NDP's election promise of improving affordability for taxpayers. If the government, instead of BC Hydro, absorbed the $4 billion write-off, the province would likely face a credit downgrade. Most importantly, it would erase the government's ability to borrow for building all the new schools, hospitals, and transportation projects it had promised during the election. The idea of cancelling Clark's dam held a powerful symbolic significance for New Democrats. But not at the cost of having to abandon the rest of their agenda.

"We have listened, we have deliberated, and we have debated," Horgan announced on December 11 at a press conference in the same legislature library rotunda where Clark had announced Site C three years earlier. "And at the end of the day, we've come to the conclusion that although Site C is not the project we would have favoured, and it's not the project we would have started, it must be completed to meet the objectives our government has set through mandate letters to ministers and commitments to the people of BC during the election campaign."

Adding salt to the wound, Horgan also revealed that the budget had jumped from $8.9 billion to $10.7 billion. And there were still considerable risks it could be delayed beyond its 2024 completion date.

Clark had long said that she would get Site C past the point of no return. She succeeded. One mischievous reporter even asked Horgan if he thought Site C should be named after Clark, given the circumstances.

"I'll leave that up to whoever is around here when the dam is finished," Horgan replied, curtly.

One person hoping to be around when the dam is completed is Andrew Wilkinson. The man with many titles, from doctor to lawyer to former Liberal advanced education minister and attorney general, was elected as the new BC Liberal leader to replace Clark on February 3, 2018.

Wilkinson had entered the race as one of the establishment candidates, along with Mike de Jong and Todd Stone, and left the Sheraton Wall Centre in Vancouver as the leader on convention night. From sitting in third place after the first ballot of the vote, he leaped over Michael Lee and then beat former MP and Surrey mayor Dianne Watts on the fifth and final ballot.

Moments after being declared the new leader of the BC Liberals, Wilkinson spoke to the media. He was asked about the prospect of facing Horgan in the legislature.

"My task is to make sure we hold the NDP to account with smart incisive questions that will make their skin crawl," he said.

But the new NDP premier has proven to have much tougher skin than expected.

SITE C WAS the toughest decision faced by Horgan early in his premiership. He took immediate blowback from supporters, who promised to carry the consequences into the next election. His Green partner, Weaver, was sharply critical as well and suggested a recall campaign against Energy Minister Mungall (though others pointed out that Weaver had inadvertently helped Site C survive by choosing not to make its cancellation a binding condition of his power-sharing deal with the NDP).

Overall, most New Democrats felt the new premier had acquitted himself well in explaining the decision. He'd appeared contrite and genuine.

"Family members of mine, friends of mine, will be very, very disappointed with this," Horgan admitted. At one point, Horgan mentioned how his wife, Ellie, also disagreed. And he choked up when he mentioned his brother Pat, who opposed the dam. (A father figure in Horgan's life, Pat died of cancer on January 6, 2018.)

Horgan's agreeable public image only grew during his first six months in charge. Some of it could be attributed to the honeymoon period that any new government enjoys, but much was also due to Horgan's continued personal growth since the election. There were few traces now of the chippy and hot-headed former Opposition leader. The calmer, friendlier, more professional Horgan easily handled the Liberal Opposition's top critics during his first legislative session.

"People have asked me why I seem so changed," Horgan said in a year-end interview with the *Times Colonist*. "It's the change in responsibility. I was obliged as an opposition critic to be negative every day, and it was counter to who I am as a person. I've always considered myself positive and upbeat. And I get an opportunity now in this new role as premier to lead a government and be positive and upbeat about the extraordinary place where we live."

INDEX

ABOUT THE AUTHORS

ROB SHAW has covered the BC legislature since 2009, first as the legislative reporter for the Victoria *Times Colonist* and currently as the legislative columnist for *The Vancouver Sun*. His stories have appeared in local and national newspapers through the Postmedia News chain. He lives in Victoria, BC.

RICHARD ZUSSMAN has covered the BC legislature since 2014, first as the legislative reporter for the CBC and currently as a reporter based at the legislature for *Global News*. His stories have appeared on local and national television, radio, and online. He lives in Victoria with his wife, Liza Yuzda, and two children.